A SECRET HISTORY OF TORTURE

Ian Cobain

A Secret History
of Torture

COUNTERPOINT
BERKELEY

Copyright © 2012 by Ian Cobain

Library of Congress Cataloging-in-Publication data is available.
ISBN 978-1-61902-109-9

Cover design by Charles Brock, Faceout Studio

COUNTERPOINT
1919 Fifth Street
Berkeley, CA 94710
www.counterpointpress.com

Printed in the United States of America
Distributed by Publishers Group West

1 2 3 4 5 6 7 8 9 10

To Jack, Max and Kate, with thanks for your patience

Contents

Introduction

It was on New Year's Eve 2007, quite late in the evening, when I first began to wonder just how much I'd failed to see. I was sitting in the office of an Islamabad lawyer, Hashmat Ali Habib, discussing one of his clients, a young man from Birmingham. Outside, the last of the rush-hour traffic was quietening; overhead, a single bulb spread an unsparing light over the cluttered room.

Habib's client was a man called Rashid Rauf, who was said to be a senior figure in al-Qaida. He had been picked up in Pakistan the previous year after police and MI5 officers in London had concluded that a number of his associates in the UK were plotting to bring several airliners down over the Atlantic.

A few days earlier the Pakistani authorities had announced that Rauf had gone on the run. According to the official version of events, the police officers who were driving the terrorist mastermind from court to a maximum-security prison on the northern outskirts of Rawalpindi had taken him to a mosque and told him that he was to be allowed to pray, alone. He then vanished.

Nothing about the official account rang true and my newspaper had asked me to try to make sense of Rashid Rauf's strange disappearance.

'Was your client tortured?' I asked.

Habib burst out laughing. I didn't yet realise that when a terrorism suspect is detained in Pakistan, torture isn't just likely, it's a given: *an absolute given.*

Habib stopped laughing at me. 'Of course he was tortured.'

There was a pause and I thought back to the other stories I'd heard in the past year about British Muslims, all suspected jihadists, who had been detained by one of Pakistan's notorious intelligence agencies. Each of the three men claimed to have been asked a series of questions by the Pakistanis while suffering appalling violence. They said that they were then asked the same questions, over a glass of water, by British intelligence officers, well-spoken young men who introduced themselves with names like Matt and Richard.

'Was your client questioned by anyone other than Pakistanis after being tortured?'

'Yes.'

'Americans? . . . British? . . .'

Habib looked up at the light fitting, directing my gaze there. He then gave me a little smile. He wanted me to understand that we were not alone: others were interested in our conversation. As we stared at the light fitting, the answers hung in the air, unspoken and unsettling.

Two years earlier I had started making inquiries about the UK's support for the US rendition programme. It had become increasingly apparent that the CIA was using aircraft based in the United States to fly terrorism suspects around Central Asia and the Middle East, to be tortured. Those aircraft needed to refuel somewhere. That somewhere was, of course, the UK.

The Foreign Office had told me that it knew nothing about the use of UK territory or airspace during rendition operations, and the Foreign Secretary even went so far as to dismiss the whole matter as a conspiracy theory. It would, however, later emerge that between 2001 and 2005 the CIA's rendition planes had flown in and out of more than a dozen British airports on hundreds of occasions.

One Saturday morning, at the time when I was investigating the rendition claims, two words in a book review in *The Times* caught my eye. The article referred to a wartime detention centre I'd never heard of: the London Cage.

My Internet search for more details drew a blank, but an out-of-print book led eventually to some yellowing cuttings at the British Library's newspaper library, which in turn led to a handful of declassified files at the National Archives in Kew, to the south-west of London. Freedom of Information requests led to more government files being reluctantly handed over and I began to learn more about the torture centre that the British military had operated throughout the 1940s, in complete secrecy, in a row of Victorian villas in one of the most exclusive neighbourhoods in the capital.

The files at the National Archives also contained a couple of oblique references to another interrogation centre that the British had run during the Cold War, this time in the village of Bad Nenndorf, near Hanover. The taking of life there was not unknown. There were further hints in the files that other such facilities may have existed, not just in post-war Germany but also in North Africa, the Middle East and beyond. Throughout the post-war period, it seems that there had been a network of secret prisons, hidden from the Red Cross, where men thought to pose a threat to the state could be kept for years and systematically tormented. And what about later? In the early twenty-first century, a group of ageing former Mau Mau fighters had started proceedings against the British government, alleging that they had been systematically tortured in prison camps in Kenya in the 1950s. Their claims had been resisted every step of the way. And the more I probed, the more it seemed that there were other colonial misdeeds still deeply buried, both in the archives of the Foreign Office and in the memories of Britain's former subjects.

While it may be a commonplace of history that each generation interprets the past according to the anxieties and fashions of the present, these discoveries had a stark resonance in the post-9/11 era. As I continued to discover more about the way the British had conducted themselves in previous conflicts, I kept wondering about the way we were conducting ourselves today in the 'war on terror'. The British government may have been offering passive support to the CIA's rendition programme, but were they aware of how these terrorism suspects were being treated when they reached their destination, or did they choose not to know? And were 'Matt' and 'Richard' just making it up as they went along, or were they following orders?

None of this squared with Britain's reputation as a nation that prides itself on its love of fair play and respect for the rule of law. After all, the UK government had been among the first to sign the 1929 Geneva Convention on the treatment of prisoners of war, and the British were a driving force behind the European human rights agenda that was forged in the aftermath of the Second World War, becoming one of the first states to sign the European Convention on Human Rights in 1950. We had claimed the moral high ground when rallying the West against Iraq following the 1990 invasion of Kuwait and the first Gulf War that followed, and during the Kosovo conflict eight years later. Surely the British avoid torture, if only because it is British so to do?

Shortly after returning from Islamabad, I arranged to see a man who knows something of the darker workings of Britain's secret state and who, from time to time, has helped me with my inquiries, usually with some cryptic comment, a hint, a raised eyebrow.

I met this man – let's call him James – at a cafe near Liverpool Street Station in London and we shared a pot of Earl Grey. I mentioned the meeting I'd had with Rashid Rauf's lawyer. After studying the couple at the next table for a moment, James asked two questions that went far beyond those I'd been willing to ask myself: 'Do you think it's possible that the British government has a secret torture policy, one that it's determined nobody should ever know about? And if so, do you think it's possible that responsibility for that policy goes right to the very top?'

I paused, then told James that I tended to avoid conspiracy theories; that there was usually a better explanation for anything that we didn't fully understand.

James stared at me before pouring the tea.

The conversation moved on, but as we said goodbye I realised that there were a bewildering number of questions competing for my attention – questions that I'd been trying to avoid formulating for months. I had no idea where any of the answers might lie. I certainly had no notion of the enormous difficulties I would encounter as I started to look for those answers: the lies and the threats of people with monstrous secrets to hide; the silence of the victims, who were terrified that their torturers could return. But I knew I had to ask.

This is what I found.

Acronyms

CAC	Conduct After Capture
CIA	Central Intelligence Agency
CSDIC	Combined Services Detailed Interrogation Centre
DGFI	Directorate General of Forces Intelligence, a Bangladeshi intelligence agency
DRS	Département du Renseignement et de la Sécurité, Algerian intelligence agency
EITs	enhanced interrogation techniques
FBI	Federal Bureau of Investigation
ISC	Intelligence and Security Committee
ISI	The Directorate for Inter-Services Intelligence, a Pakistani Intelligence agency
IRA	Irish Republican Army
JFIT	Joint Forward Interrogation Team, a British military intelligence unit
JIC	The Joint Intelligence Committee of the British Cabinet Office
JSIO	Joint Services Intelligence Organisation, a British military intelligence unit
KGB	Committee for State Security, the Soviet intelligence and security service
LIFG	Libyan Islamic Fighting Group
MI5	The British Security Service
MI6	The British Secret Intelligence Service
MI8	The Radio Security Service, a WWII division of the War Office
MI9	A division of the British WWII Directorate of Military Intelligence
MI19	Division of British military intelligence responsible for obtaining information from prisoners of war
MOD	The Ministry of Defence
NATO	The North Atlantic Treaty Organisation
NKVD	The Peoples' Commissariat for Internal Affairs, predecessor of the KGB
POWs	Prisoners of War
PWIS	Prisoner of War Interrogation Section, a WWII British army unit
RAB	Rapid Action Battalion, a Bangladeshi paramilitary police unit
RUC	Royal Ulster Constabulary
R2I	Resistance to Interrogation

1

The Secrets of My Prison House:
The Second World War and Its Aftermath

'Never strike a man. It is unintelligent, for the spy will give an answer to please, an answer to escape punishment. And having given a false answer, all else depends upon the false premise.'

Colonel Robin Stephens,
Commandant, Camp 020, 1946

When Lionel Johnson Wood, a full colonel in the British Army, strode into his office in Horse Guards Avenue on the morning of 17 June 1954, he had every reason to assume that he was about to enjoy a pleasantly uneventful sort of day. Elsewhere in Britain's War Office, Johnson Wood's colleagues would be anguishing over the latest intelligence reports from Kenya and the increasingly bloody Mau Mau rebellion, or finalising the details of the mass redeployment of troops from the Suez Canal as a prelude to British withdrawal from Egypt.

But Johnson Wood's role at the War Office had nothing to do with the increasingly tricky business of the retreat from empire. His job was to read the small number of manuscripts submitted to the War Office each year by former soldiers, sailors and airmen who had served in the British armed forces during the Second World War. These were the literary efforts of men and women whose heroics, just a few years earlier, had been largely forgotten, and who hoped to find a new and lucrative market for their war stories. The colonel vetted their work from what he described as 'the security aspect' prior to publication.

After his secretary had brought him a mug of tea, Johnson Wood hoped to snatch a few cosy minutes with that day's *Times* crossword – '17 across, military formation, seven letters' – and make plans for the weekend. It was raining outside, but who knew what Saturday might bring?

At some point during that day the War Office messenger boys brought Johnson Wood a new manuscript to read. It was about the size of a telephone directory and had been wrapped in brown paper. Accompanying the manuscript was a letter from Messrs John Farquharson Ltd, Literary Agents, of Red Lion Square, London WC1.

Not long after Johnson Wood had reached the last page of the proposed book, perfect pandemonium erupted at the War Office. The manuscript and its disturbing contents were referred rapidly upwards through the chain of command. Before long the document was being examined by the Army Council, the supreme decision-making body of the British Army. The Council sought the advice of the Attorney General, the Director of Public Prosecutions, the Foreign Office and even MI5.

The author of the manuscript was Alexander Scotland, a retired colonel who had been commanding officer of a clandestine wartime torture centre that the British military operated in a row of Victorian mansions in Kensington Palace Gardens, one of the capital's most exclusive addresses. During the course of the war, thousands of Germans has passed through this secret prison, known as the London Cage, where they were beaten, deprived of sleep and forced to assume stress positions for days at a time. Some were told that they were to be murdered and their bodies quietly buried. Others were informed that they were to be subjected to unnecessary surgery, carried out by people with no medical qualifications.

The manuscript made clear that these horrors did not end with the cessation of hostilities: the centre continued to operate for more than three years after the end of the war. Among those interrogated during the post-war years were members of the German military and police who were accused of war crimes. Many were hanged on the basis of their 'confessions'. More disturbing, Scotland's manuscript disclosed that junior German soldiers who were to be called as prosecution witnesses at the war crimes trials of their superiors were sent to the torture centre, where they spent months, even years, being prepared for their day in court.

The War Office and Foreign Office officials, the men from MI5 and the government lawyers who read the manuscript were all in agreement: police must be dispatched at once to raid Scotland's home, and more men must be sent to the offices of John Farquharson Ltd and the proposed publishers, Evans Brothers. Every copy of the manuscript must be seized immediately. All those who knew of its contents must be silenced, if necessary through threat of prosecution and imprisonment under the Official Secrets Act.

This is exactly what happened. But among the War Office and MI5 officials who had seen the manuscript were a number who knew that the potential problem did not end with Colonel Scotland. They knew that his was not the only secret interrogation centre that the British had operated during the Second World War and in the early days of the Cold War. There had been others, many others, in the London suburbs, in North Africa and the Middle East, in Delhi, in liberated Belgium and in post-war Germany and Italy. And within these secret places, men had suffered far worse torments than anything Scotland had managed to devise.

By late 1938, when it was clear that war with Germany was inevitable, the British armed forces devoted considerable thought to the four means by which intelligence about the enemy would be gathered. These were espionage; aerial reconnaissance, particularly photography; signals intercepts; and intelligence flowing from direct contact with the enemy, which meant captured documents and, critically, information extracted during interrogation.

There was no real knowledge of what direction the war would follow, of course, nor of the numbers of prisoners that would fall into British hands. Certainly, nobody could have foreseen that around 960,000 enemy prisoners would be under British control by the end of the war, 535,000 of them imprisoned in Britain itself.

At the outset of the war, two military organisations specialised in the interrogation of enemy prisoners. They were an army unit called the Prisoner of War Interrogation Section, or PWIS, and a War Office organisation known as the Combined Services Detailed Interrogation Centre, or CSDIC. Both were ultimately controlled by MI9, and later by MI19, divisions of the Directorate of Military Intelligence at the War Office.

A third body also came to be deeply involved with interrogation after the war began. This was the Security Service, or MI5, a civilian organisation, albeit one that worked closely with the War Office and which was largely staffed by former military men.

PWIS established nine so-called 'cages' around the country at which enemy prisoners would undergo an initial interrogation, to establish whether they should be subjected to further examination before being packed off to a prisoner of war camp. Three – at Doncaster in South Yorkshire, at Kempton Park, south-west of London, and at Lingfield, Surrey – were hastily converted racecourses. Another was the ground of Preston North End football club in Lancashire.

Some of the guards at the cages were drawn from the ranks of the estimated 10,000 Germans and Austrians who had enlisted in the British armed forces after fleeing the Nazis. Most of these men and women were Jewish, but many were non-Jewish political opponents of the regime, while some were artists who had fled after being branded 'degenerates' at home. After questioning at the cages, prisoners thought to possess valuable information that needed to be extracted through further questioning would be passed either to the PWIS interrogation centre known as the London Cage or to CSDIC.

CSDIC was created in March 1939, bringing together a small number of German-speaking officers and NCOs from all three branches of the armed forces. It would be their responsibility to extract both military and technical information from captured prisoners of war.

Initially the organisation was housed at the Tower of London, where cells were set aside for just ten prisoners. On 29 August, five days before Britain declared war on Germany, a directive issued by Air Commodore Kenneth Buss, head of intelligence at the Royal Air Force, showed just how modest an organisation CSDIC was at that time. 'Two RAF intelligence officers for interrogation purposes and one clerk will be attached to this organisation,' Buss ordered.[1]

CSDIC expanded rapidly once the war began, however, and a new home was found at Trent Park, a mansion near Cockfosters on the outskirts of north London. Post Office engineers fitted microphones in the light fittings of many of the rooms and cells, allowing the British to listen to prisoners talking to each other between interrogation sessions. The microphones were so sensitive that they could pick up even whispered conversations. Later, this eavesdropping technique was refined through the use of stool pigeons, prisoners who had been 'turned' by their captors and who could lure their comrades into interesting areas of conversation. These devices, and the intelligence derived from them, were given the codename 'M Cover' and became a feature of every British interrogation centre.

★

Before the war began, MI5 had viewed the prospect of dirtying its hands through the actual conduct of interrogation with some disdain. In May 1939, Harry Allen, a senior Security Service officer, wrote to the Directorate of Military Intelligence to inform it that 'as a general principle interrogation of enemy prisoners who have fallen out of the sky or who have been landed from ships' would be a War Office matter.[2] MI5 was unable to remain aloof from such matters once war was declared, however. Soon it was being called upon to question non-Britons detained under the Aliens Registration Act; next it was expected to turn its attention to refugees from Europe.

MI5 commandeered the Royal Victoria Patriotic School, an orphanage in Wandsworth, south London, for the screening of refugees,[3] as well as opening outstations in Glasgow, Bristol and Liverpool, and in Poole, Dorset, from where a seaplane service to Lisbon and back operated throughout the war.

The screening operation was run by MI5's B Division, which was responsible for counter-espionage. Guy Liddell, the head of B Division, was assisted in this unfamiliar work by Dick White, the first university graduate to join MI5, and one of the first without a military background. White – who considered the screening to be 'distasteful'[4] – would go on to be head of both MI5 and MI6, a unique achievement. On the basis of his experiences during the war, White also became a firm believer in the utility of interrogation. Over the next three decades he would play a significant role in its use by the British.

By late 1939, PWIS, CSDIC and MI5 were all in the interrogation business.

The following summer, following Allied military failure in Norway and with German forces racing across France and the Low Countries towards the English Channel, the British government was slow to comprehend the simple reasons for the enemy's stunning series of victories: better equipment, superior tactics and a martial spirit that was simply superior to that of either the British or the French. Instead, ministers and many members of the public convinced themselves that more devious forces were at work. They believed the advances could be attributed to fifth columnists operating behind the lines, legions of spies and saboteurs who were aiding the German advance.

And if fifth columnists had been in place on the Continent, they reasoned, they must be lurking in Britain also, waiting for the signal to strike.

Before long, MI5 was receiving up to 8,200 calls each week from increasingly nervous government departments wanting help with suspected spies and suspicious activities.[5] Birds of prey were trained to intercept the carrier pigeons that were feared to be bearing messages across the Channel to Nazi spies in the south-east of England. One unfortunate new recruit to MI5 was given the task of inspecting every telegraph pole along the south coast, with orders to report on any coded messages that he found scratched upon them.[6] Stretched beyond its capacity, the service came close to collapse.

It was all a disastrous waste of MI5's time; it soon became clear that there were no fifth columnists at work in Britain. The only people who could with any certainty be said to have posed a security threat were a young cipher clerk at the US embassy in London who was passing copies of secret telegrams to a Russian émigré with links to the Italian secret service, and a forty-two-year-old German woman in Hampshire, married to an RAF sergeant, who encouraged two local members of the British Union of Fascists to arm themselves in advance of an invasion.

Nevertheless, spy fever continued to sweep the county, and among the many who succumbed was Winston Churchill. Within days of succeeding Neville Chamberlain as prime minister on 10 May, Churchill reached the conclusion that Vernon Kell, the sixty-six-year-old who had been director general of MI5 since its inception in 1909, was no longer fit to lead the organisation. Kell was summarily dismissed and a senior MI5 officer, Jasper Harker, given the rank of acting director general. In reality, however, the service came under the control of a highly secretive Whitehall committee, the Security Executive, which had been established within a month of Churchill entering Downing Street.

The Security Executive was chaired by Philip Cunliffe-Lister, the 1st Earl of Swinton, a prominent Conservative politician who had been Air Secretary before the war. Lord Swinton appointed as his deputy Sir Joseph Ball, head of the Conservative Party's research department, who had served as an MI5 interrogator during the First World War. Ball in turn brought on board a London solicitor and insurance industry investigator called William Crocker, who was appointed a deputy director of MI5. The executive's secretary was a young Oxford-educated barrister called Kenneth Diplock.

Over the next few months, under Lord Swinton's control, MI5 underwent a period of rapid expansion. Regional liaison officers were appointed to work alongside the twelve regional commissioners who would be responsible for governing areas of the UK in the event of an invasion. B Division drafted in a remarkable array of playboys, army officers, journalists and academics. Other divisions preferred to recruit lawyers. Typical of these new recruits was Richard Butler, a London solicitor who became private secretary to Sir David Petrie, who was appointed director general of MI5 in April 1941 and would lead the organisation for the rest of the war. Butler would never have been tolerated at MI5 while Kell was director general: he was a Roman Catholic and Kell would not employ Catholics. As he was fond of explaining, the Vatican had the finest intelligence service in the world and he was not going to give it an opportunity to infiltrate his Security Service.[7]

Lord Swinton was deeply sceptical of MI5's ability to

interrogate suspects, arguing, for example, that its officers did not know how to talk to working-class people.[8] Encouraged by Crocker and Ball, he pressed the Home Office for permission to open an MI5 interrogation centre and the Home Office reluctantly agreed. A number of locations were considered and rejected before MI5 decided upon Latchmere House, a Victorian mansion near Ham Common, south-west of London, that had been purchased by the War Office during the 1914–18 war for use as a hospital for officers suffering from 'shell shock'.[9]

The centre was given a codename, Camp 020, adopted from an internment centre, Camp 001, that had been established in the hospital wing of Dartmoor Prison in Devon.[10] In theory, the Home Office was responsible for Camp 020; in practice its management was delegated entirely to Liddell and White of MI5's B Division. A former officer of the Indian Army, Robin Stephens, who had joined MI5 at the outbreak of war, was appointed commandant. Thirty rooms were turned into cells, with strong doors and hidden 'M Cover' microphones. Two rows of barbed-wire fencing were erected around the grounds.

By June 1940, MI5's secret interrogation centre was ready for its first customers, most of whom were not captured Germans but Britons who had fallen under suspicion.

A few days before the outbreak of war, Parliament had passed emergency legislation that included Defence Regulation 18B, which suspended the right of habeas corpus for those considered too sympathetic to Nazi Germany. By July 1940, 1,373 men and women had been detained under Defence Regulation 18B, many of them members of Sir Oswald Mosley's British Union of Fascists. A small number were selected for special treatment at Camp 020.

One of these guinea pigs was the BUF's director of policy, Alexander Raven Thomson, a forty-year-old philosopher and industrialist. Thomson was awakened early one morning in his cell in Brixton Prison, south London, marched along the wing and through a back gate, and handed over to a military escort waiting in the courtyard.

After the war, Thomson explained what had happened next: 'Packed in an army van we were driven through Richmond Park to Ham Common, where we found a large house and out-buildings completely surrounded by a double row of barbed wire with patrolling guards carrying fixed bayonets.'[11] For the next five weeks he was kept in solitary confinement, fed on rations so meagre that his weight plummeted, and woken frequently at night. He and his fellow inmates were allowed two half-hour periods of exercise, morning and night, but were threatened at gunpoint if they attempted to talk to each other.

'Week after drear week passed. Some of us were pulled from our beds in the middle of the night, brought before a secret tribunal of men sitting at a table behind glaring lights.' The BUF men were questioned about their links with Nazi Germany, their party's finances and the location of a number of pro-German English-language radio stations broadcasting to the UK. Most of the interrogations centred on the command structure, strength and disposition of the non-existent fifth column.

The army guards, who were armed with revolvers, appeared largely to be conscripted coal miners from West Yorkshire. The MI5 interrogators all wore military uniforms. A group of people detained under the Aliens Registration Act were held in another part of the building. Thomson was placed in a cell in this wing for a while, where he was 'kept awake the greater part of one night by the broken-hearted sobbing of one little man' in the next cell.

Some of the British fascists were held in cells that were brightly lit twenty-four hours a day, while others were in cells kept in total darkness. They would be moved from one location to another without notice. All were threatened with being shot or hanged. Charlie Watts, a BUF organiser from London, came to believe it might happen: 'The possibility of a brick wall and a firing squad didn't seem quite so remote.' Most of the men assumed that if the Germans did invade, they would not be permitted to leave Camp 020 alive.

Around twenty-seven BUF members were interrogated at Camp 020, among them a Brighton police officer, a London cab driver and a number of journalists. The interrogation of British nationals at Camp 020 all but ended in November 1940, however, when the Home Office, alarmed at what it was learning about the methods employed, ordered that MI5 must obtain special authorisation in future.

Alexander Raven Thomson later dismissed the interrogation regime as a 'theatrical display of tawdry imitation of what they presumably conceived to be Gestapo methods'. He and the others had been manhandled by the guards, but never assaulted during interrogation: 'Our whole experience of Ham Common was one of crass stupidity and brutal callousness.' Nevertheless, by the time Thomson was returned to Brixton Prison he had lost two stone in weight and he later suffered a nervous breakdown.

Another of the BUF detainees, Compton Domvile, the son of an admiral, found that his memory was badly damaged: 'Certain periods of my life completely disappeared from my mind. Others who shared my experiences at Ham Common have since remarked on similar symptoms in themselves. The resident doctor . . . stated to me plainly that the treatment was intended to produce a state of "mental atrophy and extreme loquacity".'[12]

After their release from Camp 020, the BUF men were interned for the remainder of the war. Some went to Stafford Prison or to one of two camps on the Isle of Man. Many languished for years at Camp 020R at Huntercombe Place, near Henley, west of London, a private prison that MI5 had established without the authority of the Home Office, much to the concern of some in Whitehall.[13]

Only once the war was over were the first inmates of Camp 020 able to explain what had happened there. Few people listened, however, and even fewer cared. After all, they were fascists.

Shortly after the fall of France, and the chaotic evacuation from Dunkirk of the British Expeditionary Force and some 140,000 French troops, Anthony Eden, the Secretary of State for War, convened a meeting at a hotel in York to discuss the impending German invasion. Sir John Dill, the new Chief of the Imperial General Staff, was there, along with the commanding officers of every army unit based in the north of England.

There was, according to one of those present, 'an almost audible gasp all around the table' when Eden asked these officers whether their men could be relied upon to continue the fight following an invasion.[14] Some thought the question impertinent. But Eden explained that the government had decided it would be 'definitely unwise' to ask poorly armed troops to continue a futile struggle against a well-equipped enemy once that enemy was firmly entrenched in the south of England. As one historian has commented, it seems the British would have fought them on the beaches, but not as far north as Yorkshire.

Eden had a second question. Would British troops follow an order to embark at a northern port, such as Liverpool, while it remained in British control, in order to be withdrawn to Canada? All those present were of the opinion that while a large proportion of regular officers and NCOs would agree to be evacuated, along with unmarried men, they could not be sure that officers and men who had recently joined the armed forces or men with families would agree to leave. There was every chance that the majority of British troops would refuse to carry on the fight from overseas, just as most French troops had not left for Britain earlier that month.

It was all the more important, therefore, that the enemy be

prevented from landing in the first place. And the interrogators at CSDIC, PWIS and MI5 would be expected to contribute to that effort.

A little after 9 a.m. on 3 September 1940, Mabel Cole, the landlady of the Rising Sun pub in Lydd, a small town on the south coast in Kent, was slightly surprised to see a young man step through the door and stride up to the bar. Her surprise turned to suspicion when the man asked in a foreign accent for a bottle of sparkling cider and a pack of cigarettes. Only someone with very little knowledge of Britain and its licensing laws would assume they could buy alcohol at that time of the day. Mabel told the young man he could buy cigarettes in the shop across the road. As he turned to leave, he smacked his head on the bar's traditional, low-beamed ceiling.[15]

The man with the sore head was twenty-three-year-old Carl Meier, a Dutch-born Nazi Party member who had spent some time in Birmingham before the war. He was one of four agents that the German military intelligence service, the Abwehr, had landed in Britain the previous night. The team had slipped across the English Channel aboard a trawler before being put into a pair of dinghies to paddle the final few miles to the coast. The bungling Meier was quickly arrested. His three comrades were also soon located and taken into custody, along with their food supplies and a radio transmitter.

Meier and his three comrades, Jose Waldberg (thirty-five), a German Abwehr veteran, Charles van den Kieboom (twenty-five), a Dutch-Japanese dual national, and Sjoerd Pons (twenty-eight), a Dutchman, were rushed to Camp 020 for interrogation.

Eventually, all four were charged under the Treachery Act, legislation introduced a few months earlier to deal with anticipated foreign spies. They were tried in camera at the Old Bailey. The jury accepted Pons's defence that he had agreed to join the Abwehr only when threatened with deportation to a concentration camp after being arrested for currency offences. On being freed by the court, he was immediately detained under Defence Regulation 18B. Meier, Waldberg and van den Kieboom were found guilty and hanged at Pentonville Prison on 10 December 1940. Shortly afterwards, a statement about the case was released to the press and the BBC, in order that the British public should learn of the measures that MI5's B Division were taking to protect the nation, and the Abwehr understand the fate that had befallen the first of their spies to attempt to operate in the UK.

While at Camp 020 the four men had all made long state-ments to their interrogators.[16] These were extracted at speed, suggesting that MI5 had employed methods other than the patient starvation and disorientation techniques used against the British fascists. As a result of these interrogations, MI5 began to learn about Operation Lena, which was to be the Abwehr's contribution to Hitler's plan for the German invasion of Britain. The four spies had been ordered to reconnoitre beach defences and possible landing strips for gliders. They had supplies for a week or two at most and had received no training to enable them to blend into British society. One, Waldberg, could not speak a word of English.

Clearly, the four spies were expecting German forces to join them at any time. MI5's interrogators realised that their opposite numbers in the Abwehr believed the invasion to be just days away.

The first phase of the Battle of Britain had opened on 10 July 1940 with the bombing of British shipping and ports. Six days later Hitler ordered the preparation of a plan for the invasion of the British Isles. Codenamed Sealion, the plan called for the RAF to be largely eliminated. Invasion barges began to gather at the Channel ports and Alfred Jodl, Chief of the Operations Staff of the German Armed Forces High Command, drew up plans for the landing of twenty divisions between Ramsgate in Kent and Lyme Regis in Dorset.

On the afternoon of 7 September, four days after the capture of the four Abwehr spies, a 350-bomber attack on London's docks signalled the start of the Blitz. That night the Luftwaffe returned with 247 aircraft, 352 tons of high explosive and 400 incendiary bombs. The raid was so enormous that the Chiefs of Staff issued a coded alert, the word 'Cromwell', to indicate that they believed the invasion to be imminent.

Despite the scale of the attacks, the RAF enjoyed extraordinary advantages over its foe. It had radar and a ground-to-air radio telephone system, Spitfire fighters that could perform tighter turns than any German aircraft, and the fuel-saving advantage of fighting close to home.

CSDIC was determined to give it another advantage: intelligence on the enemy's plans, equipment and tactics. By the time the battle reached its zenith in mid-September, the British claimed to have captured 967 downed German air crew. They proved to be a rich source of intelligence for CSDIC. The interrogators quickly produced reports not only about the Luftwaffe's order of battle but also on general areas such as morale, training and tactics, perceptions of the RAF's strengths and weaknesses, and technical matters such as new German tracer ammunition.[17]

There is little doubt that the interrogators were using brute force to extract some of this information. Sir Harry Hinsley, the official historian of British intelligence during the war, wrote that, after being placed under army guard, captured German air crew would be encouraged to become aggressive. At this point, the guards would become 'rough and ready', and the interrogators would issue various threats.

The POWs would then be taken to Trent Park. Before long there were so many prisoners crammed into the old house that CSDIC needed more space. Additional facilities were eventually found at Latimer House, a large mock-Jacobean country house overlooking a valley near Chesham in Buckinghamshire, and at Wilton Park, another grand country house six miles to the south near Beaconsfield.

With hindsight, it is possible to see that Britain was unlikely to have been invaded. Hitler was surprised by his rapid success in France and, rather than immerse himself in the details of Operation Sealion, he chose to go sightseeing in Paris, before returning to his Alpine retreat at Berchtesgaden. He told Jodl that the British would understand that their war was lost if he gave them time to think about it.[18]

In any case, the flat-bottomed barges that the Germans plan-ned to use for the invasion had been designed for navigating the Rhine, not for crossing open water. The Royal Navy could have sunk them with the wake from its passing ships. By October the weather ensured that the Channel could not be crossed in such craft.

By that time, the handful of people who were privy to German cipher decrypts were aware that the invasion had been postponed, but the British government chose to keep the country on a state of high alert.

Unaware of this intelligence at this stage, and without the benefit of hindsight, Britain's interrogators believed they were grappling with an existential threat to the nation. These remained desperate days that demanded desperate measures, they thought. And desperate measures called for determined men.

If interrogation is an art, Alexander Scotland, the man who ran the London Cage and whose post-war literary ambitions would trigger such panic at the War Office, considered himself to be something of an old master.

A retired military intelligence officer, Scotland was fifty-seven when war was declared. Nevertheless, the following year he was recalled to duty and asked to assist with the interrogation of the small numbers of German troops being captured during the British retreat to Dunkirk.

After the First World War Scotland had been awarded the Order of the British Empire 'for valuable services rendered' interrogating German prisoners of war. He had found himself in this role because he not only spoke German but had for a number of years served in the German Army.

Born in Middlesbrough, one of nine children of a railway engineer, Scotland had left school at fourteen. He worked as an office boy in London, spent a year in Australia and then decided to sail to South Africa in the hope of serving in the British Army during the Boer War. By the time he arrived the war was over and instead he found work as a trader on the border with the German colony of Deutsch-Südwestafrika, which is now Namibia. His biggest customers were locally based German troops and, in order to get round a regulation stipulating that certain supplies must be provided only by the German Army itself, it was suggested that he should join up and be given a uniform and rifle.

He spent almost four years serving in the German Army under the name Schottland. During this time, German forces were waging what was then known as the Hottentot Wars. A century later, the German government would admit that these had not been wars, but the twentieth century's first act of genocide, an attempt to wipe out the Herero and Namaqua peoples, who were resisting colonisation of their land. Scotland later claimed to have taken part in what he described as 'a number of battles' during this episode.[19]

Scotland left the German Army at the end of this campaign but remained in the colony and, according to one British military intelligence report compiled after he had submitted his manuscript to the War Office, 'gave some assistance to the British authorities from time to time'.[20] On the outbreak of war in 1914, the Germans, quite correctly suspecting there to be a spy in their midst, arrested Scotland and detained him for a year in the colony's capital, Windhoek.

This period of incarceration gave Scotland his first experience of interrogation, albeit on the receiving end. 'During the long, arduous questioning I was given by the staff officer attached to the German colonial troops, I learned perhaps the most valuable lesson of my career in South Africa,' he later wrote. 'From that officer, a Lieutenant Hepka, I acquired some of the techniques of interrogating an enemy subject.'[21] What those techniques were, Scotland chose not to say.

Finding himself back in the interrogation business two decades later, Scotland assisted with the establishment of the chain of PWIS interrogation centre cages. He then took command of the cage that was being established in London.

The London District Cage was located at 6, 7 and 8 Kensington Palace Gardens, a row of grandiose Victorian villas built in the 1840s by a developer called John Marriott Blashfield. The road was, quite possibly, the most exclusive address in the city. The interrogation rooms, the cells and Scotland's office were located in numbers 6 and 7, while number 8 became the guardroom. It appears that several prisoners were also held and interrogated at number 8 and it is likely that this is where some of worst torture took place.

Nine officers and twelve NCOs served under Scotland's command at the Cage. Most of the officers were interrogators, while the NCOs, who included a number of Germans, were interpreters, translators and typists.[22] There was room for sixty prisoners at any one time and five interrogation rooms. Security was provided by soldiers from Guards regiments, selected, one War Office record noted, 'for their height rather than their brains'.

Initially the prisoners were to be interrogated in an attempt to extract military intelligence, but from 1945 onwards they were questioned about war crimes.

In his unpublished manuscript, Scotland recalled how he would muse, on arriving at the Cage each morning: '"Abandon all hope ye who enter here." For if any German had any information we wanted, it was invariably extracted from him in the long run.'[23]

Colonel Scotland's opposite number at Camp 020 was Colonel Robin Stephens. If Scotland was the old master of British interrogation, Stephens regarded himself as a pioneer, a representative of the avant-garde.

Born in Egypt to British parents in 1900, Stephens was educated at Dulwich College, the south London public school, before being commissioned into the Indian Army. He fought in a number of campaigns and was mentioned in dispatches. On returning to London he studied law, but failed to qualify and dabbled in journalism before joining MI5.

Stephens was known to all as 'Tin Eye', because of the monocle that was permanently fixed to his right eye. It is unlikely to have been a term of affection: he had a fearsome reputation as a temperamental bully.

A widely travelled man, he could speak Urdu and Arabic as well as German, French and Italian. His travels had not led him to respect foreigners, however: his post-war writings show him to have been an extraordinarily xenophobic individual. Spaniards, for example, were 'obstinate, stubborn, immoral and immutable', while Italy was 'a country peopled by undersized, posturing folk'. Two of his prisoners, he said, had been 'abnormally intelligent for Icelanders, but still not over-intelligent', while of another he noted: 'Because he was a good Frenchman, he accepted the German's money.' He disliked 'shifty, Polish Jews'. Most of all, however, he loathed 'the Hun'.[24]

Stephens arranged for an additional ninety-two-cell block to be added to Camp 020 and more 'M Cover' to be installed. There was also to be a punishment room, the notorious Cell 13, which was completely bare, with smooth walls and a linoleum floor.[25]

Camp 020 had a resident medical officer, Harold Dearden, who had been recruited by Lord Swinton's Security Executive and asked to help devise an interrogation regime.

Dearden had served as a medical officer in the Grenadier Guards during the First World War, being wounded twice and losing both an eye and his speech. Following the war he taught himself to speak once more and appears to have built upon this experience to apply himself to psychiatry without any formal training.

During the 1930s, he specialised in the treatment of what he described as 'functional disorders of the nervous system'. Many of his patients were members of the leisured classes, people 'immune from vulgar financial anxieties', as he put it, and he supplemented his handsome income by penning popular psychology and self-help guides for the *Daily Mail* and the *Home Journal*.

Dearden dreamed up the regimes of starvation and of sleep and sensory deprivation that were intended to break the will of Camp 020's first inmates.[26] At Camp 020 he would test the effectiveness of his theories by participating in interrogations himself, bewildering inmates by appearing alongside the immaculately uniformed Stephens in a crumpled civilian suit, often with a smudge of tobacco ash down the front.

Dearden experimented in techniques of torment that left few marks, methods that could be denied by the torturers and that civil servants and government ministers could disown. The seeds Dearden sowed at Camp 020 would take root and bear fruit during Britain's post-war colonial conflicts around the globe and closer to home in Northern Ireland in the early 1970s. Almost seventy years later, in 2008, the British Army in Iraq was still employing some of the techniques that Dearden pioneered.

By the time Camp 020 closed, six months after the end of the war, a total of 480 people had passed through its gates. Seventy-seven of them were German, sixty-eight Belgian and sixty-four French, but there were prisoners from thirty-four different countries, including Canada, Ireland, Japan and Egypt.[27] The object of their interrogation, Stephens told his officers, was simple: 'Truth in the shortest possible time'.[28]

Although the British fascists incarcerated in Camp 020 had nothing of interest to say to their interrogators, many of the subsequent inmates were of the highest-possible intelligence value. Principal among them were the Abwehr spies who followed in the footsteps of the four captured at Lydd, many of whom were 'turned' and persuaded – or maybe forced – to work for MI5 in one of the most stunning intelligence coups of the war.

Agents who fell into British hands would, before long, relay back to Germany a series of radio messages that contained a blend of misinformation and genuine intelligence. A group of intelligence officers and academics, established at the suggestion of Liddell and White in November 1940 and known as the Twenty Committee – from the Roman numerals XX, or Double Cross – decided what real secrets should be divulged. If a spy refused to cooperate, messages would be sent back to Germany on his or her behalf. The messages not only sowed disinformation in the mind of the enemy but also encouraged the Abwehr to send more spies, by boat or by parachute, each of whom was then captured and put to use. Some of the double agents were so trusted by their German masters that generous funds were supplied to reward networks of newly recruited local spies, which, of course, did not exist. In this way, MI5 tricked the Nazis into paying for the entire Double Cross operation.

MI5 was never completely sure that it controlled all German spies sent to Britain, although as the conflict progressed German cipher decrypts suggested this to be the case. And after the war it was established that all but one German agent had been intercepted and either turned or neutralised by MI5. The exception was a Dutchman, Englebertus Fukken, who shot himself in an air-raid shelter in Cambridge in March 1941 after working undercover in Britain for five months.

The Twenty Committee was chaired by John Masterman, an Oxford history don who had been Dick White's mentor at Christ Church and who had been recruited to MI5 at White's suggestion. Writing twenty-five years after the war, Sir John, as he was by then, noted that few spies are of a 'Spartan breed' and that 'many, perhaps a majority, of them are ready and even willing to commit treachery either under pressure or for simple reasons of self preservation'. He added that the British did more than simply practise large-scale deception through Double Cross. 'By means of the double agent system *we actively ran and controlled the German espionage system in this country*.'[29] The italics are Sir John's and no doubt he was entitled to them.

The interrogators at Camp 020 had the benefit of the intercepts of Abwehr signals from the Ultra programme at Bletchley Park, although none were informed of the source of this intelligence until the spring of 1941. But this cannot fully explain their success. What was the nature of the pressure that was, according to Masterman, applied to persuade German spies to commit treachery? Were they subjected only to the regime inflicted upon the BUF prisoners, with sleep deprivation, starvation, threats and prolonged periods of isolation? The spies needed to be turned quickly after capture, to prevent their Abwehr masters becoming suspicious about prolonged radio silence and to ensure that their subsequent messages were trusted. How was this achieved?

Sir John chose not to say.*

---

* Writing about the Double Cross system in the 1970s, Masterman dropped a heavy hint that British intelligence also controlled a secret prison in Lisbon during the war.

★

From its humble beginnings at the Tower of London, meanwhile, CSDIC grew rapidly, as Luftwaffe and Kriegsmarine prisoners were joined by enemy soldiers captured in Norway, France and North Africa. Those in the know pronounced the acronym as Sizdik. Few were in the know, however. CSDIC succeeded in protecting more than its methods from prying eyes: its very existence was a closely guarded secret.

In October 1941, for example, a full five months after he was appointed vice-chief of the Imperial General Staff, General Henry Royds Pownall was handed a secret briefing paper that disclosed the existence of CSDIC and explained the organisation's work. It read: 'CSDIC is administered by the War Office on behalf of all three services and has the duty of extracting all forms of information from enemy P/W by special methods of interrogation. It is no exaggeration to say that the results achieved are of the greatest operational importance to all three services.'[30] The paper had nothing further to say about the 'special methods of interrogation' that were being employed.

CSDIC's use of 'M Cover' required large teams of technicians, translators and typists to assist with the work of the interrogators. Recordings were made on wax or shellac discs before being labelled and archived. Many of those involved in this work were Germans and Austrians serving in the British Army. The monitors were all sergeants and the rooms where they worked always had a letter M on the door. These rooms were nicknamed Mother, and Mother, the joke went, was always listening.[31]

Violence was often not needed, of course: there were plenty of prisoners who cooperated willingly, either because of their anti-Nazi convictions or a desire to ingratiate themselves with their captors. On occasion, the intelligence gathered through the 'M' devices appears to have been far more valuable than that extracted through direct interrogation.

But although CSDIC's methods were at times highly

sophisticated, violence was also employed. The speed at which its interrogators were able to compile extremely detailed reports based upon the interrogation of submarine crews, for example, despite the extraordinary resilience of the men who served on U-boats, must have left those receiving the intelligence with little doubt that coercion was involved.

Shortly after the war, events in Germany would show that the methods used at a CSDIC prison could be even more brutal than those employed at the Cage. And once again, steps would need to be taken to prevent the truth about Britain's use of torture from seeping out into the world.

By August 1940, the War Office decided that CSDIC was so effective that a new branch should be established in Egypt. A suitable location was found at Ma'adi, six miles from the army's Cairo headquarters, and by the end of the year an interrogation centre was processing up to sixty prisoners at a time.

CSDIC's Middle East operation expanded over the next two years and a number of mobile units were created, equipped with huts that could be quickly erected and fitted with 'M' devices. By the end of the war, more than 200 officers, 100 NCOs and around 2,000 men had served with CSDIC in the Middle East. Their work took them to Iraq, Palestine, Syria, Sicily, Italy, Malta and Greece, as well as North Africa.[32]

CSDIC interrogators in Cairo began to experiment with the use of drugs, such as amphetamines and thyroxine. One interrogator, Alexander Kennedy, went further and combined these with hypnosis and 'ambiguous sounds and visual stimuli' in an attempt to trigger hallucinations.[33]

Before the war, Major Kennedy had trained in London as a physician and psychiatrist. His studies had taken him to Johns Hopkins University in Baltimore, where he had conducted research into the interrogation methods of the city's police department. An amateur boxer and keen rugby player, he had been commissioned into the army in 1939 and assigned first to the Special Operations Executive before being sent to Cairo.

Kennedy soon began to attract a number of visitors eager to learn more about his work. Among them was Dick White of MI5's B Division, who witnessed Kennedy's interrogation of a German spy called Elie Haggar. White was less than impressed and made clear that he favoured more direct methods, not least because Kennedy was taking weeks to extract information that White believed could be obtained in hours.[34]

When the United States entered the war in December 1941, it formed a similar organisation called the Combined Services Detailed Interrogation Center. Declassified British records show that its officers travelled to the UK to study CSDIC's methods, and some of its trainees were also admitted to the London Cage. From 1943, it was agreed that prisoners sent to any CSDIC prison were available for joint British and US interrogation, irrespective of the nationality of their captors.[35]

As the war progressed, CSDIC outposts were established across the Mediterranean: at Beirut, Algiers and, later in the war, Naples and Rome. One unit operated from the Red Fort in Delhi. Teams of interrogators travelled to the front from Delhi, searching for Japanese prisoners to interrogate, but they found precious few subjects. Those who could be found were difficult to crack, the interrogators told London, becoming 'surly and uncommunicative' following harsh treatment. After a while, they decided to concentrate on those prisoners who were dying.[36]

By early 1945, CSDIC was so well resourced that the many thousands of recordings of captured POWs that it made onto wax and shellac discs at its interrogation centres around the globe were flown back to Britain by its own small fleet of aircraft. CSDIC guarded these recordings jealously and had no intention of entrusting them to the RAF.

★

With the end of the war in sight the London Cage was redesignated a War Crimes Investigation Unit and its interrogators switched from extracting military intelligence to securing convictions. Of the 3,573 prisoners who passed through Kensington Palace Gardens, more than 1,000 were persuaded to either sign a confession or give a witness statement for use during war crimes prosecutions.

Among those processed at the Cage at this time were several individuals accused of shooting fifty RAF officers who had been recaptured after a mass breakout from Stalag Luft III in Lower Silesia in 1944. The murders – which were later the subject of the 1963 Hollywood film *The Great Escape* – aroused enormous public anger when word reached Britain. Of the twenty-one accused, fourteen were hanged after a war crimes trial in Hamburg. The remainder were sentenced to lengthy terms of imprisonment. Many of them had confessed only after being interrogated by Scotland and his men. One of the suspects died at the Cage, with Scotland informing the War Office that he had hanged himself.

Throughout the war, the existence of the London Cage had been carefully concealed from the International Committee of the Red Cross, but early in 1946 the ICRC became aware of its location after a British officer inadvertently included its name and address on a list of POW camps sent to the organisation. In a lengthy memo to the War Office, Scotland explained that he had identified the officer responsible and the man had promised 'that this blunder would not be repeated'.

A Red Cross inspector, Frederick Bieri, called twice at the Cage in March 1946 but was turned away. Scotland argued that the Red Cross need not be admitted because his prisoners were either civilians or 'criminals within the armed forces', and neither, he claimed, were protected by the Geneva Convention. Should the Red Cross be allowed inside the Cage, he added, he would instruct the RAF to stop sending him prisoners suspected of involvement in the Stalag Luft III murders. 'The interrogation of these criminals must proceed in Germany under conditions more closely related to police methods than to Geneva Convention principles,' he wrote.

It was a further eighteen months before the Red Cross was given permission to enter the Cage. Its inspector found little evidence of ill-treatment but, as he noted in subsequent reports, he later discovered that the ten prisoners who had been in the worst physical condition had been spirited away to other POW camps shortly before his arrival. The inspector added that he feared that any prisoner who lodged a complaint in his presence would suffer reprisals. What he did not know was that he had inspected only 6 and 7 Kensington Palace Gardens; nobody had informed him that number 8 was also part of the prison.

Despite the growing number of complaints it was receiving about the London Cage, the Red Cross eventually decided to do nothing 'through official channels' as it had been assured that the prison's closure was imminent. It also feared that any intervention could result in the prisoners suffering even worse treatment.[37]

In due course, Scotland was called to appear as a prosecution witness at a series of war crimes trials in Germany, where he was repeatedly questioned about his interrogation methods. During the two trials of the Stalag Luft III defendants, the accused protested that they had been starved, whipped and systematically beaten at the Cage. They said that they had also been confined in specially constructed showers that fired jets of icy water, not only from above but also from the sides. Some said they had been menaced with red-hot pokers and 'threatened with electrical devices'.

The defendants said the guards at the Cage boasted that they were 'the English Gestapo'. Starvation and sleep deprivation were said to be routine. When being questioned, they would be expected to kneel, upright, with their thumbs held in line with the seams of their trousers. While maintaining this position, they would be beaten around the head. The trial also heard allegations that men held at the Cage were told that if they did not cooperate their 'families would be handed over to the Russians and taken to Siberia where the wives would be common property'.[38]

A number of the complaints led to investigations by British Army courts of inquiry. But these panels were expected to weigh up the claims of Nazi prisoners and alleged war criminals against the word of British officers: the judgments were never going to be objective.

One of the cases examined was that of Fritz Knöchlein, a former lieutenant colonel in the Waffen SS. Knöchlein was sent to the Cage for interrogation about the massacre of 124 British soldiers, including ninety-eight men of the Royal Norfolk Regiment, in May 1940. Having surrendered to troops of the 3rd SS Totenkopf Division at La Paradis in the Pas-de-Calais, the British soldiers had been lined up against a barn and mown down by machine guns. According to the two survivors, dying men were finished off with bayonets.

The inquiry into Knöchlein's complaints was shelved, however, and in October 1948 he was prosecuted at Hamburg, accused of having been the officer who gave the order to open fire on the Norfolks. His defence was simple: he was not there. He insisted that he had been the commander of another unit with the Totenkopf Division and that on the day of the massacre he had been a number of miles away. He also told the court that at the Cage 'one specific interrogating officer had told me that Gestapo methods are not only used in Berlin at the Alexanderplatz, but we can do that much better in London here'. He added: 'I personally and quite a number of my other comrades were in a most brutal and gruesome fashion tortured in the London District Cage. My personal complaint I made to Colonel Scotland only achieved that the tortures became worse.'

Knöchlein gave a written statement to his defence lawyer in which he set out his allegations about the Cage. A certified translation of this statement was passed to the War Office and declassified in 1973.[39] In it, Knöchlein describes how he was deprived of sleep for four days and nights after his arrival at the Cage in October 1946. He says he was allowed a small amount of food each morning and thereafter only tea or water during the rest of the day. He was allowed to wear nothing but a thin pair of trousers. On his first day at the Cage, he said, he was forced to perform around 100 sit-ups before being compelled to walk in a tight circle for four hours, being kicked by a guard at each turn. After this he was interrogated for the first time.

Some of the torments Knöchlein describes were based upon disciplinary measures that were meted out in the British Army at that time. But at the Cage they were taken to great extremes. Thus he was put to work cleaning stairs and lavatories with a tiny rag, for days at a time, while buckets of water were poured over him. Any attempt to rest would result in a blow to his back from a cudgel. On occasion, he said in his statement, he and two other men would be pushed into cupboards, crammed in so tightly that they were unable to move.

Among other declassified War Office papers about the Cage are copies of statements signed by three British Army privates, named Ballantyne, Johnstone and Sugden, who confirmed that their orders had been to enter Knöchlein's cell every fifteen minutes, around the clock, depriving him of sleep.[40]

After lodging his complaint with Scotland, Knöchlein says he had been forced to stand next to a large gas stove before being escorted to a bathroom. 'Doors and windows were wide open. I had to undress and, in my heated state, I had to step under the icy shower (a special shower which does not drop water on the body from above but also throws it from the sides!).

When I had cleaned myself and wanted to get dry, freezing and shivering, three men who were standing around me prevented me from leaving the shower. They smeared my body with coal to force me to remain under the cold shower "for reasons of cleanliness". Finally they poured an additional bucket of cold water over me. Owing to this treatment I got bad bronchitis, and my rheumatic disease got worse.'

He and another man, one Oskar Schmidt, were then forced to run in circles in the grounds of the house while carrying heavy logs and barrels full of lubricating oil. 'Since these tortures were the consequence of my personal complaint, any further complaint would have been senseless. One of the guards who had a somewhat humane feeling advised me not to make any further complaints, otherwise things would turn worse for me.'

In addition to his own suffering, Knöchlein added that he had heard one fellow prisoner begging, in German, to be killed, as he could endure the mistreatment no longer; that men were repeatedly beaten about the face and had hair ripped from their heads; that they were threatened with a South African sjambok whip; and that they were informed that 'there were sufficient possibilities in England to have a man disappear without trace, and he would not be the first one to disappear from this house'.

All this was happening just a few hundred yards from Hyde Park and less than three miles from Downing Street.

During Knöchlein's trial, a number of men who had been processed at the Cage were called to give evidence against him. The key eyewitness, a former Waffen SS section commander called Theodor Emke, had identified Knöchlein as the officer who gave the order to shoot the Norfolks. Knöchlein's lawyers were convinced that he made the accusation after he too had been tortured. Under cross-examination, Emke confirmed that he had been a prisoner at the Cage. He denied, however, that he had been mistreated.[41] The Red Cross declined to assist Knöchlein's defence, saying it could pass any evidence of mistreatment at the Cage only to the British government. Knöchlein was found guilty and sentenced to hang.

Perhaps inevitably, copies of Knöchlein's statement began to be circulated outside the War Office, in both Britain and Germany. A number of prominent figures became interested in his case, among them Basil Liddell Hart, a historian and former soldier, and Lord Pakenham, the junior government minister later better known as the prison reformer Lord Longford.[42]

Even the commander-in-chief of the British Army in Germany, General Sir Charles Keightley, expressed the view in a letter to the War Office that the allegations were 'of such a serious nature that . . . they should be investigated'.[43]

Some disquiet about Scotland's methods had already been voiced at the headquarters of the British Amy of the Rhine, but the matter was never pressed, possibly because the information that he extracted was considered so useful; possibly because his prisoners were thought to deserve ill-treatment.

Eventually a decision was taken that both sealed Knöchlein's fate and ensured that the authorities would not be required to shine any further light on the dark secrets of the London Cage. On 4 January 1949, in a three-paragraph memo, Manny Shinwell, the Secretary of State for War, ruled: 'I have reached the conclusion that there are no grounds for either quashing or commuting the sentence. The decision must stand. As regards the matter of an Inquiry into the allegations of ill-treatment at the London District Cage, I do not propose to take further action.'[44] Sir Harry Legge-Bourke, a Conservative MP and war veteran who was campaigning on behalf of the condemned man, was told the sentence would be carried out at once, 'because of public feeling'.[45]

Two weeks later, Knöchlein went to the gallows.

Having told one war crimes trial after another that the allegations of torture being levelled by men like Knöchlein were lies, it is difficult to understand why Alexander Scotland was suddenly willing to reveal, in 1954, the truth about the techniques that he and his men had employed at the London Cage. Unsurprisingly, others did not share his eagerness to boast about what had gone on.

After seizing all four copies of the manuscript, the War Office gave a simple reason why Scotland's writing should never be permitted to see the light of day: 'The book discloses methods used in interrogating prisoners of war.'[46] The Foreign Office view was equally terse: 'Publication of this book would cause considerable embarrassment to HMG.'[47]

MI5 asked its legal adviser, Bernard Hill, to examine the manuscript carefully and provide a review highlighting the crimes that it disclosed. Hill concluded that Scotland and his interrogators had been guilty of a 'clear breach' of the Geneva Convention and had employed methods that were 'completely contrary to the express terms' of international law.

The examples of war crimes cited by Hill were forcing prisoners to stand to attention for more than twenty-four hours at a time; forcing them to kneel while they were beaten about the head; threatening to have men shot for failing to disclose information; using the bucket-and-mop treatment for three days at a time until prisoners were broken; and threatening to have an unnecessary appendix operation conducted on a prisoner by another inmate with no medical qualifications.

Hill pointed out that Scotland was also proposing to disclose that a number of men sent to the Cage for interrogation after the war were forced to incriminate themselves during war crimes trials. One man, a naval officer, was sentenced to ten years' imprisonment on the basis of a confession that Scotland said he had signed only after being 'subject to certain degrading duties'. Another, General Nikolaus von Falkenhorst, commander of German forces in occupied Norway, had been sentenced to death in 1946 after signing a confession at the Cage. The general,

Scotland noted, 'had become acutely depressed and miserable after the various examinations'. His sentence was commuted to twenty years' imprisonment.

Hill was also concerned that several of the men accused of the Stalag Luft III murders had not confessed until being interrogated by Scotland and his men. The only evidence against Erich Zacharias, a sergeant in the Gestapo's frontier police, for example, had been a confession that Scotland was now acknowledging had been signed because 'he had been worked on psychologically'. At trial, Zacharias insisted that he had also been 'worked on' physically. He was one of the men who went to the gallows.

Another of those sent to the Cage was Friedrich Wilhelm von Lindeiner-Wildau, the commandant of Stalag Luft III. Hill pointed out that Scotland knew this man to be 'entirely innocent of the murders', but was admitting in his manuscript to having threatened him with prosecution as a murderer and war criminal in order to coerce him into cooperating. Lindeiner-Wildau spent two years at the Cage and was freed only once he had given evidence against the men who were subsequently hanged.

Two years after Scotland submitted his manuscript to be vetted, the War Office decided to strike a deal with him. The old man had been threatening to publish his book in the United States and the War Office knew that a prosecution under the Official Secrets Act could not be sustained, despite the threats that had been issued. Scotland was told he would be allowed to publish in the UK, but only after a rewritten manuscript had been vetted and every line of incriminating material expunged. He was also told that he would never be allowed to recover his original manuscript.

A heavily censored version of *The London Cage* duly appeared in the bookshops in 1957. But officials at the War Office, and their successors at the Ministry of Defence, remained troubled for decades by the events at Kensington Palace Gardens.

Many years later, in September 1979, John Farquharson Ltd wrote to the Ministry of Defence out of the blue. They introduced themselves as representatives of the late Colonel Scotland's literary estate and explained that they wanted to lodge one of the original manuscripts with the company's archives. The panic that this letter triggered at the MOD was reminiscent of events twenty-five years earlier. The department's lawyers begged for the help of the Treasury Solicitors, asking whether they could think of a reason – any reason – other than national security grounds, for refusing to hand the manuscript back. 'The straw we are grasping for is perhaps something in the law of property or succession,' the MOD wrote, adding nervously that they were hoping Farquharson Ltd 'will not press the matter'.[48] Early in 1980, the Treasury Solicitors replied that it would be improper to retain the manuscript.

So the MOD quietly deposited a copy at the Public Record Office (now the National Archives) at Kew, where it went unnoticed for almost a quarter of a century. Such was the MOD's sensitivity about the Cage, however, and about the awful candour of the manuscript, that its exchange of letters with Treasury Solicitors remained classified until 2011.

Even now, some of the MOD's files on the Cage remain beyond reach. One set of papers, concerned specifically with interrogation at the Cage, was deliberately withheld from the public archives. When, in 2005, the MOD received a request for its disclosure under the Freedom of Information Act, it replied that it could not release the documents as there was a possibility that they were contaminated with asbestos.[49] Three years later, the MOD informed the National Archives that the 'contaminated' file had been destroyed. It had not been possible to have the documents scanned before destruction, officials said, because 'severe water damage made scanning impossible'.[50]

★

And what of the London Cage itself? Scotland, his interrogators, technicians and typists, and the towering guardsmen, packed up and left the building in January 1949. The villas were unoccupied for several years. Eventually, numbers 6 and 7 were leased to the Soviet Union, which was looking for a new embassy building. Today they house the chancery of the Russian embassy.

Number 8 remained empty, however. It was too large to be considered as a family home in the post-war years and in too poor a state of repair to be converted to offices. There seemed also to be a vague understanding that something unthinkable had happened there, something that was perhaps best avoided.

By 1955, the building had fallen into such disrepair that it needed to be demolished and a developer was found who agreed to buy the house from the Crown Estate, knock it down and build an apartment block. In 1964, three luxury flats were built on the plot; when one went on the market in 2006, it was valued at £13.5 million.

What had happened inside the Cage was not completely erased from memory, however. Twenty years after Knöchlein's death, his widow, Kathe, was still writing letter after letter to the Foreign Office, complaining that her husband was a decent soldier who had been nowhere near the scene of the massacre at La Paradis and had fallen victim to the most cruel miscarriage of justice. She begged that the case be reopened.

Each letter was diligently filed away and no action was taken.

Camp 020 closed at the end of 1945. Two years later, after being refurbished, it reopened as a civilian prison under its old name, Latchmere House.

After the war, when writing an account of his work, Colonel Stephens maintained that those under his command were forbidden from employing physical violence. 'Figuratively,' he wrote, 'a spy in war should be at the point of a bayonet.' But only figuratively. 'Violence is taboo, for not only does it produce answers to please, but it lowers the standard of information. Never strike a man. It is unintelligent, for the spy will give an answer to please, an answer to escape punishment. And having given a false answer, all else depends upon the false premise.'[51]

In time, 'Tin Eye' Stephens and his men became the stuff of legend: the interrogators who never turned to torture, even during the nation's darkest days. Their stance was hailed as evidence that torture is not only morally repugnant and un-lawful but unnecessary. For decades afterwards, senior MI5 officers would quote Stephens approvingly, and cite Camp 020 as proof that the agency always maintains its moral authority while defending the realm.

So how was pressure brought to bear on inmates, pressure so intense that it quickly turned enemy agents into compliant tools in the hands of MI5? The prize, as John Masterman pointed out, was that the agency controlled the entire German espionage network in Britain.

By using information provided by signals intercepts and stool pigeons, interrogators could persuade prisoners that they already knew a great deal and that it was pointless to remain silent. In addition, the inmates of Camp 020 could be threatened with execution under the Treachery Act. Fifteen of them were hanged after being tried during the course of the war and a sixteenth was shot after court martial. Decisions about who should be prosecuted were taken by a group of the interrogators and such was the certainty that the men they chose would be convicted – only one spy was acquitted – that the group referred to themselves as the Hanging Committee. Those who were selected for the drop included men who refused to cooperate or whose help was no longer needed, spies whose capture had been witnessed by too many members of the public, and four British citizens whose crimes were considered particularly unforgivable. But is this enough to explain Stephen's remarkable success?

The experiences of Alexander Raven Thomson and his British Union of Fascists colleagues showed that people were abused at Camp 020. As well as sleep deprivation and a starvation diet, several prisoners were subjected to mock executions and were knocked about by the guards.[52] There is also good reason to believe that some prisoners were left naked for months at a time. But would this be enough to turn so many enemy agents, so quickly, after capture?

In 1979, while Latchmere House was undergoing further modernisation, workmen made an odd discovery in one of the cable ducts above a cell. A prisoner, writing in Flemish, had penned a harrowing plea for help and then hidden his letter. Clearly, he had suffered terribly at the hands of his captors.

When William Crocker, the Security Executive official who had pressed for the establishment of an MI5 interrogation centre, wrote his memoirs more than twenty years after the closure of Camp 020, he expressed enormous pity that he could disclose nothing about the place, as it had been decided that it was not in the public interest for him to do so. 'That means', he wrote, 'that like the Ghost in *Hamlet*, I also "am forbid to tell the secrets of my prison-house" . . .'[53]

The truth about those secrets, the techniques that underpinned what is undoubtedly MI5's greatest achievement – the Double Cross network – lay behind the door of Cell 13, the punishment cell of Camp 020. And the secrets of Cell 13 were expected to remain concealed for ever.

2

For Purposes of Revenge: The Cold War

'Mental pressure but not physical torture is officially allowed.'

Standing orders for No. 74 CSDIC,
Bad Nenndorf

December 1946. The war in Europe had been over for more than eighteen months and Dr Wolfgang Günther could turn a blind eye no longer. Günther was the chief medical officer at what was known to the British authorities as the Civilian Internee Hospital in the small medieval town of Rotenburg. A growing number of his patients, mostly fellow Germans, had fallen ill while imprisoned in one of the post-war internment camps that the British had established across north-west Germany to incarcerate those considered a threat to the Allied occupation.

Every few days British soldiers would arrive at the hospital with desperately ill prisoners from one particular camp, the interrogation facility that CSDIC operated at Bad Nenndorf, west of Hanover. These sick men and women arrived not in an ambulance, but in the back of three-ton army trucks from which they were dumped, sometimes quite literally, at the hospital entrance.

The Nenndorf patients were of grave concern to Günther and his staff. They were filthy, confused and were usually suffering from multiple injuries. Frostbite was not uncommon and a number had identical circular wounds on their shins. Every one of them arrived at the Internee Hospital painfully emaciated after months of starvation. All were utterly terrified of being compelled to return. And they were extremely reluctant to describe what had happened to them.

On 12 December Günther sat down to write a report in which he complained about the condition in which prisoners were arriving from Nenndorf. He then handed it to a hospital clerk employed by the British military.[1] A week later, the clerk returned to Günther with a message from British Army intelligence officers: saying anything in public about Bad Nenndorf was a serious affair; writing reports about the place was extremely dangerous and Günther should be careful not to make the same mistake again.

During the early months of 1947, the hospital received, on average, one new patient from Bad Nenndorf every three days. A glance at these people showed Günther and his colleagues that the conditions endured by the inmates of the secretive interrogation centre were, if anything, becoming worse.

In mid-February, British soldiers delivered a prisoner called Franz Osterreicher, a man of thirty-eight who was in a particularly poor state, unable to speak and too emaciated to be placed on scales to be weighed. Osterreicher had frostbite on both feet. 'He was very cold and his pulse was rapid, about ten above normal, and weak, his respiration was made with great effort,' Gunther wrote in his notes. 'His body was without the slightest reserve of resistance against infection, lacking any fat and muscle.' Within a few hours, Osterreicher was dead.

Four days later, Walter Bergmann, a twenty-year-old, arrived in the back of another British Army truck. 'The patient was suffering from very serious malnutrition,' Günther recorded. He was also too weak to be placed on the scales, but appeared to weigh about 40 kilos. 'He was unable to speak or move his limbs, his body was cold, his face was pale and white, his forehead and upper parts of his cheeks were blue-coloured. His body was thick with dirt.'

Günther and his colleagues struggled to raise Bergmann's temperature. The following day, after the young man recovered consciousness, they gave him a blood transfusion, Günther himself donating the blood. Despite their efforts, Bergmann died at 10 p.m. that evening.

There were others mentioned in Günther's notes: Adolf Galla, aged thirty-six, a dental technician weighing 43 kilos, with open sores on his back and frostbite on both feet; Erich Gutschmidt, also 43 kilos, with 'no fat or muscles under his skin'; Albertus Hommen, a Dutchman, 48 kilos, his teeth falling out; Liselottie Uhe, aged twenty, a secretary, 52 kilos, diseased, with acute appendicitis; Anna Hausmann, aged twenty-eight, weighing 55 kilos; Robert Buttlar-Brandenfels, aged twenty-six, frostbite so severe that the toes of his right foot needed to be amputated, transferred to the hospital after swallowing a spoon, such was his desperation to escape Bad Nenndorf; Franz Nornack, aged twenty-six, weighing 56 kilos, 'both legs paralysed, vomiting blood'.[2]

After the deaths of Osterreicher and Bergmann, Günther resolved to take action, regardless of the threats from the British Army's Intelligence Corps. He contacted James Morgan-Jones, a major in the Royal Artillery who was the commandant of the internment camp at Fallingbostel, twenty-five miles to the south. Morgan-Jones agreed to drive up to Rotenburg to see what the fuss was about.

Morgan-Jones was shown Buttlar-Brandenfels, who explained what had happened to him at Bad Nenndorf. 'I asked him if he realised the seriousness of his allegations, and he replied that he did,' Morgan-Jones recorded. 'I further asked if he was prepared to give me a written statement confirming what he had said, which he did.'

Günther asked for permission to speak about other cases and for Morgan-Jones's assurance that there would be no repercussions. 'He then began reciting the symptoms and conditions of case after case of CSDIC transferees. I was appalled.'

Even then, Günther was too terrified to show Morgan-Jones his other Nenndorf patients, or to hint at what horrors they had said were being perpetrated there. It was only on a subsequent visit that Morgan-Jones was shown Adolf Galla. Morgan-Jones, who had six years of war behind him, subsequently submitted to his superiors a report marked 'Top Secret' in which he said that the spectacle of Galla was 'one of the most disgusting sights of my life'.

'Notwithstanding the fact that he had been in Rotenburg hospital for five weeks, he was still a figure which may well have been one of the Belsen inmates,' Morgan-Jones wrote. 'This man literally had no flesh on him, his state of emaciation was incredible. The doctor, on my instruction, turned him over gently. At the base of the spine above the buttocks was a huge festering sore, the size of a man's hand. This, I understand, was the result of lying on bare boards at CSDIC.' Galla was petrified of being sent back. 'If ever a man showed fear – he did.'[3]

The Internee Hospital at Rotenburg was not the only place where CSDIC was dumping its human waste after squeezing out every last drop of useful information. Other unwanted inmates were driven south to an internment camp that the British had established at Eselheide, north of Paderborn.

That camp's commandant, a former Royal Navy officer, complained to his superiors that between December 1946 and April 1947 he had received several batches of starving prisoners. On occasion, men who were gravely ill arrived handcuffed to others who were dying. In March, for example, he received a party of four, named Menzel, Bracke, Winter and Durbajlle. 'I ordered them to the bath, they were in such a dirty state.

On seeing them stripped I was shocked by their conditions, especially Menzel. He was merely a living skeleton.'[4]

The commandant ordered the camp doctor, Hans Rinner, to prepare detailed medical reports on prisoners recently admitted from Bad Nenndorf and arranged for a number of the men to be photographed.

Rinner reported that Gerhard Menzel weighed just 49 kilos on arrival, his lungs were diseased and there were signs that he had attempted to slash his wrists. He was unable to stand unassisted. A twenty-six-year-old admitted to the internment camp under the name of Morice Marcellini and claiming to be French weighed 53 kilos and had few teeth. Hans Habermann, aged forty-three, was similarly toothless and had 'two round cicatrizes on both shin bones'. Habermann was Jewish and had survived three years in the Buchenwald concentration camp before being incarcerated by the British at Bad Nenndorf. Rinner predicted that one man, Heinz Biedermann, aged twenty-three, who weighed 52.8 kilos and was 'unsteady, irresolute and fearful', would soon die.

As Rinner's report filtered slowly upwards through the Control Commission, the British military government then governing north-west Germany, it was decided that a British physician should be sent to Eselheide to verify the complaints. This doctor, one J. H. Jordan, reported that dying men were being sent to the camp from Bad Nenndorf and that the scars on the prisoners' shins appeared to be 'the result of some instrument to facilitate questioning'.[5] CSDIC had recovered a number of 'shin screws' from a Gestapo prison in Hamburg and had put them to use at Bad Nenndorf.

Jordan's report eventually found its way onto the desk of Major General Sir Alec Bishop, the deputy chief of staff to the head of the British Army in Germany, Sir Brian Robertson. Bishop in turn wrote to Major General John Lethbridge, the head of the Control Commission's Intelligence Division, observing that as Dr Jordan was British his report was 'quite a different matter than evidence gathered from German sources'. Bishop drew attention to the doctor's concern that dying men were being shipped out of Bad Nenndorf and to the comments about the wounds on the prisoners' shins. 'Sooner or later,' Bishop warned Lethbridge, 'these stories are bound to come to the notice of the Press or Parliament.'[6]

CSDIC's presence in Germany had been planned long before the end of the war. In September 1944, three months after the landings at Normandy, with Allied troops in eastern France closing in on the German border, the British government's Joint Intelligence Committee had begun to consider what sort of intelligence organisation would be required in an occupied Germany. The chairman of the JIC, Victor Cavendish-Bentinck, predicted that a large part of the German Army would form into guerrilla bands, while Stewart Menzies, head of MI6, declared that some 275,000 Germans would need to be incarcerated. The JIC considered whether some form of 'Black and Tan force' would need to be raised, a reference to the notorious auxiliary units deployed in Ireland twenty-five years earlier in an attempt to suppress revolution, so known because initially they wore mismatched dark police tunics and khaki army trousers. The committee eventually concluded that what it described frankly as 'repression' in post-war Germany should be a little more discreet.[7]

The JIC had initially envisaged an organisation with around 1,200 intelligence officers and created an Intelligence Division of the Control Commission under the command of Lethbridge. Before long, however, Lethbridge's Intelligence Division had outgrown both MI5 and MI6.[8] Many of its officers were attached from those two organisations, given military ranks and placed under military command.

MI5 and MI19 were asked to join forces to establish

interrogation centres in areas of Europe being liberated by the Allies and, ultimately, in Germany itself.[9] In March 1945, a 'Ham-cum-CSDIC' interrogation centre, as Guy Liddell described it, was established at a castle in Diest, east of Brussels. There were twelve intelligence officers and 105 other ranks. Most of the interrogators were MI5 officers from Camp 020, but others came from CSDIC, or from Colonel Scotland's PWIS. 'Tin Eye' Stephens adored the location. 'It was a medieval sort of place with dungeons and moats,' he wrote, 'and excellently suited for the purpose.'[10]

Early in 1945, Lord Cherwell, Churchill's special adviser, had penned a report that set out his grand vision for a post-war Germany. Those exasperated Foreign Office officials who read it were not slow to point out the limits of his lordship's vision. 'The paper says nothing about the difficulties of administering a desert traversed by swarms of unemployed nomads. This is not Lord Cherwell's responsibility but it will at some time become that of the Foreign Office.'

And so it proved. When the Potsdam Conference of July 1945 carved up the western portion of defeated Germany between the three Western Allies, it was said that the Americans got the scenery and the French got the wine, while the British got the ruins.

In the immediate aftermath of the war, British officers annotated their maps with landmarks that were little more than the largest piles of rubble. Their patrols walked in the middle of the streets to avoid the tumbling masonry. By day, the roads were teeming with foreign slave workers trying to find their way home, children and parents trying to find each other, Nazi officials trying to find a place to hide. By night, after the air-raid sirens had sounded the curfew, there was silence.

In many places there were no food supplies, no running water, no electricity, no medicines, no pots or pans. Stretching alongside the main roads were enormous barbed-wire pens, one after another, inside which the disarmed men of the Wehrmacht waited for whatever defeat would bring. Five million men were taken prisoner by the Western Allies alone and held, initially, in the most wretched conditions.

Meanwhile, there were no police, no coal miners, no train drivers, no mechanics. In the year that the Germans came to know as Year Zero, millions of citizens of a once-great nation were living and dying in holes in the ground.

Within the British zone of occupation, it was perhaps inevitable that the victors would come to see themselves as imperial masters. In Westminster, MPs spoke of the Germans being trained to take responsibility for themselves following the imposition of a colonial form of government; some talked of viceroys and governor-generals. The newly elected prime minister, Clement Attlee, told the wives of British officers and administrators as they joined their husbands that the Germans would look upon them as 'representatives of the British Empire'.[11]

Among their new subjects were a large number of people who would be considered, in the words of the Potsdam Agreement, as 'dangerous to the Occupation or its objectives' and could be arrested and interned. British military commanders conducted sweeps at addresses across the British zone and also began deciding which prisoners of war should be transferred to internment camps. Luftwaffe pilots and technicians were particularly prone to internment, as they were deemed to possess expert knowledge that posed an 'international menace'. During the four years following the end of the war, around 95,000 people were interned in the British zone.[12] A number of these internees would eventually find themselves undergoing interrogation at the hands of the Intelligence Division.

By this time, the Intelligence Division had four clear if overlapping responsibilities: combating any threat from Nazi guerrillas; investigating war crimes; assisting in the search for technical and scientific booty to be carried back to the UK; and locating agents whom the Germans had trained for use against the Soviet Union. Later, it would begin more aggressive actions against the Soviets, as it appeared increasingly likely that a Third World War was inevitable. Interrogation played a critical role in achieving these aims.

Dick White, who had been given the rank of colonel and attached to the Allies' joint headquarters, wrote to Sir David Petrie, the head of MI5, to say that plans for an interrogation centre in Germany itself were well advanced. The army wanted Colonel Stephens to run the place, White said, and he suggested that as many German-speaking interrogators as possible be transferred from Camp 020 to Germany. 'The sound principles upon which Camp 020 and Camp 020R have been run will be preserved in the new Interrogation Centre,' he said.[13] And nobody would hand down any written instructions about what would, or would not, be allowed to take place there.[14]

The war had been relatively kind to the stately old spa town of Bad Nenndorf in Lower Saxony. It had escaped the massive bombing raids that had devastated Hanover, eighteen miles to the east. Its principal business, the grand Badehaus where visitors bathed in sulphur springs, had limped along. And, surrounded as it was by good farmland, fresh produce could usually be had. American troops occupied the town shortly before the end of the war; the townspeople found the GIs to be easy-going young men. Bad Nenndorf's main problem was that it remained crowded by refugees from Hanover, and every public building, spare barn or cellar was crammed with people with nowhere else to go.

Early in the morning of Wednesday 1 August 1945, Bad Nenndorf was awoken by the noise of a large convoy of trucks rumbling through the streets. There followed the sound of slamming doors, shouted orders and the pounding of running boots. Peering from their windows, the townspeople could see that the commotion was being caused not by American but by British soldiers, Tommies, and their aggressive behaviour triggered immediate alarm. A small number of them had been seen around the town for some weeks, and they had seized control of the Badehaus and the grand nineteenth-century hotel next door, surrounding both buildings with sturdy fencing topped with barbed wire. Now, it appeared, they wanted more.

The Tommies hammered on the doors of houses close to the Badehaus, telling the occupants that they had ninety minutes in which to pack their belongings and clear out. The British were taking over a third of the town. More than 1,000 people were to lose their homes. Walter Münstermann, then a fourteen-year-old schoolboy, recalled years later: 'We thought everyone would be allowed back in a few days. Then the soldiers started putting barbed-wire fences around the centre of the village, and slowly we began to realise that this was going to be no ordinary camp.'[15]

Bad Nenndorf had been chosen as the site for the new 'Ham-cum-CSDIC' camp to replace the one at Diest. The town was about to fall within the boundaries of the British zone and 'Tin Eye' Stephens, having visited in June, realised that the small bathrooms inside the solidly built bathhouse would make excellent prison cells once the baths were removed and steel doors fitted. 'M Cover' was installed, the interrogators were billeted in the hotel next door and local streets were renamed: George Street, Elizabeth Street, Ham Avenue and Latimer Lane.[16]

The outer perimeter was guarded by men from T Force, an army 'exploitation unit' which had been formed to locate and seize Germany's technical and scientific assets – machinery, designs, research papers, even people – for removal to Britain. The inner warden force was created largely of men from different army units who were sent to Bad Nenndorf after receiving suspended sentences for offences such as assault or desertion. Most were barely out of their teens and had already endured more than a year of war. Some were taken first to see the Bergen–Belsen concentration camp and then told, falsely, that they were going to be guarding the men responsible for the horrors perpetrated there.

The new interrogation centre was officially designated No. 74 CSDIC. There the techniques of interrogation that Stephens and his team had devised in great secrecy at Camp 020 during the fifth-column hysteria of 1940, then honed to deal with the very real threat posed by invasion spies, were to be employed with utter ruthlessness. The experience gained around the world by the interrogators of CSDIC would also be brought to bear, along with the propensity for extreme violence of the men arriving from the London Cage.

No. 74 CSDIC would cast its net wide. Not only would former members of the SS be incarcerated there, but civilian Nazi Party officials, former Abwehr officers, diplomats, scientists, journalists and industrialists. Increasingly, from 1946, in an attempt to prepare for the Third World War that many were convinced was inevitable, it would concentrate on members of the Germany Communist Party, Red Army defectors, East Europeans discovered in the British zone and anyone caught crossing from the Russian zone in what appeared to be suspicious circumstances. Over the next two years, 372 men and forty-four women would pass through its gates. And for each of them Bad Nenndorf was to be a perfect hell.

As a seven-year-old local child, Ingrid Groth would watch as the prisoners arrived in the back of British Army trucks. After dark, she and other children would creep as close as they could to the Badehaus. 'Often it was quiet,' she said. 'But sometimes, you could hear the screams.'[17]

★

One of those who experienced Bad Nenndorf from the inside was Robert Buttlar-Brandenfels, the man who eventually swallowed a spoon in his desperation to be transferred to hospital. A minor aristocrat, he had worked for a while in the German administration in occupied Norway before returning to Berlin, where he turned his hand to journalism. Throughout this time he was also working as an agent for the Russian intelligence service, the NKVD.[18] In February 1943, on returning from a meeting with his handlers, he was arrested by the Gestapo, interrogated and, after two years in Plötzensee Prison in Berlin, sentenced to death. Two months later he was freed when the advancing Red Army burst open the prison gates. The NKVD asked him to continue his services. 'I didn't say yes, and I didn't say no.' Instead, he made his way to the British zone, where he offered to spy against the Soviets. He was sent to London, detained on arrival at Croydon aerodrome, interrogated for ten months by police and War Office officials – whom he described as 'quite proper' – and then dispatched to Bad Nenndorf. After MI5's experiences of running wartime double-agents to devastating effect, Buttlar-Brandenfels's interrogators were determined to establish whether his offer to spy for Britain was genuine, and they were prepared to use the cruellest of methods to test him.

I entered Bad Nenndorf on 27th November 1946. We were compelled to run at the double through corridors. I was made to undress and everything was taken from me. I was given a pair of boots, a jacket, a pair of trousers and a shirt. I asked for socks and for underwear but was refused this. I was taken to cell No. 2, with a concrete floor, no heating, with burst window panes. I stayed in this cell before being interrogated for the first time. The officer told me: 'The intelligence authorities of this place are not bound by any rules or regulations. We do not care a damn whether you leave this place on a stretcher or in a hearse. The only thing for you to do is to tell us what we want to know.' Three interrogations took place on 9th December. At the third interrogation there was a woman typist present.

From my cell I could hear the noise of the scrubbing. I did not know what the meaning of this noise of the scrubbing was. I sometimes heard the guards ordering in broken German to 'go on scrubbing', and the prisoners were abused. I could distinguish from the orders of the sentries that there was some method behind these scrubbings. I did not know what it was.

I was called again for interrogation on 3rd January. I assured the officer that I could not tell him anything else. He told me: 'Well I warned you. Now you will have to bear the consequences.' I was taken to cell No. 12. My jacket was taken from me, and my shoes. The cell had no furniture whatever, no bedstead, no heating. There was a radiator but it was turned off and there were no panes in the window. I was given a bucket of water and a brush and told to scrub the cell walls. There was a temperature of about 20 degrees below freezing outside. That is Fahrenheit. I was told this by one of the guards. My feet were bandaged. Both my feet were soaked. At 9 o'clock I was given two blankets and told to lie down. I pointed out to the Corporal that I could not because the floor was too wet. Later on, because I was getting too tired to stand I lay down. I could not sleep. I had lost the feeling in my feet. Next morning . . . my feet were still more swollen and they were getting of a blue colour. I was so despairing to get out of this cell I swallowed a spoon. I stayed in this cell, under the said conditions, exactly 72 or 73 hours.

I was called again to see the officer who interrogated me. Not only my feet were swollen but my legs as well, so I had literally to crawl on the floor to the interrogation room. The sentries were ordered by one of the Corporals not to help me. The officer asked me whether I had had enough. I told him that I had been a prisoner for two years of the Gestapo in Germany, and sentenced to death by the German People's Court, but that I had never in all those two years undergone such treatment. Then he told me that apparently I did tell him the truth and that I should write another statement. He told me I would be taken to a warmer room.

My feet did not get better. Four toes of my right foot have been amputated. Those of my left are stiff now and I cannot yet walk.[19]

An operation was also carried out to remove the spoon.

The entire regime at Bad Nenndorf was intended to weaken, humiliate and intimidate. The prisoners were forced to wear clothes that were too small and boots that were too large. 'We looked like bizarre clowns,' one recalled, and they would trip and fall while being made to run at the double to and from interrogation. Weak tea would be served every few hours, sometimes with oatmeal or boiled potatoes. Proper meals were served only on Sunday. The prisoners all became emaciated.

Five years after the end of the war, *Quick*, a popular German magazine, published an account of prison life written by a former inmate called Stille:

At 4.30, the prisoners had to get up. During the day, no one was allowed to lie down, or sit down. If an internee was unfortunate enough to break down in exhaustion for a couple of seconds, his food allowance would be restricted. The prisoners spent their days walking up and down their cells, or standing against the walls. Days lasted for ever: from 4 a.m. to 9.30 p.m. Prisoners would stand against the walls of their cells, and think that they were going crazy.

If a prisoner complained to Captain Smith, the camp doctor, that they feared they were going to starve, Smith would reply drily: 'Yes, it looks like you are.'

Each evening, prisoners were ordered to place their trousers and jackets outside their cells and stand in their underwear, awaiting the evening inspection. 'Tin Eye' Stephens was said to have taken particular enjoyment from this ritual.

> He liked to have some fun. He was a tall bloke, square-shouldered, with a dark red face. He would stroll from cell to cell and examine the inmates – miserable, half-frozen creatures – with a chilling stare. Every now and then he would yell at an inmate. The unarticulated yelling usually contained a question that was very hard to make out. The prisoner would be unable to answer properly. Not that the colonel expected an answer, really. Most of the time he would immediately after asking his question plant a punch on the prisoner's chin.

A small number of inmates would then be ordered to fetch pails of sewage water, which were then dumped on the prisoners' clothes.

At 9.30 p.m., the prisoners were given two blankets each and allowed to lie down, on bare wooden beds from which several boards had been removed. The lights would remain on and twice a night prisoners would be ordered to stand by their beds for twenty minutes while each man in turn recited their name and number. 'In the morning, the prisoners had to put on wet, half-frozen, and utterly disgusting rags.'[20]

★

Prisoners were beaten, whipped and forced to sit in baths of cold water for hours. Men were handcuffed back to back and shackled against the open windows. Any prisoner thought to be uncooperative during interrogation was taken to Cell 12 and forced to scrub the walls and floor for days at a time. Sometimes, despite sub-zero temperatures, they were repeatedly doused in water. One man, Kurt Parbel, a director of the film division of the Nazi's propaganda ministry, is said to have spent eight days standing in the cell in cold water. A guard, taking pity, allowed him to wear boots and occasionally to sit on a lavatory to get some rest.[21]

Horst Mahnke, a professor of philosophy at Berlin University who became a captain in the SS, said after his release that he had been beaten and whipped in-between interrogation sessions, during which he would be forced to stand to attention for up to twelve hours at a time, threatened with execution and told that his wife was to be brought in to be tortured.[22]

Morice Marcellini, who was eventually admitted to the internment camp at Eselheide, claiming to be French, said that he would be suspended by his wrists and beaten by NCOs wielding rubber truncheons while the interrogating officers went for lunch. Perhaps significantly, in the light of the way in which British torture techniques were to develop in the years ahead, he also said that he would be forced to spend long periods standing against a wall, his legs spread and his hands above his head, his weight borne on his outstretched fingers.

This man believed he was tortured because the British could not accept his story: that far from being French, he was actually named Alexander Alexandrevitch Kalkowski, and was a half-Russian, half-Norwegian officer in the NKVD who had spent the entire war behind German lines without being detected, despite once spending a short period in a German prison. Eventually, the War Office files show, CSDIC accepted that he was telling the truth.

★

The question of what should be done with prisoners once they were no longer needed for interrogation quickly became a problem for Stephens and his officers. They were fully aware that they could continue to inflict medieval torments on helpless men and women only so long as the wider world knew nothing about it.

They favoured dumping unwanted inmates at internment camps, in the belief that they would be held indefinitely. Senior officials of the Control Commission agreed that those who had passed through interrogation centres were 'in possession of knowledge which is harmful to the Allies and constitute a dangerous security threat to the Occupying Forces'. By the end of 1946, however, the Control Commission lawyers had had a change of heart and informed the Intelligence Division that this practice was no longer considered lawful. Instead, they proposed to convene a series of military courts, sitting behind closed doors, where 'a severe sentence should be imposed'. This plan was blocked by the Commission's Political Branch, however, with officials protesting that it was contrary to accepted principles of British justice that sentences of any kind should be imposed on people 'whose only crime is that they have had the misfortune to acquire a too detailed knowledge of our methods of interrogation'.

Despite their misgivings about arbitrary detention by secret courts, the Political Branch officials did offer an alternative solution, one based on the measures that the Nazis had taken to guarantee the silence of those small numbers of concentration camp inmates who had been released back into the general population. Bad Nenndorf inmates to be freed were warned that they would be rearrested, along with their wives and children, and that they would suffer far worse mistreatment if they ever uttered a word of what they had experienced.

★

I discovered for myself just how effective this system of intimidation could be after travelling to the small town of Lindau, on the eastern side of Lake Constance, to meet Gerhard Menzel, the man who had been described as being 'merely a living skeleton' when admitted to the Eselheide camp in March 1947.

When I met Menzel in July 2006, he was a man of eighty-three, with three children and two grandchildren. He had a highly successful business career behind him, having owned a forklift-truck firm for many years. He was a vigorous, intelligent man, level-headed and full of original thoughts and humour. That evening, Germany was to play Italy in the semi-final of the World Cup and the streets of Lindau were crowded with young people on their way to one of the giant screens in the town – young people for whom the Nazi era was a matter for history lessons and for whom German nationalism was something to be expressed through football chants.

But after all those years Menzel was still petrified. He demanded proof that the interview was not a trick by MI5 and that the interpreter I had brought with me was not from British intelligence.

Menzel had joined the Waffen SS in 1940, at the age of seventeen, serving in a tank unit within a joint German-Dutch division. He fought in Czechoslovakia and Italy, spending the last eight weeks of the war as a non-commissioned officer, an *Unteroffizier*. He says he was captured on the Italian-Austrian border and imprisoned near Salzburg in a camp which was so poorly managed that one day he simply walked away.

The British were convinced that he had been taken prisoner by the Red Army. When he was pointed out to them in a street in Hamburg, in the British zone, in 1946, they assumed he had been freed early from Soviet captivity because he had agreed to become a spy. Menzel was detained by Captain Richard Langham, a CSDIC interrogator, and taken straight to Bad Nenndorf.

Menzel's account of the interrogation centre suggests he had found himself in a place where all sense of reason and proportion had evaporated; where the interrogators were capable of believing everything and nothing at the same time; where there was so little outside oversight that any excess, any crime, was possible; and where the thirst for 'intelligence' and an underlying desire for revenge meant there was no limit to the inmates' suffering.

He told me: 'They had different methods for different prisoners. The main thing with me was starvation. You would lose consciousness, you couldn't think clearly, you became very confused. I thought I was going to die. We all thought we were going to die.

'The Russians had the worst time when they were being interrogated. They beat them up. They really beat them up. When they came back from being interrogated you couldn't see where their eyes were. They wouldn't talk about what happened to them. A lot of people wouldn't have survived such treatment, but the Russians seemed able to bounce back.'

Menzel shared a cell with five other men, including a deserter from the Red Army, a major named Vladimir Denisov. 'I was very, very surprised. Here was I, an SS officer, and I was in a camp with Red Army officers. I could never understand why the British were treating their allies in this way.'

He recalled that the guards were convicts. 'Some of the reasonable ones used to say: "We're prisoners, just like you."' He was usually interrogated by Captain Langham and a Dutchman, Captain Kees van Rije. Both appeared to be keen to persuade their superiors that they were uncovering an important conspiracy. 'Their stories changed by the week. They would tell London that they had something important, that they had uncovered some big plot, and you would be expected to go along with it.'[23]

Menzel fell foul of Bad Nenndorf's punishment regime after

agreeing to escape with another prisoner called Dieter Albrecht, who turned out to be a stool pigeon. Menzel spent the next sixteen days with his hands cuffed behind his back. Once that was over he was consigned to Cell 12 for three more days and buckets of water were thrown over him every thirty minutes. There appears to have been no intelligence value to any of this: the camp authorities had arranged for Menzel to be tricked by Albrecht simply in order to provide a pretext for tormenting him further. Shortly afterwards, Stephens lost interest in Menzel, at which point the emaciated and confused former *Unteroffizier* was shipped out to an internment camp.[24]

Like Menzel, other inmates soon understood that Bad Nenndorf's interrogators would sometimes be desperate for intelligence about threats that were either non-existent or negligible. Operation Nursery, for example, an attempt to track down members of a Nazi guerrilla organisation called Wehrwolf, saw large numbers of young men and women rounded up and sent to No. 74 CSDIC.

The operation's codename reflected the fact that most of the targets were boys, some as young as fourteen. Eventually, the Intelligence Division accepted that the threat from Wehrwolf was largely illusory: the organisation had barely existed beyond its mention in a few febrile broadcasts by Joseph Goebbels before the end of the war.

Other Intelligence Division operations in which Bad Nenndorf played a role are detailed in a briefing paper submitted to Clement Attlee in 1948. It was meagre fare.

At the head of Bad Nenndorf's list of achievements, according to the paper, were the interrogations that proved, beyond doubt, that Hitler was dead. The Intelligence Division was also proud that 'a detailed history of German espionage in Ireland between the wars and during the 1939–1945 period was disclosed by the interrogation of a man named Haller'.

In fairness, the officials also pointed to some interrogations at Bad Nenndorf that may have had real value: the investigation of 'Russian methods of recruiting and training German agents in the Western Zones', for example, and 'the scientific and technical work that is being carried out by German scientists under Russian direction'.

But other examples they cited suggested that Stephens and his team were subjecting men and women to great suffering while in pursuit of the blindingly obvious. For example, the interrogation of one Otto Dietrich, a secretary of state under Goebbels, is said to have 'produced a most detailed account of the manner in which the Nazis controlled all information, news and propaganda'.[25]

Some within the British military hierarchy in Germany appeared to have harboured their own doubts about the value of the intelligence being extracted at Bad Nenndorf. T-Force, the army exploitation unit, asked Stephens to hand over all prisoners who were scientists or technicians, adding that if he wished he could hold the remainder 'for purposes of revenge'.[26]

If the nature of the intelligence being gathered was of dubious importance, so too was the quality of it. The experience of historian Hugh Trevor-Roper showed all too clearly the difficulty of distinguishing the accurate and worthwhile information that was being extracted from the false tales told in the hope of satisfying the torturer and bringing the pain to an end.

During the war, Trevor-Roper worked for the Radio Security Service, or MI8, a signals intelligence division of MI6, and travelled regularly during 1945 to the headquarters of Field Marshal Montgomery's 21st Army Group. Often he would stay with Dick White, who by now had the rank of brigadier and was the Intelligence Division's head of counter-intelligence. White had requisitioned a comfortable eighteenth-century stately home near Herford in North Rhine-Westphalia, where, over lunch accompanied by several bottles of hock, he would explain that he was deeply concerned about the fate of Hitler. He asked Trevor-Roper to undertake a systematic study in order to nail a lie being spread mischievously by the Soviets that Hitler was alive and well and being harboured by the British. The assignment was to lead, eventually, to Trevor-Roper's most famous work, *The Last Days of Hitler*.

Trevor-Roper established that Hitler was indeed dead, and his findings were published in a press release that was issued in November 1945.[27] Eventually he would locate copies of the Führer's will. However, he also questioned captured high-ranking officers held at Bad Nenndorf, among them Nicolaus von Below, Hitler's Luftwaffe adjutant. Von Below had remained at the Führerbunker until the end. After being captured in February 1946, he had been sent to Bad Nenndorf, later recording in his memoirs: 'Bad Nenndorf was the most wicked and nasty thing I experienced whilst a prisoner of the British.'

Von Below was subjected to the standard sleep deprivation and isolation regime. 'At night I often heard the screams of my fellow inmates.' Eventually he was interrogated, being forced to stand to attention for hours while questions about Hitler's final, secret orders were screamed at him. When he insisted there were no such orders, his food ration was reduced still further. 'Since I never received or heard of any such orders, I had to make them up, to get myself out of the bad situation I was in. Now that I was ready to talk, the commander summoned me to his office, where he and two of his officers were waiting for me. The commander was in ridiculously formal uniform, complete with belt and hat, I assume to underline the importance of his mission. A couple of days later the conditions of my detention went back to normal.'[28]

Von Below's fabrication was to be incorporated into *The Last Days of Hitler*. Trevor-Roper recounted how Hitler had appointed Admiral Karl Dönitz as his successor, having lost faith in both Himmler and Goering, and, shortly before his suicide, had heaped praise on the navy and Luftwaffe while condemning the Army General Staff. The historian also immortalised Hitler's 'last message to the world', with its pan-German dream: 'The efforts and sacrifices of the German people in this war have been so great that I cannot believe that they have been in vain. The aim must still be to win territory in the east.'

'All bullshit,' von Below insisted later, adding, however: 'It has given me much pleasure to read it in Trevor-Roper's book.'

During the early months of 1947, it was not only Wolfgang Günther and the staff at the Internee Hospital who were becoming increasingly alarmed by the state of former Bad Nenndorf inmates. Many were being dumped at civilian internment camps and the British officers who ran those centres eventually decided to meet to approve a course of action. They sent a statement to the Control Commission's Penal Branch, complaining that these 'security suspects . . . were in a deplorable condition which indicated serious ill-treatment'.

Control Commission officials, having interviewed a former inmate called Nikolaus Ritter, who had served as an officer in the German Army and Abwehr and who 'seemed to be an honest man', expressed their concern over the torture of prisoners 'by the application of thumb and shin screws and by hot and cold water treatment'.

The commander-in-chief of the British zone, Air Marshal Sir Sholto Douglas, appointed a court of inquiry to investigate. After hearing evidence at both the Internee Hospital and Bad Nenndorf, the court concluded that the allegations of the former inmates were substantially correct and that Stephens should bear overriding responsibility for the punishment cell system, which should be abolished.

The court heard that although standing orders were that 'mental pressure but not physical torture is officially allowed' to extract information from prisoners, at least three of the interrogators, Captain Richard Langham, Captain Kees van Rije and Major Frank Edmunds, 'had conspired to extract information from internees at all costs'. The guards had 'apparently been instructed to carry out physical assaults on certain prisoners with the object of reducing them to a state of physical collapse and of making them more amenable to interrogation'.

Finally, the court concluded that while Stephens was responsible as commandant for everything that happened at the interrogation centre, 'it is the opinion of the Court that the Intelligence Division' – meaning Major General Lethbridge and Dick White – 'must themselves bear the major share in the ultimate responsibility for the treatment meted out at Bad Nenndorf'.

The court ordered that Stephens, the medical officer, Captain John Smith, and Langham and Edmunds be suspended – van Rije had already left the army – and that control of Bad Nenndorf pass from the Intelligence Division to a branch of the Control Commission's Legal Division. Finally, it ordered that a further investigation be mounted by the Control Commission's civilian police force in view of the fact that 'considerations of manslaughter arose in the case of two internees'.

In July 1947, the wire around Bad Nenndorf was ripped down, the sentry posts were dismantled and the prison closed as abruptly as it had opened. Slowly, the spa began to return to the familiar business of catering for the health needs of well-heeled elderly German tourists.

For years to come, however, Bad Nenndorf would be known across the region as *das verbotene Dorf*, the forbidden village.

In London, the government realised immediately that the political fallout from the events at Bad Nenndorf could be deeply damaging to the nation's reputation. Ernest Bevin, the Foreign Secretary, passed the papers from the court of inquiry to the Chancellor of the Duchy of Lancaster, Frank Pakenham, and also to his close adviser Hector McNeill, Minister of State at the Foreign Office, asking what they believed should be done.

Pakenham highlighted 'the fact that we are alleged to have treated internees in a manner reminiscent of the German concentration camps' and was in no doubt that those responsible ought to be prosecuted.

McNeill was so disturbed that he told Bevin he needed a few days to think before replying. When he was ready to respond, he was all for hushing things up:

> Apart altogether from any normal emotional reaction to the incidents, I still think that if the substantial facts are given any currency it will cause us grave trouble in the House, will be a propaganda stick with which the Russians will beat us for a long time and will damage heavily the reputation of our Intelligence Services.
>
> I doubt if I can put too strongly the parliamentary consequences of publicity. Our friends will be uncomfortable and our enemies will exult. Whenever we have any allegations to make about the political police methods in Eastern European states it will be enough to call out in the House 'Bad Nenndorf', and no reply is left to us.[*]

Most alarming for McNeill was that the papers made clear that Bad Nenndorf was not the only interrogation centre of its sort that the British were operating in Germany. What other hidden horrors, he wondered, might come tumbling out into the light?

---

[*] McNeill's hopes that Moscow would not discover the secrets of Bad Nenndorf were in vain: his secretary was Guy Burgess, the Soviet spy, who regularly smuggled his papers out of the building to be photographed by a handler before returning them early next morning.

Above all, I should like to be assured that no rough methods were applied to women. I note again from the papers that there were women at Bad Nenndorf. It would be frightful if there were any female skeletons in the cupboard. Next to children and animals the British public, most properly, go into hysteria about the ill-treatment of women.[29]

McNeill suggested that the best solution was for Langham and Edmunds to be quietly dismissed, and that Stephens's and Smith's commissions be terminated.

But by this time the Control Commission, at the request of the court of inquiry, had already put its best detective on the case.

Tom Hayward, a tall, well-built man of forty-seven, had twenty-two years under his belt as a police officer by the time he arrived in Germany in February 1947. He had spent most of his career as a detective with Scotland Yard's Criminal Investigation Department, rising through the ranks to become a detective chief inspector, and with fifteen commendations to his name he could no doubt expect further promotion. But when he heard of an opening for an investigator with the Control Commission's Public Protection Branch he jumped at the chance. During the previous war he had served in the Household Cavalry from the age of eighteen, but spent it at a barracks in London. Perhaps he relished the opportunity for some travel and adventure. Bad Nenndorf was his first major German case.

After studying the medical reports on the survivors, Hayward interviewed Stephens, his deputy, Lieutenant Colonel Raymond Short, the medical officer, Captain John Smith, and all the interrogators. The interrogators were an intriguing group. Around half were middle-aged former German-language lecturers from British universities. The other half were

German or Austrian, many of them Jews who had joined the British armed forces after emigrating to the UK, some of them arriving as boys more than a decade before. Major Hans Kettler, for example, who had been at the London Cage before Bad Nenndorf, had grown up near Dortmund, arriving in Britain in 1925 to study at Magdalene College, Cambridge. Kettler was said to be 'regarded as outstanding for his rough treatment of prisoners'. Frank Edmunds, who had been born in Nuremberg in 1912, had settled with his family in Wembley, to the north-west of London, before the war. The interrogator known to inmates as Richard Langham had been born in Munich in 1921, arrived in Britain as a thirteen-year-old orphan and was commissioned into the Royal Armoured Corps in 1944. The inmates were never aware of this. Sixty years later, Gerhard Menzel was rendered speechless on learning that his torturer had been a fellow German.

Hayward also interviewed forty-six guards and orderlies, who gave clear accounts of the abuse once they were offered immunity from prosecution. A Private Wood, for example, made a statement about Heinz Biedermann, the inmate who had been expected to die on discharge to the Eselheide internment camp. 'He was a big hefty lad when I saw him first. I saw him again about four or five weeks later and he had wasted like a candle. When he took his shirt off I could see every bone in his back.'[30]

Hayward tried, without success, to recover the torture implements, such as the shin screws.[31] He did, however, discover one damning piece of evidence: the inmates had been weighed on arrival and again on leaving the prison, and a careful record kept of their weight loss. In the case of some prisoners he also found written interrogation plans that showed a determination 'to extract information . . . at all costs'.

Hayward's 130-page report remained secret for almost sixty years, until the Foreign Office declassified it following my

Freedom of Information Act request. Many of the photographs of the emaciated inmates were missing by the time it was released and the Ministry of Defence tried, without success, to persuade the Foreign Office to withhold those few that were still in the file.

In his report, Hayward described how inmates remained at Bad Nenndorf for an average of seven months. Some were held as long as a year, however. Information extracted from them was supplied to MI6, the War Office and many other departments.

Hayward found the allegation of widespread intimidation to be 'overwhelmingly corroborated'; that of prolonged solitary confinement to be 'well established'; and the allegation of inadequate medical attention to be self-evident. He also found that the food was insufficient to sustain the prisoners. The combination of dousing with cold water and enforced scrubbing was not a punishment but an aid to interrogation, with the warders all emphasising 'the cruel manner in which it was enforced'.[32]

Hayward also discovered that a significant number of the inmates had found themselves at Bad Nenndorf because they had offered to act as informers. One of the men who starved to death, Walter Bergmann, had offered to spy for the British, but fell under suspicion because he spoke Russian. Bergmann had been ordered to the punishment cell when he was caught stealing scraps of food. Hayward's anger at this man's death could not be concealed behind the formal prose of his report: 'There seems little doubt that Bergmann, against whom no charge of any crime has ever been made, but on the contrary, who appears to be a man who has given every assistance, and that of considerable value, has lost his life through malnutrition and lack of medical care.'

The other man who died of malnutrition was Franz Osterreicher, who had been arrested while attempting to cross from the Russian zone with forged papers. Osterreicher, a teacher, was gay – or, as Hayward put it, 'throughout his life has had to suffer because of homosexual tendencies' – and had been entering the British zone to find a man with whom he had 'made an intimate friendship'. One of the interrogators satisfied himself that this account was true, but had been overruled. Osterreicher was slowly starved to death. If Hayward appears outraged by the death of Bergmann, he was deeply distressed by the manner in which Osterreicher died. 'He was obviously the type of man who would not complain,' he wrote, 'and in his struggle for existence or to get extra scraps of food he stood a very poor chance.'

Hayward noted that Stephens's deputy, Short, had admitted that half the people at Bad Nenndorf had nothing of interest to say under interrogation. As a result of his own inquiries, he concluded that the majority of the prisoners were 'persons of little Intelligence value, several being innocent of any offence whatsoever'. One inmate had been sent there as a result of a clerical error, and was incarcerated for eight months, while another, a former diplomat, remained locked up because he had 'learned too much about our interrogation methods'.

Hayward also came across a number of mysterious deaths at Bad Nenndorf, but appears to have been reluctant to delve too deep. A former SS man called Abeling died shortly after his arrival and Hayward was informed that he had been shot while resisting arrest. He was buried nearby, with the local gravedigger being told he was a British officer who had died of natural causes. A firing party was on hand to ensure that the dead man was buried with full military honours and a white wooden cross with a false name was erected over the grave. Sixty years later the wooden cross had been replaced with a gravestone bearing the name of the British officer local people believed to be buried there: John White, born 1.8.1911, died 17.1.1947.[33]

Another inmate was said to have hanged himself with a pair of underpants. His corpse was buried nearby, then exhumed in the middle of the night six months later and spirited away. Hayward concluded cryptically that 'it is obvious it would be undesirable to make further inquiries'.

A few days after Hayward submitted his report, the new commander-in-chief, General Sir Brian Robertson, ordered that Colonel Stephens be placed under close arrest.

Courts martial were inevitable. Too many people in Germany and the UK knew what had happened at Bad Nenndorf. A brief report on the scandal had even appeared in *Berlin am Mittag*, a newspaper published in the Russian zone. The only question remaining was how much, if any, of the proceedings should be held in public? It was not just the manner in which the inmates had been treated, there was also the fact that some of them were Russian. Less than three years earlier, the Soviet Union and the UK had been allies. As Lord Pakenham said in a note to Ernest Bevin: 'There are two main points on which publicity could fasten in this case: the fact that Bad Nenndorf was used *inter alia* for obtaining intelligence on the Russian Zone and that Russian as well as German nationals were held there; the fact that we are alleged to have treated internees in a manner reminiscent of the German Concentration Camps.'[34]

There was another concern as well. The British government was anxious that nobody should discover that there were other CSDIC interrogation centres in Germany. Already there had been complaints from German clergymen about the methods employed at an interrogation centre at Plön, near Kiel, where inmates were said to have been shackled for weeks at a time, some with wet hoods over their heads. There had even been complaints that a pregnant woman had been tied up inside a sack.[35]

There were other such places. Unknown to the Red Cross, the British were operating interrogation centres at three intern-ment camps, while in Berlin there was a fourth within a former Gestapo detention centre on the Lehrter Strasse. And these were just a small part of the network of prisons that CSDIC operated across Europe, North Africa and the Middle East.*

Ivone Kirkpatrick, deputy under-secretary at the Foreign Office, warned that Stephens's solicitors were threatening to highlight the responsibility that the Intelligence Division bore for events and, more worryingly, 'they may wish to call evidence . . . that other similar centres still exist in the British Zone'. On the other hand, he said, at least an open court martial would show that it was not a matter of gratuitous brutality, 'but of brutality designed to extract information from people sent there for the specific purpose of interrogation'.[36]

General Robertson, meanwhile, said that 'the possibility of public scandal' was not his direct concern; he was more worried that Russians would stop defecting to the British if they knew what fate was in store for them.

A decision was taken to prosecute Stephens, Smith and Langham in open court, with the courts martial sitting behind closed doors at certain points in the proceedings. This was not merely to prevent the Soviets from discovering that defectors were being interrogated at Bad Nenndorf, but also to ensure that the world knew nothing of the methods that the British were employing there.

Frank Edmunds was never brought to justice. By the time he had been charged with two counts of disgraceful conduct of a

---

* After Bad Nenndorf's closure, a purpose-built replacement called No. 10 Disposal Centre opened at Harsewinkel, east of Münster, a location chosen because it was a twenty-minute drive from the comforts of the officers' club at the RAF base at Gütersloh. Surviving lists of inmates' names suggest they were mostly Russian and East European. There was closer medical supervision of interrogation, but starvation diets for some. Most of the interrogators had served at Bad Nenndorf and there were frequent complaints about brutality. After this centre closed in January 1951, the British established yet another interrogation facility, the No. 1 Special Disposal Unit, at Werl Prison, east of Dortmund.

cruel kind he had already left the army. He was ordered back to Germany, but the charges were dropped when his court martial had not commenced three months after his last salary payment, at which point he ceased to be subject to military law. Because he had been subject to military law at the time the offences were committed he could not be prosecuted in the Control Commission's courts.[37] Edmunds returned to London and embarked on a successful business career.

Richard Langham went on trial in March, denying two counts of disgraceful conduct of a cruel kind. Despite attempts to prevent anything shameful from emerging in open court, Stephens's deputy, Lieutenant Colonel Short, blurted out that although the interrogators were forbidden to actually carry out murders, they were permitted to threaten to kill prisoners' wives and children, and that such threats were considered 'quite proper'. If the threats did not work, the prisoner would be 'interrogated until he was broken'. 'MI5 Methods told to Court,' read the *Daily Express* headline the following day. 'Quite Proper to Threaten Wives.'[38] One former inmate told the court that Langham had burned him with lit cigarettes. The court martial accepted Langham's claim that he was not responsible for the 'curious things' that had happened at Bad Nenndorf and he was acquitted. Shortly afterwards he moved to the United States, where he found work as a hospital administrator.

Captain John Smith was charged with the manslaughter of Bergmann and Osterreicher, and also faced a string of charges of professional neglect.[39] In his defence, he described Bad Nenndorf as a 'beastly place' but said that he had had no idea that people were being brutally treated, placing the blame firmly at Stephens's door.[40] He was cleared of manslaughter, but convicted on five of eleven charges of neglect. His punishment was to be dismissed from the army. He was fifty years old.[41]

Colonel Stephens went on trial on 8 June 1948 in Hamburg, charged with four counts of disgraceful conduct and ill-treatment of prisoners. The first charge related to the torture of Gerhard Menzel, the second and third to Dieter Albrecht, and the last concerned eight forms of mistreatment, including starvation, beatings, the use of extreme cold, the scrubbing punishment and the handcuffing of prisoners back to back. Stephens denied all the charges.

The judge advocate was Gerald Thesiger, a High Court judge and serving army officer. The president and members of the court martial – the jury, effectively – were a major general, five brigadiers and a colonel. After Stephens pleaded not-guilty to each charge, the court martial heard a submission, in secret, from Major General Douglas Packard, Director of Military Intelligence. It was then announced that the entire hearing would be held behind closed doors on the grounds that an open court martial 'might prejudice the administration of justice'. It would be another sixty years before the transcript was declassified.

We now know that behind closed doors Packard told the court martial about the role CSDIC played during the war and the belief that 'so far as is known our results were superior to anything obtained by the interrogation procedures of our enemies'. It was vital, he said, that nothing about CSDIC and its methods – or the existence during the war of Camp 020 – be disclosed in open court.[42]

There was never any chance of a conviction on the first count, as Menzel would not be giving evidence. The court martial was told that he had escaped from an internment camp; in fact, he decided to escape – by walking out of the front gate – after being warned by a British sergeant that he would spend the rest of his life behind bars if he gave evidence against Stephens.[43] Nor was there any chance of a conviction on counts two and three: Albrecht, the subject of those charges, was a stool pigeon at Bad Nenndorf, working for the British. The prosecution withdrew those charges. Everything now hinged on the final, catch-all, charge.

'The charges cover a campaign of cruelty pursued with unremitting zeal and energy,' said the prosecutor, Charles Henderson, KC, in his opening speech. 'The question, yea or nay, was a man handcuffed behind his back by day and handcuffed in front by night for inordinate periods of time, was he kept in a waterlogged cell under Arctic conditions . . . was he made to stand naked before a window for any purpose other than to lower the dignity of man?'[44]

Many of the British guards gave evidence. They explained that they had been ordered to beat the prisoners and said the inmates were frequently handcuffed back to back. The court martial also heard evidence that orders consigning a man to the punishment cell were put in writing and that Stephens had read those orders.

One former inmate after another appeared in court to testify, some angry, assertive and eager for justice, others needing to be pushed into court in wheelchairs. One of those who testified was Adolf Galla, the frightened inmate who had been in such a dreadful condition on admission to Rotenburg Internee Hospital that a British officer described him as 'one of the most disgusting sights of my life'. Galla gave an insight into one of the purposes behind the brutality of the Intelligence Division's secret prisons. Asked his occupation, and assured he could speak openly as no members of the public were present, Galla replied: 'I am working for the intelligence centre at Kiel. I am working as a senior official in the Communist Party . . . to receive information from the Russians.' Some of the prisoners had been broken under torture before being put to work as double agents.[45]

On several occasions former inmates attempted to give evidence about the use of 'the Gestapo implements'. Each time, Stephens's counsel, Aubrey Melford Stevenson, KC, rose quickly to his feet to silence them, pointing out that the use of such instruments played no part in any of the charges against the defendant.

Stephens did not deny any of the horrors of Bad Nenndorf. His defence was, quite simply, that he had no idea that the prisoners for whom he was responsible were suffering such torments. This was the very defence that had been offered – unsuccessfully – by countless concentration camp commandants at war crimes trials over the previous three years. This time the court martial was prepared to take such a defence seriously. It was, after all, a British officer on trial.

Although he was the commandant of Bad Nenndorf, Stephens claimed to have been too busy writing the official history of Camp 020 to be aware of the mistreatment of the prisoners. It was in this volume that he had written that interrogators must 'never strike a man' and that 'violence is taboo' – mantras that MI5 was still quoting sixty years later.[46] Despite describing himself in court as a strict disciplinarian and a stickler for detail, he had been so preoccupied by his literary task that he had not realised that men under his control were being beaten, whipped, frozen, deprived of sleep and starved to death.

While being questioned about his wartime work at Camp 020, Stephens repeatedly evaded questions about the use of punishment as an aid to interrogation. Eventually, under increasingly ill-tempered cross-examination by Henderson, he admitted that prisoners had been confined to Camp 020's notorious Cell 13 as a 'punishment' intended to assist their interrogation; that Cell 13 was unfurnished, with smooth walls and a linoleum floor; that Cell 14 was an identical punishment cell; and that their occupants could be handcuffed and kept in 'a certain amount of discomfort'. But he stressed that Sir David Petrie, the head of MI5, was fully aware of this, and that such information was included in intelligence reports to government ministers. 'Cell 13 was a well-known device,' he said.[47]

Stephens was acquitted of the two outstanding charges,

allowed to leave the service of the War Office and told he was free to rejoin MI5.

At the Foreign Office, there was a firmly rooted suspicion that the War Office had never wanted to see Stephens prosecuted at all; that, as one senior official said, 'there has been a lack of resolution in the Judge Advocate–General's Department to see that justice is done in this case'.[48]

What would explain such a lack of resolve? Why were the 'Gestapo implements' excluded from the prosecution, despite the medical records that corroborated testimony about their use? Why was Menzel, the main witness, allowed to walk out of an internment camp? Why did half the charges relate to a stool pigeon, resulting in their inevitable collapse?

Before the court martial began, Stephens's solicitor, Richard Butler, had written a series of letters to the War Office in which he warned that he would need to bring forward evidence about activities at Camp 020. 'I cannot believe that the Security Service, or indeed the Home Office, will view, save with feelings of considerable alarm, the disclosure in public of the detailed history of Camp 020,' he wrote, adding that it might be 'in the country's interests' for senior civil servants to meet him to discuss the matter further.[49] But what was it about 'the detailed history of Camp 020' that could cause such alarm to MI5 and the Home Office?

The answer to this question can be found inside a file of official correspondence about the case that remained classified until 2001, before being quietly deposited with the UK's National Archives. Buried deep within the file are two letters that the Attorney General of the day, Sir Hartley Shawcross, wrote to the Prime Minister, Clement Attlee, shortly after the court martial began.

Shawcross knew Stephens: they were contemporaries at Dulwich College. He also knew something of the activities of

MI5, having worked closely with the agency during the two years he served as regional commissioner for the north-west of England during the war.

In his first letter, Shawcross informed Attlee that the prosecution had been warned by the defence that it planned to assert 'that if cruelties did occur at Bad Nenndorf they were of the kind systematically adopted as the practice at MI5 Interrogation Centres during the war, and at Camps in Germany subsequently and authorised by Ministers through Sir David Petrie', the head of MI5.

Shawcross dashed off his second handwritten letter later the same day. He enclosed a list of twenty-one witnesses whom Stephens's lawyers were planning to call to corroborate this line of defence. They included Lord Swinton, the man who had set up Camp 020, Major General Lethbridge, Dick White, Sir Alexander Maxwell, permanent under-secretary at the Home Office throughout the war, and Sir Herbert Creedy, who succeeded Lord Swinton as chairman of the Security Executive.[50] The list was a Who's Who of the British security establishment, and they were queuing up to attest that government ministers had permitted MI5 to 'systematically' adopt cruelties at Camp 020.

For good measure, Shawcross informed Attlee that the defence was 'being conducted on the instructions of a Mr Butler'. Richard Butler was the London solicitor whose Roman Catholicism would have barred him from joining MI5 had Vernon Kell not been sacked. After being recruited to MI5 he had – as Shawcross reminded Attlee in his letter – served as Petrie's private secretary during the war. If anybody knew where the bodies were buried, it was Richard Butler.

The Attorney General's anxious letters explain why so many punches were pulled when Stephens was prosecuted. They also explain MI5's ability to quickly turn the wartime invasion spies into compliant double agents, resulting in perhaps the agency's greatest-ever achievement: the wartime Double Cross system.

The claim that violence was taboo at Camp 020 was a lie. It had been run on the same brutal lines as Bad Nenndorf. It too had been a torture centre.

3

Soiling the Honour of the Country: Colonial Conflict, 1945–67

'All those concerned in the preservation of order in Aden, both civil and military . . . are conscious, as I am, of the need to do so with restraint and humanity.'
George Brown, Foreign Secretary,
November 1966

'If India becomes free,' Gandhi predicted in a letter to President Roosevelt in 1942, 'the rest must follow.' And so it came to pass. With the end of the Raj, first Burma and then Ceylon slipped quietly away from the British Empire, barely noticed. And then came Palestine.

When the British Mandate for Palestine had been established in 1922, it represented the first Christian government in the Holy Land for a thousand years and had been a moment for the British to savour: it appeared to be the pinnacle of imperial achievement. Instead, it was to be the point at which the British discovered their impotence. Over the next quarter-century, as Jewish impatience and Arab anger mounted, the British-run Palestinian Police Force resorted to increasingly brutal methods in a losing battle to maintain order.

The police in British Palestine were a curiously Anglo-Irish affair, modelled on the Royal Irish Constabulary and including in their ranks hundreds of former Black and Tans.[1] One of them was Douglas Duff, who had served in Galway before travelling to Palestine, where he became a superintendent and head of police in Jerusalem, as well as the eponymous source of the expression 'duffing up'.

In his memoirs, Duff could not resist boasting that he frequently employed what he described as 'third degree' methods, such as the beating of the soles of feet and the practice now known as waterboarding. 'This latter method had the merit, from the investigator's viewpoint, of leaving no traces for doctors to detect,' he wrote. 'The victim was held down, flat on his back, while a thin-spouted coffee-pot poured a trickle of water up his nose, while his head was clamped immovably between cushions that left no marks of bruising. Usually we British officers remained discreetly in the background, not wishing to have the skirts of our garments soiled.'[2]

By 1947, two divisions of British troops were supporting the police in a doomed task, one that was costly in terms of lives and deeply unpopular both at home and abroad. At the end of that year the British, tired and dispirited, announced that they had had enough. Five months later the last British soldiers were marching up the gangways and onto their troop ships at Haifa.

After Palestine, the subjects of the British Empire began, one by one, to awaken to a new sense of national identity, a patriotism that owed nothing to king or mother country, and everything to a belief that in the mid-twentieth century the imperial ideal of the British was not only anachronistic but absurd. Often this awakening resulted in a bloody revolt. And usually the British were ill-prepared for it. In the early 1950s there were more police officers serving in Britain than in the whole of the Empire, and colonial intelligence-gathering machinery tended to be rickety and underfunded. All too aware of the fragility of their state apparatus, colonial governments turned quickly to the use of exemplary force. But post-Palestine, the rebels knew that the British would not fight to the end. In the eyes of one historian, 'it was the Easter Rising magnified a thousand times, and dispersed across the Empire: the same passions, the same ironies, the same waste, sometimes the same poetry, always, in the long run, the identical conclusion'.[3]

Frequently a brief rearguard action was mounted, usually in an attempt to determine the nature of the government that followed, but sometimes motivated by little more than pride. Just as brutality often accompanied the establishment of empire, so it attended on the dismantling. There would be interrogation of insurgents and with that interrogation came torture. It ranged from the barbaric cruelties and disfigurements inflicted upon countless Kikuyu people in Kenya to the brutal reaction to the Eoka campaign in Cyprus, and the vicious and cynical use of torture in an attempt to maintain a toehold in the Middle East in Aden. And always, because torture was such an un-British affair, it would be partnered with concealment, denial and lies.

The Kenyan rebellion which became known as the Mau Mau Uprising had started quietly during the mid-1940s, but quickly gathered impetus after the Second World War when men from Kikuyu and other communities who had served in the British forces returned home demanding economic and social justice. The Kikuyu were Kenya's most populous ethnic group, for whom the arrival of British settlers in the early years of the century had been a disaster.

At the start of the twentieth century the government in London had been eager to encourage British people to settle in Kenya. A few years before, in order to protect the source of the Nile from colonial rivals, the British had laid 582 miles of railway line from Mombasa, on the coast, to Kisuma, on the eastern shore of Lake Victoria, at a cost of £6.5 million. The rapid agricultural development of the new possession appeared to be the only way of paying the crippling bill.

Over the next thirty years, settlers from Britain and other

European countries expropriated swathes of African land with the full support of the British authorities. Their arrival had a particularly harsh impact on the Kikuyu, most of whom had the choice of labouring on European-owned farms for poor wages or migrating to the quickly expanding cities, seeking insecure work in unfamiliar places.[4] Some settlers, meanwhile, acquired vast estates and indulged in hedonistic lifestyles that became notorious across the Empire and beyond. By the early 1950s, the best agricultural land, the White Highlands, supported about two Europeans per square mile, while the poorest land supported up to 300 Kikuyu per square mile.

The first significant Mau Mau attack came in October 1952. It claimed the life of a prominent pro-British chief and caused the colonial government to declare a State of Emergency. The uprising that followed was a confused and confusing affair, one that has been the subject of many conflicting explanations over the years. Even the term Mau Mau has yet to be definitively interpreted. But what is not now disputed is that the Kikuyu's hunger for land was the compelling force behind the insurgency; nor that over seven years both sides would wage a dirty, merciless war.

The settlers could not fail to recognise the depth of Kikuyu anger, but mistakenly believed it to be rooted in the so-called spell of the Mau Mau oaths which the insurgents were expected to take. One settlers' leader described Mau Mau as a 'mind destroying disease'. When the words and acts of the oathing ceremonies became more widely known, they encouraged the view among Europeans in Kenya that they were witnessing a savage form of mass hysteria, a psychosis sweeping through a tribe destabilised by the civilising forces that had overtaken it.

Murders committed by Mau Mau certainly did appal: people were hacked to death and burned alive; tied in sacks and dropped down wells; decapitated and disembowelled. The overwhelming majority of the victims were African, although a small number of settlers, including elderly people and children, were also attacked and killed. The nature of the killings reinforced the settlers' belief that they were confronting not just another anti-colonial phenomenon but a fanatical, anti-civilising force, one that needed to be thoroughly expunged. Their response was, in some cases, influenced by a belief that Africans were biologically inferior; even that they were less capable of feeling pain.

In their ignorance, their racism and their terror, the British colonial authorities resorted to measures that were unprecedented in their barbarity and almost unimaginable in scale.

Shortly after the Emergency was declared, Harry Cross, a south London detective constable recruited as an inspector in the colonial police, wrote to former colleagues to describe the 'Gestapo methods' that were being employed to interrogate the insurgents. 'After persuasion they usually confess something,' he wrote. 'It's not uncommon for people to die in the cells.'[5] Despite this sort of conduct, some settlers accused the newly appointed governor, Sir Evelyn Baring, of being too hesitant and too weak, and insisted that only the whole-scale extermination of the Kikuyu would solve their problems.[6]

Years later, Terence Gavaghan, a colonial district officer based in central Kenya, would tell the American historian Caroline Elkins that Mau Mau was 'a seething mass of bestiality' that needed to be exterminated: 'We had to go to extraordinary lengths to get rid of this thing.'[7]

In colonial Kenya the authorities spoke not of interrogation but of screening. Such was the fear generated by Mau Mau that every Kikuyu was considered suspect, and women and children as well as men were at risk of being taken to specially designated screening camps. The work there was carried out by settlers' militias and bands of Kikuyu loyalists known as Home Guards, as well as police, district officers and men of the King's African Rifles, an East African force with British officers. As a consequence of what these units did, screening is a memory that holds particular horror for the Kikuyu.

Men were whipped, clubbed, subjected to electric shocks, mauled by dogs and chained to vehicles before being dragged around. Some were castrated. The same instruments used to crush testicles were used to remove fingers. It was far from uncommon for men to be beaten to death. Women were sexually violated with bottles, rodents and hot eggs.[8]

It was not long before Christian missionaries were condemning the screening centres as 'cruelty camps'. Kenya's Attorney General, Eric Griffiths-Jones, documented the use of torture in several memoranda.[9] Duncan McPherson, an assistant commissioner of police who opposed the brutality, complained: 'I would say that the conditions I found existing in some camps in Kenya were worse, far worse, than anything I experienced in my four and a half years as a prisoner of the Japanese.'[10]

Among those who were tortured was Barack Obama's grandfather, Hussein Onyango Obama. Having served in the British Army in Burma during the Second World War, he returned to Kenya, where he was accused, possibly incorrectly, of being an insurgent. In his memoir *Dreams from My Father*, Barack Obama refers briefly to his grandfather's imprisonment: 'Eventually he received a hearing, and he was found innocent. But he had been in the camp for over six months, and when he returned . . . he was very thin and dirty. He had difficulty walking, and his head was full of lice.' In 2008, Sarah Onyango, Hussein Onyango's third wife, told journalists that 'white soldiers' had visited the prison every few days to inflict what was described as 'disciplinary action' upon inmates suspected of subversion. 'He said they would sometimes squeeze his testicles with parallel metallic rods,' she declared. 'They also pierced his nails and buttocks with a sharp pin, with his hands and legs tied together with his head facing down.' Onyango is said to have been left permanently scarred and, not surprisingly, bitterly anti-British.[11]

The violence, far from abating as a result of the torture, reached fever pitch. Kikuyu and other Kenyans mounted attacks on police stations in the cities, while more guerrillas retreated to the forests, dodging army patrols and the bombs of the Royal Air Force to carry out raids on rural police posts and settlers' farms.

In May 1953, General Sir George Erskine, a personal friend of Sir Winston Churchill, was asked to fly to Nairobi to restore order. Erskine was bewildered by the phenomenon of Mau Mau. 'They are not normal human beings,' was his conclusion. But he saw too that the Kikuyu had real grievances that would one day need to be addressed. And he loathed the settlers, confiding in one letter to his wife: 'I hate the guts of them all, they are all middle-class sluts.'[12]

Later that year in a progress report for Antony Head, the Secretary of State for War, Erskine could not have been more frank about the killings and torture:

> In the early days ... there was a great deal of indiscrimin-
> ate shooting by Army and Police. I am quite certain
> prisoners were beaten to extract information. It is a short
> step from beating to torture, and I am now sure, although
> it has taken me some time to realise it, that torture was a
> feature of many police posts. The method of deployment
> of the Army in the early days in small detachments
> working closely with Police ... had evil results.
>
> As you know I have set out to clean up and not cover
> up ... I very much hope it will not be necessary for
> HMG to send out any independent inquiry. If they did
> so they would have to investigate everything from the
> beginning of the Emergency and I think the revelation
> would be shattering.[13]

Erskine's report remained classified until 2005.

Under Erskine, screening did not end but became more

disciplined. It was soon incorporated into the new policy of concentrating the Kikuyu population into Emergency Villages, large compounds surrounded by guards and barbed wire where they could be prevented from providing support to Mau Mau fighters. Between mid-1954 and late 1955 more than a million Kikuyu were herded into around 850 villages, where public meetings were held at which individuals would be goaded into confessing their 'sins', or encouraged to 'unburden themselves'. The screening teams were aided by *gakunia*, or 'little sacks', the feared hooded informants who would identify prominent Mau Mau. Those who were identified would be taken away by the screening teams for further interrogation.[14]

Inmates who attempted to inform the outside world of what was happening in the screening centres could expect harsh retribution. After smuggling a series of letters to Church leaders, to members of the opposition Labour Party in London and to the colonial government itself, Josiah Mwangi Kariuki was paraded before thousands of fellow detainees. 'The Commandant shouted in Swahili . . . "Mwangi, take off your clothes and lie down on the bench." I was then given 12 strokes by a Jaluo sergeant-major. I was then taken to Compound 6 where there was a European who gave me another twenty-eight strokes.'[15]

The letter-writing campaigns of Kariuki and others like him were doubly dangerous for the authorities. Their accounts of life in the camps contradicted the official assertion that the detainees were being humanely treated, while their literacy challenged the government's portrayal of the Mau Mau insurgency as an atavistic, uncivilised cult. It appeared, Kariuki wrote, 'that the colonial government of Kenya had lost its soul, and was no longer capable of distinguishing between right and wrong'.

By the end of 1955 Erskine and his troops had gained the upper hand and Mau Mau no longer posed a serious military threat. Nevertheless, the State of Emergency was not lifted until January 1960, during which time thousands of Kikuyu remained detained and the abuses continued as the colonial authorities attempted to cleanse an entire people of their rebellious tendencies. By now, the systematic brutality had a new name, 'dilution technique', which was intended to force most Mau Mau to confess and obey orders, leaving only a 'hard core' to be dealt with.

'We would be asked whether we had taken the oath,' one detainee, Ndiritu Kibira, explained. 'Those who denied having taken it were beaten badly until they were forced to confess or at least gave them some information. Many died from the beatings.'[16]

Police and troops did not enjoy complete immunity. By February 1954, 130 prosecutions had been brought against police officers accused of brutality, and seventy-three were convicted.

Nevertheless, the chances of investigation and prosecution were remote, and many men were candid about their crimes and their contempt for the victims. One auxiliary police officer, speaking two years after the Emergency was lifted, described his attempts to persuade three Mickeys – slang for Mau Mau – to talk:

They wouldn't say a thing, of course, and one of them, a tall coal-black bastard, kept grinning at me, real insolent. I slapped him hard, but he kept right on grinning at me, so I kicked him in the balls as hard as I could. He went down in a heap but when he finally got up on his feet he grinned at me again and I snapped, I really did. I stuck my revolver right in his grinning mouth and . . . I pulled the trigger. His brains went all over the side of the police station. The other two Mickeys were standing there looking blank. I said to them that if they didn't tell me where to find the rest of the gang I'd kill them too. They didn't say a word so I shot them both. When the sub-inspector drove up, I told him that the Mickeys tried to escape. He didn't believe me but all he said was: 'Bury them and see the wall is cleared up.'[17]

The response of Griffiths-Jones, the Kenyan Attorney General, showed the willingness of colonial law officers to draft legislation that accommodated rather than prohibited the abuses. Griffiths-Jones was well aware of the torture and the killings. As the use of the dilution technique spread, he drafted emergency regulations that authorised what was termed 'compelling force' against any individual who failed to comply with a lawful order.[18]

Few members of the colonial administration raised any concerns about the violence. One of the exceptions was Colonel Arthur Young, a former commissioner of the City of London Police who had been sent to Nairobi with instructions to bring the colonial force under more disciplined control. Throughout 1954, Young, a Christian and a socialist, repeatedly complained to Governor Evelyn Baring that 'unjustified and abhorrent' crimes were being committed by forces not under his command. After less than a year in post, realising that Baring had no interest in bringing the torture and killings to an end, Young resigned.

Questions about Young's resignation began to be asked in the House of Lords and a small number of backbench Labour MPs travelled to Kenya, investigating and complaining, albeit with little support from their party's leaders. In September 1955, the MP Barbara Castle wrote in the Labour-supporting *Tribune*: 'In the heart of the British Empire there is a police state where the rule of law has broken down, where the murder and torture of Africans by Europeans goes unpunished and where the authorities pledged to enforce justice regularly connive at its violation.'

The government in London and the colonial administration in Nairobi responded with a series of blanket denials. Whenever they were presented with evidence – including the testimony of prison guards – officials and ministers dismissed each case as an isolated incident, an understandable reaction to the horrors of Mau Mau. Alan Lennox-Boyd, the Secretary of State for the Colonies, became particularly adroit at denying what was becoming increasingly clear. The recriminations and denials became bitter and partisan. The liberal British press reported on the allegations of widespread brutality and abuse of power; the right-of-centre press focused resolutely on Mau Mau attacks. Between Castle and Lennox-Boyd, the dispute became highly personal.

As pressure mounted for an independent inquiry, the colonial authorities began gradually to release the detainees. A few thousand, however, supposedly the 'hard core' Mau Mau who had not been broken by the dilution technique, were to be kept behind barbed wire indefinitely in a camp at Hola, in the south-east of the country. In February 1959, a Commons motion in favour of an inquiry resulted in a vote split along party lines and was soundly defeated. A number of commentators hailed the outcome as a vindication of British colonial rule.

A few days later, on 4 March, news began to reach Nairobi and London that a number of men had died at Hola the previous day. The colonial government issued a press release stating that ten men had died 'after they had drunk water from a water cart'. The clear implication was that the water was contaminated. It was a crude lie: the men had indeed drunk from the water cart, but it was clean water. Shortly afterwards, eleven of them had been deliberately clubbed to death by their warders after refusing to obey a 'lawful order', as defined by Attorney General Griffiths-Jones. There had been two separate attacks: when the camp commandant, Michael Sullivan, discovered that only six men had died in the first, he ordered the second. Scores more had been injured, twenty-three eventually receiving hospital treatment.[19]

In London, the *New Statesman* compared Hola to the Nazi

concentration camps and the British people's apathy to that of Germans under Hitler. In New York, *Time* magazine reported that the investigation into 'the brutal slaughter' appeared to be 'strangely half-hearted, often clouded by deceit and outright lies'. Baring and Lennox-Boyd denied everything and leapt to the defence of their local officials. There was no judicial inquiry, no vote in the Commons, and the local coroner said he could find no witnesses prepared to talk about what had happened. Eventually the colonial authorities ruled that there was insufficient evidence to support any prosecutions. Sullivan was ordered to retire, with no loss of income.

The growing worldwide awareness that Britain's 'civilising mission' in East Africa had descended into barbarism led directly to British withdrawal from Kenya. Even Conservative MPs were admitting publicly that the affair had been hugely damaging to the country's reputation and began to accept that, while the British may have won the battle against the Mau Mau, they had lost the war to maintain control of the country. One MP, Enoch Powell, from the right wing of the party, declared that a nation that behaved in this manner did not deserve an empire.

Shortly before retiring from the Colonial Office, Lennox-Boyd declared British rule in Africa to be a triumph. His successor, Iain Macleod, immediately began taking steps towards withdrawal and, by 1963, Kenya was an independent nation.

There is some dispute among historians over the numbers of people incarcerated during the State of Emergency and the numbers who died during the uprising. The official estimate is that around 71,000 people were detained in late 1954 and that the figure fell steadily from then. Some estimates have put the number far higher. Similarly, some historians believe the official death toll of 12,000 to be far too low.

What is clear is that the abuses of the screening and detention camps caused lasting trauma, suffering that many former inmates felt unable openly to discuss until the ban on Mau Mau membership was finally lifted in 2003.

Shortly after this, a group of five ex-prisoners who had endured physical and sexual abuse brought civil proceedings against the British government in the London courts. Two of them had been castrated, while a third man spent two years in manacles before being taken to Hola, where he was among the group badly injured during the attacks that left eleven dead. Two of the claimants were elderly women. One, Jane Muthoni Mara, had been fifteen when she was arrested. She recalled that after a white army officer ordered her torture, a black soldier forced a bottle into her vagina while demanding she reveal the whereabouts of her brother, a Mau Mau fighter. 'He filled the bottle with hot water and then pushed it into my private parts with his foot,' she said. 'I screamed and screamed. Other women held at the camp were raped the same way. I have never forgotten it.'[20]

In court, five decades after these events, the British government made no attempt to deny what had happened in the camps. Instead, it invoked an obscure legal principle in an attempt to continue to deny responsibility. Its lawyers argued that the claim should not be allowed to proceed because of the law of state succession, insisting that it was the Kenyan government formed after independence, not the British government, that bore legal responsibility for the acts of the colonial administration.

The court dismissed this line of defence as 'dishonourable' and ruled that the former prisoners had the right to sue the British government, as there was 'ample evidence' of systematic torture and 'substantial' evidence that the authorities in both London and Nairobi had known what was happening.

During the court proceedings, it emerged that the British government had secretly spirited sixty-three boxes of documents out of Nairobi on the eve of Kenya's independence. When other Kenyan records were being declassified, these papers remained in storage at Hanslope Park, a secretive government research centre that develops technical aids for MI5, MI6 and GCHQ.

The papers contained descriptions of torture that the colonial officials themselves were providing to their superiors: accounts of the use of pliers, stress positions and solitary confinement, of torturers who dealt with detainees by pushing 'pins into their sides, buttocks, fingers and, on at least one occasion, the head'.

Among the cache was a letter from Baring to Lennox-Boyd in which he informed the Secretary of State that eight European officers were facing accusations of a series of murders, beatings and shootings. They included 'One District Officer, murder by beating up and roasting alive of one African.'

There was also a secret memorandum in which the Kenyan Attorney General, who had drafted changes to the colony's laws to authorise violence, described the dilution technique in practice. Blows were aimed mostly to the upper body, Griffiths-Jones wrote, although those meting out the beatings were aware that 'vulnerable parts of the body should not be struck, particularly the spleen, liver or kidneys'. Anyone who protested would have 'a foot placed on his throat and mud stuffed in his mouth . . . in the last resort knocked unconscious'.

While Griffiths-Jones expressed no concern for the legal or human rights of the detainees, he did worry about those carrying out the attacks: 'The psychological effects on those who administer violence are potentially dangerous; it is essential that they should remain collected, balanced and dispassionate.'

At the end of his secret memo, Griffiths-Jones urged Baring and Lennox-Boyd to ensure that as few people as possible should know what was happening. 'If we are going to sin,' he wrote, 'we must sin quietly.'

There was an intriguing postscript to the Mau Mau court case. When Foreign Office officials discovered the sixty-three boxes of files that had been flown out of Nairobi before independence, they found that Hanslope Park had been the hiding place for sensitive papers from across the British Empire. There were 2,000 boxes of files from more than three dozen other former colonies. According to a report on the affair, staff at Hanslope Park had been fed a 'canard' that the files did not belong to the Foreign Office and so were 'out of bounds'.[21] These were the most sensitive files from Britain's former colonies: those that documented the depths to which its officials had sunk and demonstrated that ministers in London had been fully aware of what was happening.

The Victorian historian Sir John Robert Seeley famously commented that the British seemed to have 'conquered and peopled half the world in a fit of absence of mind'. It would appear that the conquerors were anxious that a certain forgetfulness should also accompany the imperial endgame, and the savage manner in which it was sometimes played.

Blow your nose loudly in Cyprus, the writer Lawrence Durrell once joked, and someone in the next town would know about it within minutes. From the moment that the Eoka campaign against British rule was launched on 1 April 1955, however, the gossips fell silent.

'It was fantastic in an island where everyone was related to everyone else, how little general intelligence was coming in,' Durrell wrote. 'Partly the silence was due to fear of reprisals; but mostly because the sympathies of the general public were engaged, and even the non-combatant's door was always open to shelter a bomb-thrower.'[22]

The first attacks were on a broadcasting transmitter and army barracks in Nicosia, Famagusta, Larnaca and Limassol. Eoka, the Ethniki Organosis Kyprion Agoniston, or National Organisation of Cypriot Fighters, set out their objectives in manifestos scattered around the streets. 'Liberation from an occupier always comes through blood. We hereby take on the struggle to rid us of the British yoke,' the leaflet declared. It was signed 'Digenis', the nom de guerre of Georgios Grivas, a Cyprus-born former officer of the Greek Army.

Grivas, a veteran of a right-wing paramilitary group that had fought against Greek Communists after the Second World War, was a driven, obsessive man. He had slipped quietly back to the island the previous year with a promise from Athens that it would fund a nationalist guerrilla army. What Grivas's manifesto did not state – but the island's large Turkish-Cypriot population understood clearly enough – was that he sought not only an end to British rule but *enosis*: union with Greece.

The attacks should have come as no surprise to the British. The previous January, a Greek caique loaded with arms, ammunition and 10,000 sticks of dynamite had been intercepted by a Royal Navy frigate as it attempted to land at a remote bay on the west of the island. The smuggling of arms to Cyprus was assessed by the British authorities to represent a threat to more than just the peaceful administration of a small colony: Cyprus had become, since the loss of Palestine and the Suez Canal zone, Britain's military and intelligence headquarters for the Middle East. As a result of some curious feature of the ionosphere, listening stations on Cyprus could pick up signals from the Soviets' main missile-testing centres in central Asia. The island was also home to heavy bombers that, in the event of war, would attempt to penetrate deep into the Soviet Union. Cyprus was of the highest-possible strategic importance to the UK and NATO.

But the British intelligence apparatus was focused on regional rather than local concerns. Grivas, cooperating closely at times with Archbishop Makarios III, the astute and popular politician-priest who was primate of the Cypriot Orthodox Church, built up a well-armed and apparently well-organised guerrilla band under their noses.

The April attacks sent shock waves through Whitehall and the colonial administration. Blame quickly attached to the police Special Branch, which had been established only a year earlier and remained disorganised and under-resourced: a 'right royal muddle', in the view of MI5 and MI6.[23] So little did Special Branch know about Grivas that they assumed he was a Communist.

A senior MI5 officer was sent to Nicosia as director of intelligence, with instructions to take a firm grip on matters. Military interrogators and police were flown in from the UK, with helicopters provided to take suspects to the nearest interrogation centre. Eventually, John Prendergast, who had served as a senior colonial police officer in both Palestine and Kenya, was appointed to the same role on Cyprus. His officers were in no doubt what he expected from them: find Grivas and his commanders, capture or kill them, and smash Eoka.

It wasn't long before serious allegations began to be made against the British. In March 1957, David de Traz, a forty-year-old Swiss lawyer and representative of the International Committee of the Red Cross, was sent to investigate. After being admitted to Nicosia Central Prison, de Traz began to hear what he would describe as 'deeply distressing' stories from the inmates.

He interviewed around sixty men accused of being insurgents, all of whom had been transferred to the prison from the interrogation centre at Omorphita in the city's northern suburbs. These men told him that they had suffered appalling mistreatment during interrogation. Many had been beaten, some burned, others immersed in icy water. Some complained that they had been strapped down with a towel folded over their faces and that water, or sometimes kerosene, had been poured onto the towel to give them the impression they were drowning. 'Here is a brief list of the signs that I saw,' de Traz wrote in his report to Geneva. 'Broken jaw, cracked ribs (in great number), broken fingers, broken wrists, injuries to the skull, blows of a bayonet in the back, traces of whip marks on the back, traces of burns on legs . . .' He told the ICRC that he had heard the name of the interrogation centre at Omorphita mentioned 'frequently and with much rancour'.

Among those he interviewed was Nikos Sampson, a twenty-one-year-old press photographer. A number of fingernails were missing from Sampson's left hand. According to de Traz:

> I spent ten minutes alone with him in his cell. I offered him a cigarette, which allowed me to see that certain of his nails were missing. He suddenly told me about all sorts of torture that he been inflicted on him and showed me scars on his legs that he said were caused by burns. The official explanation given for Nicos losing his nails is that police had to hit his hand when he was arrested to disarm him.[24]

Sampson had been arrested following a series of Eoka assassinations in central Nicosia, after the British noticed he was always soon at the scene taking photographs. They suspected – correctly, as it turned out – that he was one of the gunmen. Samson told de Traz that a Special Branch sergeant by the name of Jeffrey Leach had used a piece of broken glass to slowly prise off his fingernails. Sampson was later tried for his role in the killings but acquitted after the court accepted that his confession may have been the result of torture. Twenty years later he would serve, briefly, as president of Cyprus.

After hearing scores of accounts to torture, de Traz was convinced that the allegations were too numerous and too well-supported by physical evidence to be discounted. 'The British policy is to break the back of Eoka by any means,' he concluded. He added that among the Eoka prisoners there was 'a real hatred that I didn't see last year'.

Three months later, and with no end to the mistreatment in sight, Dinos Constantinou, Secretary General of the National

Committee for Self-Determination of Cyprus, wrote to the ICRC to complain that the British were still committing the gravest-possible breaches of the Geneva Conventions.* Attached to his letter about 'the tortures inflicted on the Cypriot people by the British in Cyprus' was a complaint from Makarios, who had taken signed statements from 317 suspected Eoka supporters alleging torture. Among them were two clergymen, one an abbot, who complained that they had been beaten and burned. A pregnant woman was said to have miscarried after being beaten. Several men described being strapped to iron bedsteads and being subjected to what would today be called waterboarding. Others said that they had had toothpicks inserted under their nails, that their testicles were repeatedly crushed, that they had been burned with cigarettes or had had a walking stick inserted into their rectum. Most said that they had been continuously deprived of sleep.[25]

The Greek government had already lodged complaints about Britain's use of torture in Cyprus with both the European Commission on Human Rights in Strasbourg and the United Nations Secretary-General, Dag Hammarskjold, in New York. Early the following year, the Commission dispatched a six-strong delegation to Cyprus to investigate, much to the alarm of the British, who attempted to prevent it from speaking to prisoners about their experiences. The Foreign Office wrote to its embassy in Athens, instructing staff to find a means of discrediting the Greek complaints by presenting them as part of

---

* On the same day in June 1957 that Constantinou was writing his letter to the ICRC, 1,500 miles away in London the Geneva Conventions Bill was passing into law. *The Times* reported next day that there had been cries of enthusiastic support for Viscount Alexander of Hillsborough, the former defence minister, after he declared: 'I am sure it must be in our hearts and minds that if these Conventions had been ratified before the last great war a great many of the horrible actions that occurred and which disgusted humanity so much might never have been perpetrated at all. So I think we are taking a good step in the right direction.'

a smear campaign against British police and troops in Athens. Unearth 'reckless and irresponsible' Greek media reports, London urged. 'The more extravagant they are the better.'[26]

The British authorities denied everything. But this was not merely because future prosecutions might be undermined. As one historian has observed of the methods employed by the French during the war they were fighting almost simultaneously in Algeria, torture 'soils the honour of the army and the country', something the British were anxious to avoid.

By this stage it was clear that the British were fighting a losing battle. The death toll had been mounting month on month as Eoka planted bombs outside police stations, tossed grenades at passing foot patrols and mounted close-quarter assassination attacks in the towns and villages. With the loss of 156 British servicemen and police, along with a similar number of Cypriots suspected by Eoka of being collaborators, the British Prime Minister, Harold Macmillan, had given up all thought of permanent British rule of Cyprus. He began to seek a path to independence, one that would enable the UK to maintain a significant military and signals intelligence presence on the island.

As the British prepared for withdrawal, MI5 and Special Branch stepped up the hunt for Grivas. Earlier in the year, his second-in-command, Grigoris Afxentiou, had been killed by British forces who had set his hideout ablaze after a shoot-out, burning him alive. John Prendergast and a number of others took the view that it would make sense for Grivas to suffer the same fate.[27] An intense manhunt codenamed Operation Sunshine was mounted across the island, involving signals intelligence, blackmail and bribery, the creation of fake Eoka units and interrogation.

As the independence talks grew closer, the British believed the death of Grivas would weaken the Greek and Cypriot hand. Duncan Sandys, the Minister of Defence, sought assurances from the Chief of the Defence Staff that security forces had deployed 'an efficient organisation for obtaining information from Cypriot prisoners by tape-recording overheard conversations, by means of stool pigeons *and by other methods which proved effective in the last war* [my italics]'. He was assured that they had.[28]

Any Eoka activist who might possess even a scrap of information was rounded up to be interrogated in one final, frenzied episode of British brutality. On 2 February 1959, with talks in Zurich under way, British soldiers surrounded a boys' high school in Famagusta and ordered all the pupils to stand in a circle around the touchline of the football pitch. A young man with a hood over his head, with small eye-holes, made his way along the line. In Cyprus, the British called these informants hooded toads. When the informant reached a schoolboy called Petros Petrides, he made a small sign. It was shortly before Petros's sixteenth birthday.

Interviewed in 2010, Petros explained what happened next. He was taken by the soldiers to a prison in Famagusta old town. 'It was an old building, medieval. I was stripped naked and put in a pitch-black cell, one metre by three metres. Other prisoners were beaten outside my cell, so that I could hear their screams. Later I would be beaten outside other cells so that the prisoners inside could hear me.

'I was taken from the cell, along a corridor and into the second room on the right, the interrogation room. It was completely spattered with blood – the walls, ceiling, floor and the bed frame in the middle of the room were all covered in blood. To help myself get through it, I told myself that they probably slaughtered a chicken and sprayed the blood around the room, but I didn't really know.

'The interrogators were British Special Branch officers. No Turks were involved in my torture. They were men in their forties, stocky and well dressed, in shirt and trousers. They were calm, they were never angry. They knew what they were doing.

They were very good at their jobs. They spoke broken Greek. One of them was half Maltese. At one point he said: "I swear on the life of my Maltese mother I'm going to kill you."

'They kept asking me if I was a member of Eoka, who I knew from Eoka. I had been distributing leaflets around Famagusta and we used to go up on to the roofs of buildings to shout Eoka slogans through a loudhailer, but that's all. I was just a boy. I was skinny, I couldn't have weighed more than seventy pounds. I was scared. I was humiliated.

'They punched me in the stomach and grabbed my genitals. They tied me on the bed, spread-eagled and naked, and rubbed pepper into my lips and eyelids, and my private parts. They would put a piece of cloth over your nose and mouth and drip water on it and you would feel like you were drowning. Just before you passed out they would stop and take the cloth off. And then they would do it again.

'They put a metal bucket over my head and beat it. I'm still deaf in my right ear. Also, they would blindfold you with a piece of cloth that was soaked in blood and make you kneel and hold a chair high above your head. They would come from behind and punch you in the stomach. If you dropped it you were beaten more. Once I dropped it backwards and it hit one of the interrogators. I was really beaten for that.

'In the dark cell you just had a bottle to piss in. You were fed on bread and sardines. There wasn't enough water. They would rattle the latch on your door and you would jump up thinking they were coming to take you for interrogation. You couldn't sleep. Sometimes they did take you for interrogation. And when you were returned to your cell, you felt happy to be there, in this tiny pitch black cell, thinking "I'm back in my own cell", because you weren't in the other room being interrogated. And then they would rattle the latch again . . .'[29]

A few days after Petros and other young Eoka suspects were arrested, the British called off the search for Grivas. The

Greek Foreign Minister, Angelos Averoff, had quietly warned Macmillan over dinner that the guerrilla leader was best left undisturbed, to avoid the collapse of the negotiations and a possible bloodbath.[30]

Petros was moved into what Special Branch described as one of the 'luxury cells', which had a small window, where he was allowed to wear underpants and even permitted to use a toilet. A week later he was set free.

He went on to study electrical engineering and built up a large and successful business. By 2010 he was the wealthy chief executive of a chain of media and trading companies. But he had never spoken about what had happened, not even to his grown-up sons.

'It was a turning point in my life, a milestone. Going through that at sixteen years old makes you a different person. Strangely enough, I think that if you go through that and survive, it makes you stronger. You think you can conquer the world.'

While Petros and his friends were being tortured, Greek and Turkish delegates were conducting secret talks at the United Nations, while the British were preparing for formal talks in Zurich that were intended to lead the island to independence. The European Commission quietly shelved its investigation into the Greek government's torture allegations, having learned they were going to be withdrawn as part of the negotiations. When its provisional findings were published almost forty years later, it was clear that the Commission had already concluded that detainees were being tortured.[31]

Petros remains haunted. His memories of the horrors of the blood-spattered interrogation room are still vivid, hovering just over his shoulder. 'You never forget what happened. I can remember everything; it's always there, behind me. But I'm not going to let it draw me into it. I'm not going to get sucked in by what happened.'

Only one matter still troubles him: 'The hypocrisy. The

hypocrisy still makes me angry. When I hear people say that the British never do this sort of thing, that the British are too decent to do this, I just have to turn my head away, and maybe smile to myself.'

With the successive losses of Palestine, the Suez Canal zone and then Cyprus, it was decided that Aden would be the main British military base in the region.

In Downing Street, Macmillan had made clear that he understood that a 'wind of change' was leading inevitably to independence for African nations. But he underestimated the potent force of Arab nationalism, inspired largely by Gamal Abdel Nasser of Egypt, and believed he could consolidate the UK's influence in the Arab world through the expansion of the military presence at Aden. In 1963, new barracks were being erected for 25,000 men, along with accommodation for 10,000 wives and children. Schools, medical clinics and social clubs were to follow. Britain's commander-in-chief in the Middle East, Air Marshal Sir Charles Ellsworthy, declared: 'Aden is essential for our vital oil and strategic interests. We're here to stay.'

The local population had other ideas. In December that year a hand grenade was tossed into a group of colonial officials waiting for a flight at the airport. The deputy high commissioner was killed, along with an Indian woman waiting for the same flight. Dozens were injured. London declared a State of Emergency and suspended the legislative council, appointing the high commissioner, Sir Kennedy Trevaskis, as the sole political authority.

Scores of prominent local trade unionists were rounded up for questioning, together with members of the People's Socialist Party, which was sponsored by Nasser. It was not long before the suspects' families began to hear that they were being tortured, allegations that soon began to surface in both the Arabic and the British media.

Trevaskis asked the Chief Justice, Richard Le Gallais, to

investigate. A little more than two weeks later Le Gallais reported that there had not been any 'unjustifiable' or 'brutal' treatment of detainees. This was simply untrue and Trevaskis knew it: shortly after the grenade attack, he had agreed that the Ministry of Defence in London should send a team of trained interrogators to assist the Special Branch of the Aden police, which was struggling to identify the attackers. When the International Committee of the Red Cross began expressing concern over the media reports, the British government, armed with a copy of the report drawn up by Le Gallais, was able to insist that the matter had been thoroughly investigated and the allegations found to be baseless.

The military's interrogation centre had been established in a civil servant's house at Ahwar, a village 160 miles east of Aden. The British Army's Intelligence Corps arranged for it to be staffed by seven interrogators: five from the army, including two officers, and one each from the RAF and the Royal Navy.

According to a highly classified Ministry of Defence report, eleven of the prisoners were taken to Ahwar and tortured for several weeks. They were hooded, subjected to loud noise, deprived of sleep, starved and forced to stand in stressful positions for long periods. The results of their interrogation were passed to Special Branch.[32] The Intelligence Corps concluded at the end of this process that it had been 'a negative operation in the sense that it pointed to the innocence of those arrested'. The possibility that any of the tortured men may have turned to 'terrorism' as a result of their experiences appears not to have been considered.

During 1964 the insurgency became a little more frenetic and a little more bloody. Two British servicemen and a civilian were killed, along with an Arab policeman; thirty-two people were wounded. Trevaskis, possibly at the instigation of the army, suggested to London that the suspected insurgents be identified and assassinated. Others, including MI5, insisted they should be captured and interrogated.[33] That September, another interrogation centre was established at Fort Morbut, a two-storey building inside an army base overlooking the harbour at Steamer Point. Six cells were created on the ground floor, with interrogation chambers and offices on the top floor. This time the prisoners appealed directly to the Red Cross, in a smuggled letter in which they complained that they were being subjected to 'physical and moral torment'.[34] Once again, the British insisted that there was absolutely no truth in the claims, and refused the Red Cross permission to visit the colony.

Before long, the various anti-British guerrilla groups began to merge into two distinct rebel bands, the National Liberation Front (NLF) and the Front for the Liberation of Occupied South Yemen (FLOSY), both of which were backed at different times by Egypt. Many of their targets were British servicemen or Adeni policemen, who were often shot in the back of the head at close range. A number of the wives and children of servicemen and British civil servants were also killed and injured in gun and bomb attacks, among them the wife of the MI5 liaison officer, killed when a landmine hidden inside a bookcase detonated during a drinks party at a British diplomat's home.

By 1966, the British accepted that they were not 'here to stay' after all and announced that they would leave Aden within two years. The violence only intensified, however, in part because the Adeni insurgents assumed that the British were lying and in part because the two groups began to target each other in a merciless struggle for supremacy. By now the British really were confused. They were uncertain of the identities of the leadership of the rebellion and unable to understand which group was being backed and financed by Egypt at any particular time.

Initially the authorities had two means of gathering intelligence: their Adeni Special Branch detectives and information extracted through interrogation. But after more

than two years of conflict with guerrillas who regarded Special
Branch as a serious threat, that organisation existed in name
only. Six of the twenty-five local detectives had been killed,
four more had narrowly survived assassination attempts and all
but three of the survivors had resigned, fearing for their lives.
The remaining officers were reinforced by British detectives,
men who had no local knowledge and no local contacts. In
growing desperation, the British authorities drafted in John
Prendergast, who had headed the Special Branch operations
against both the Mau Mau and Eoka.

Following Prendergast's arrival, Fort Morbut began to work
around the clock. Increasing numbers of suspects were arrested
in army raids on their homes in the dead of night and dragged
away for interrogation. And as the British built up a more
detailed picture of their enemy, they realised, with growing
alarm, that many of the colony's senior Adeni police officers
and administrators appeared to be members of either the NLF
or FLOSY.

Prisoners who were no longer of any interest to the interrogators were not prosecuted or released, but detained for long
periods at a prison on the opposite side of the town. There
they would write letters to be smuggled to the outside world
that recounted their experiences inside the fort: stories of being
beaten by British soldiers, starved, held naked in fiercely air-
conditioned rooms for days at a time, deprived of all sleep,
forced to run in circles until exhausted. They complained that
they had suffered electric shocks on their hands and necks, and
that sticks and the barrels of guns had been forced into their
anuses. Some had lost fingernails and toenails.

In public, Trevaskis's successor, Sir Richard Turnbull, continued to insist that the British authorities were upholding the
highest-possible moral and legal standards. Privately, he took
the view that the British position would be hopeless without
the use of torture. 'If effective interrogation ceased we should

have virtually no forewarning against terrorism or information on its development,' he wrote in one confidential telegram to the Foreign Office. 'You may think I exaggerate. But it is almost impossible to over-state the possible consequences of the effective neutralisation of virtually the only intelligence weapon we have.'

Turnbull argued in the same telegram that the torturers were deserving of pity, and perhaps even respect, rather than vilification: 'In the interrogation centre we depend on serving officers carrying out an exacting, unpleasant and difficult task which in the last resort they cannot be forced to do, or at all events do determinedly. They are marked men for terrorists – secrets of identity cannot be kept here – and have physical danger as well as unpleasant work to endure.'[35]

Not all British servicemen took the same view and soldiers of the Special Air Service in particular stopped handing prisoners over to the Intelligence Corps because they did not wish them to be tortured. One former member of the SAS, Ken Connor, recalled how his comrades once asked for the assistance of an interrogator and watched a few hours later as an overweight officer clambered out of a helicopter: 'He said he was Maltese, but might equally have been Egyptian or Libyan. He was carrying an officer's swagger stick, and when he was taken to the prisoner the interrogator began to beat with his swagger stick all over the body, including the soles of his feet.' The SAS troopers believed that what they were watching was both counterproductive and morally wrong. 'Some members of B Squadron were restrained with only the greatest difficulty from shooting the interrogator. He beat up the prisoner for ten or 15 minutes, then said, "He knows nothing", got in the helicopter and went back to Steamer Point. That episode made a lasting impression on B Squadron. After that no-one they lifted was ever interrogated by the intelligence side.'[36]

★

In the summer of 1966, the Swedish branch of Amnesty International, the human rights organisation set up five years earlier, agreed to investigate complaints of torture it had received from the Civil Service Association of South Arabia. The cases documented by the association included those of Adel Mahfood Khalifa, a senior civil servant, who said he was beaten, deprived of sleep and forced to spend long periods naked in a small air-conditioned cell where he would be repeatedly doused in cold water; Abdul Majid Mockbel Sabri, a prison officer, who said he was beaten, subjected to the cold-cell treatment, raped with a wooden stick, and who lost several fingernails; and Abdul Rehman Fara Salem, a council worker, who suffered two broken fingers while being beaten and who said he was forced to lean against a wall, supporting his weight on his hands for long periods.[37]

When the Swedish delegate, Dr Salahaddin Rastgeldi, arrived in Aden, the British refused him permission to see any of their 164 prisoners. They were unable, however, to prevent him from interviewing those who had been released. Among these was Hashim Jawee, aged twenty-five, a local Aden councillor, of whom Rastgeldi said: 'He seemed to be deeply shaken by the interrogation and showed feelings of shame for the humiliating treatment to which he was subjected. There was no doubt about the truth of his description of his arrest and interrogation.' Jawee, like several other former prisoners, said one of his torturers had been a Frenchman, fresh from the war in Algeria. Rastgeldi reported back to Amnesty that he believed he had heard several credible accounts of torture.

The British government decided not just to continue denying the allegations, but to smear those who were investigating. When the head of Amnesty's Swedish section, Hans Goran Franck, wrote to Harold Wilson, who had been elected as Labour prime minister two years earlier, informing him that the organisation had gathered 'reliable information on the practice of torture', the Foreign Secretary, George Brown, told Wilson that Franck was a Communist sympathiser.[40] Selected journalists were invited to an off-the-record government briefing, where they were told that Rastgeldi could not be impartial because he was of Kurdish extraction and, falsely, that he was in the pocket of the Egyptians.[38]

Meanwhile, Amnesty's head office in London appeared to its Swedish branch to be strangely reluctant to publish Rastgeldi's report. This was because Amnesty had a rather unpleasant secret of its own. Shortly after the organisation's inception, its founder, Peter Benenson, and others around him, had forged a close and undeclared collaboration with the British government. A year after the Aden investigation it would emerge, to Amnesty's enormous embarrassment, that the organisation was secretly being funded by the British. A mysterious and generous backer identified in internal correspondence only as 'Harry' was, in fact, Harold Wilson's government.

Benenson was also compromised by party allegiance. He had been one of those who had campaigned to bring the truth about the Kenyan camps into the open, and had much admired the efforts of Barbara Castle and her fellow Labour MPs. Gerald Gardiner, the Lord Chancellor, wrote a confidential memo to Wilson explaining that 'although very much pressed by their Swedish section, Amnesty held the Swedish complaint as long as they could because Peter Benenson did not want to do anything to hurt a Labour Government'.[39]

When Amnesty could hold out no longer and its report was finally published, the British government agreed to hold an inquiry of its own. Roderic Bowen, a barrister and former Liberal MP who had lost his seat in that year's general election, was invited to travel to Aden. There was no question of Bowen being asked to investigate the torture allegations – not least because the government's man on the spot, Turnbull, had already made perfectly clear that they were true – so instead he was asked to 'examine the procedures current in Aden for the arrest, interrogation and detention of persons suspected of terrorist activities'.[40]

It was a narrow brief and Bowen was determined to stick to it. Even he, however, could not ignore the fact that allegations of torture had been made. Nor could he overlook the medical records of the prisoners, which showed that after a short period at Fort Morbut they displayed injuries consistent with torture. Furthermore, he found that the colonial government's legal advisers and health directors had repeatedly complained to the deputy high commissioner that 'interrogation was assisted by physical violence'.

Bowen's report explained that the most recent complaints 'circulate round three men'. While he declined to identify them, they were named in a number of classified defence reports, which explained that they were an officer in the Intelligence Corps and two NCOs. One report by military lawyers concluded that although the men had a prima facie case to answer, the officer could not be summarily prosecuted because he had – like Frank Edmunds of Bad Nenndorf before him – simply left the armed forces. Furthermore, it would be 'unthinkable' to take action against lower-ranking men when the officer was not appearing in court.[41]

Bowen made a number of recommendations intended to assist the investigation of complaints of mistreatment, including the introduction of civilian interrogators and improvements in record-keeping. In an introduction to the report, George Brown, who had been informed by Turnbull of the truth about Fort Morbut, expressed his admiration for those struggling to maintain order in Aden and said he was confident that 'they are conscious, as I am, of the need to do so with restraint and humanity'.

Peter Benenson made his own visit to Aden shortly after Bowen. On his return, he appeared to be in turmoil, resigning the presidency of Amnesty and warning that the government was bugging its offices and opening its mail. To some, he appeared to have suffered a nervous breakdown. To others, he seemed to have experienced a moment of truth. Benenson wrote to Gerald Gardiner to say that 'during many years spent in the personal investigation of repression . . . I never came across an uglier picture than that which met my eyes in Aden. It is no exaggeration to say that I was [made] physically sick . . . by the deliberate cruelty and affronts to the human dignity of the Arab population. There is . . . a strong possibility that some if not all the rather horrifying allegations are correct.'[42]

By mid-1966, the British were determined to be out of Aden by the end of the following year. They began to withdraw closer to the town, abandoning much of the inland territory to the NLF and FLOSY. Whitehall realised that the chances of influencing the complexion of the post-colonial government were fast vanishing and instead drew up plans for a fighting withdrawal. The work at Fort Morbut continued apace. The interrogators were no longer attempting to defeat an insurgency, however; now they were looking for scraps of information that would help the British avoid a disorderly and undignified rout.

The Foreign Secretary, having agreed publicly to implement many of Bowen's recommendations, was informed privately that it 'would not be practicable' to do so.[43] Newspaper reports alleging torture continued to be published and complaints continued to be received by the High Commission, but the surviving records suggest that most cases were closed without any investigation.[44]

In January 1967, two months after the Bowen report was published, the government was embarrassed by a report in the *Observer* based on allegations made by Mohamed Ali Shamsher, who said he had spent seventy days at Fort Morbut, during which time he was kept naked, hooded, beaten, half starved and initially given water only every three days. The newspaper also described how Shamsher said he had suffered electric-shock torture: 'In the upper interrogation room twice during questioning the officer would take my hand swiftly and place it quickly on a black wire lead running parallel to the edges of the interrogation desk and I would feel the shock right through my body.'[45]

Adenis were not the only people complaining about the activities at Fort Morbut. A Corporal G. Lennox of the Royal Army Ordnance Corps wrote to the *Sunday Times* to say that while on guard duty he had heard 'screams of pain and howling of the detainees'.

At home, hundreds of students were occupying the London School of Economics, Carnaby Street was catching the eye of the fashion magazines and Engelbert Humperdinck was at number one with 'Release Me'. The Summer of Love was just around the corner, yet 3,500 miles away, in a colony that had long since been lost, British torturers were subjecting young men to unspeakable torments with whips, sticks and electrodes.

In June, the local militia, the South Arabian Army, mutinied against their British commanders. Large sections of the police also rebelled. Eight British soldiers were killed when their truck was ambushed and fourteen others died in attacks elsewhere. It was to be two weeks before the British fully regained control of the town.

An airlift was organised to remove British civilians and rear echelon troops, and step by step the British retreated into the town. Even then the interrogations continued at Fort Morbut, ending only in September, as the British withdrew to the harbour and the airfield, their barbed-wire perimeter steadily contracting, with the Royal Marines guarding against any final overwhelming Adeni assault.

When the British departed a few weeks later, they left behind 125 dead. More than 800 had been wounded. More than 1,000 civilians had died in Aden town alone. That day the correspondent from *The Times* reported: 'These gloomy statistics faded this morning, however, in the general pleasure at going, and going quietly.'

4

A Barbaric Assault on the Mind:
Scientific Advances, 1950–70

'The techniques . . . have never been used by any organisation responsible to Her Majesty's government.'
Harold Macmillan, Prime Minister,
21 March 1960

On 30 May 1951, Sir Henry Thomas Tizard walked into the Ritz-Carlton on Montreal's Sherbrooke Street and asked for a single room with a bath. A bespectacled man in his mid-sixties, Tizard was once described as resembling nothing so much as an intelligent and sensitive frog. He was also said to have one of the finest scientific minds that had ever applied itself to war. Tizard the Wizard, they called him in the RAF, forever thankful for the role he played in championing the development of radar several years before it was needed during the Battle of Britain.

Tizard held a series of powerful positions within the British scientific and military establishment. He was chairman of the Defence Research Policy Committee and the Advisory Council on Scientific Policy, and consultant to the Joint Intelligence Bureau. He was in Montreal to address the Canadian Association of Physicists.

On 1 June, in-between a morning session with the association and dinner with some of its members, he slipped away for a meeting at the hotel that was marked in his private diary as 'discussion with Solandt, etc.' 'Solandt' was Dr Ormond Solandt, chairman of the Canadian Defence Research Board; 'etc.' were Dr Cyril Haskins of the CIA's research and development board and Professor Donald Hebb, head of the psychology department at McGill University in Montreal. A second CIA representative was also present, along with three other Canadian scientists.[1]

Solandt had written to Tizard a few weeks earlier to remind him 'that you once suggested calling a meeting in Canada to discuss the possibilities of research on the uses and misuses of drugs, hypnosis, etc., in war. It occurred to us that we might usefully have such a meeting in Montreal while you were there.' Tizard replied eagerly that he would be 'glad to attend', adding: 'We recently had a meeting of experts here so I shall be glad to come over with their opinion.'

Nobody at the meeting used the word brainwashing, the expression that had been coined nine months earlier by an American journalist and former intelligence officer, moulding it from the Chinese *hsi-nao* – 'to cleanse the mind'. Those present preferred the word 'menticide'. Nevertheless, they were there to consider ways of developing scientific techniques to induce 'confessions' through the destruction of individuals' core beliefs and values. The Canadian minutes of the meeting show that they talked about 'individual factors involved in the loss of persons who are converted to Communist thinking'.

The CIA's minutes of the meeting indicate that the Americans failed to disclose the existence of Project Bluebird, a behaviour-control programme the agency had launched the previous year.[2] The subjects for the Bluebird experiments were defectors, suspected double agents and other 'individuals of dubious loyalty' whom the CIA regarded as 'unique research material' for the testing of various drugs and hypnosis.[3] The minutes also show that if Tizard was aware of the British experiments with so-called truth drugs being conducted on Communist insurgents captured in Malaya, he chose not to mention them.

The CIA appears to have been alarmed in particular by the manner in which József Mindszenty, the head of the Roman Catholic Church in Hungary, had been reduced to a compliant, almost zombie-like figure at a show trial two years earlier in Budapest. Mindszenty, a potential successor to Pope Pius XII, had pleaded guilty to all of the charges he faced, including the ludicrous accusation that he had stolen the country's crown jewels, and was jailed for life. There was also some discussion about the Moscow show trials of the 1930s, with the group concluding that it would be a good idea to question refugees who had undergone interrogation in the Soviet bloc in an attempt to learn more about Russian and East European methods. Someone suggested that Mindszenty's sister, who lived in Nova Scotia, would be a good starting point.[4]

Initially, Tizard was sceptical about the notion of menticide experiments. The CIA recorded that he 'stated at the outset that there was nothing new in the whole business from what was practised during the Inquisition days and there was little hope of achieving any profound results through research'.

The Canadians, on the other hand, were enthralled by the subject. Hebb in particular was intrigued by what he termed 'sensory isolation'. According to the Canadian minutes of the meeting, Hebb 'suggested a situation whereby an individual might be placed in a situation . . . in which by means of cutting off of all sensory stimulation . . . and by the use of "white noise", the individual could be led into a situation whereby ideas, etc., might be implanted'.[5]

The CIA recorded that Tizard changed his mind and became 'quite enthusiastic', agreeing to put some of his staff in contact with Hebb to develop joint research programmes. 'Tizard was clearly impressed by the idea and agreed to its importance from a research standpoint. The others present had been convinced prior to the meeting and had little difficulty in reaching a common understanding that this is a vital field in the defence of the Western Powers.' It was agreed that a three-way research programme should be established in pursuit of mind-control techniques.

In the Cold War, one of the key battlegrounds was to be the human mind.

Professor Donald Hebb, a neuropsychologist, had had no previous interest in interrogation or psychological torture, being chiefly interested in learning more about the structure of the brain. At McGill he had been subjecting terrier puppies to periods of isolation and recording their behaviour on release in an attempt to learn more about the development of mammals' brains. But in 1951, with the offer of substantial funding from the Canadian Defence Research Board, he was about to change direction.

Hebb's clandestine project was called Experimental Studies in Change of Attitude and given the codename X-38. He told the postgraduate students with whom he was working that it was to be top secret. Few paid any heed, talking about it openly. His team began by constructing a row of air-conditioned and sound-proofed cells, measuring four feet by six feet by eight feet, on the top floor of McGill's psychology unit. The postgraduates were paid $20 a day to lie inside while wearing gloves, opaque goggles and headphones that broadcast hissing noises. Their instructions were to remain inside the cell as long as possible. They could communicate with observers outside and were monitored through windows.

Even Hebb was surprised by the results. While a few of his subjects lasted two days and one remained in a cell for six, only half his twenty-two subjects managed twenty-four hours. Some became so disoriented that during lavatory breaks they got lost inside the bathroom and needed help to find their way out. A few began to hallucinate, one after only twenty minutes. Some reported difficulty sleeping; others said they experienced long and vivid dreams.

Hebb then experimented with the implanting of ideas. The subjects were told that they could listen to something other than white noise: the choice included recordings of a repeated chorus of 'Home on the Range', a religious message aimed at children and a series of stock-market reports. When Hebb discovered that the postgraduates would listen to anything rather than hissing, he replaced 'Home on the Range' with a series of lectures intended to persuade the listener of the reality of paranormal phenomena. The subjects were questioned about their views on such matters before entering the cell and after leaving. Most of their views changed. Some even reported a new-found fear of ghosts.[6]

The following June, a delighted Hebb reported to the Defence Research Board that X-38 was succeeding.

In June 1950, eleven months before Tizard and Hebb's first encounter at the Montreal Ritz-Carlton, the Korean War had broken out. Western governments should have expected the North Korean invasion across the 38th Parallel: a number of intelligence reports had not only anticipated it but predicted the date. Yet the West seems to have been reluctant to accept that the Cold War could turn hot so soon and was taken completely by surprise.

As the North Korean forces advanced, they captured huge numbers of prisoners. Over the next three years of war, tens of thousands of South Korean troops would be captured, along with more than 10,000 American, British, Commonwealth and Turkish troops.

The first sign that the Communists had been able to influence some of these men came six months after the Montreal meeting when a small number of American and British prisoners made broadcasts on Radio Peking. Commanders and politicians in both countries were deeply concerned about what could be happening to their men at the hands of the enemy; concern turned to alarm following the armistice of July 1953, when twenty-one Americans, three Belgians and one British prisoner said they did not want to go home.

By this time the word brainwashing was highly popular, and for many people very frightening. Rumours began to spread about the existence of 'mysterious oriental devices'. In fact, to judge by the differences in the degree of collaboration between the Western nations' prisoners, it is more likely that the level of discipline the troops were able to maintain played a far more significant role in whether individual soldiers were willing to change their allegiance. There was very little collaboration among the Turkish contingent, where order was strictly enforc-ed, at times through violence. It is thought that only one Turk perished in the prison camps, although more than half had been wounded before capture. The one who died was beaten to death by his comrades for collaborating.[7]

In comparison, significant numbers of American prisoners collaborated with the North Koreans and, later, Chinese captors, simply because morale was poor, discipline had become badly frayed and, during the first winter of the war, when supplies were scarce, many of the POWs began to starve. Those who appeared to show a positive attitude to political 're-education' lectures received better rations and so many decided to play along simply in order to survive.

Nevertheless, the US authorities were convinced that a number of returning prisoners had been brainwashed into becoming Communist spies. In 1959, the Americans claimed to have identified seventy-five such men. In London, the War Office was so concerned that it re-established MI19, the body that had governed CSDIC during the Second World War, under the new name A19. This secretive organisation, which operated within the Air Ministry, recruited a young occupational psychologist called Cyril Cunningham, who travelled around the country in the guise of an officer in the Army Dental Corps, equipped with a reel-to-reel tape recorder, interviewing former prisoners of war to try to establish why some had collaborated.

Cunningham would spend the next ten years studying the interrogation techniques employed in tens of thousands of cases in nineteen different countries. Eventually he concluded that while interrogators were interested in extracting intelligence, 'the most important task of every interrogation agency' was usually 'the selection, control and operation of secret agents and informers' – as had been the case at Camp 020. Cunningham also formed the view that while interrogators liked to stress the psychological elements of their work, 'much that has been described as "psychological" is about as psychological as a piece of 4 by 2 across the kidneys'.[8]

And certainly collaborators did exist among the POWs who returned from Korea. Andrew Condron, a Royal Marine from West Lothian in Scotland, became a committed Marxist while a prisoner of the Chinese and remained in China for ten years. And George Blake, an MI6 officer serving in Seoul who spent three years in Chinese hands after capture during the rapid advance of 1950, returned home a secret Marxist and went on to spy for the KGB for nine years.

In Montreal, Hebb and his team eventually began to lose interest in sensory deprivation experiments. One reason for this, ironically, was that they tired of the monotony of waiting outside sound-proofed cells for days at a time. But with generous funding available from the British and Canadian governments, as well as the CIA, there were plenty of other scientists willing to take up where Hebb left off.

In 1955, Jack Vernon, a psychologist at Princeton University, obtained funding from the US Army to build an isolation chamber in which he replicated Hebb's work, discovering that postgraduate students 'lost disciplinary control over the thinking process' after prolonged isolation. Vernon believed that it might be possible to change religious convictions through sensory deprivation.

At the National Institute of Health in Maryland, Professor John Lilly took the experiments one step further, with a tank filled with water at body temperature into which a subject could be lowered wearing a face mask and breathing apparatus. Lilly tested the equipment himself and began to hallucinate after less than three hours. He briefed the CIA on his work, but fell out with the agency over its insistence that his research be classified.

However, one of Lilly's colleagues, Dr Maitland Baldwin, a former student of Hebb, became an enthusiastic researcher for the CIA. In one experiment, Baldwin locked a US Army volunteer in a sensory deprivation tank for forty hours. Baldwin reported that the man eventually kicked his way out after 'an hour of crying loudly and sobbing in a most heart-rending fashion'. Baldwin told Morse Allen, the CIA officer who had recruited him, that sensory deprivation would almost certainly cause irreparable psychological damage. Nevertheless, he made clear that if the agency could provide the cover and the subjects, he would carry out what Allen's report described as 'terminal type' experiments. After a series of meetings within the CIA, an agency medical officer killed off the project, branding it 'immoral and inhuman', and suggesting that those urging such experiments might want to 'volunteer their heads for use in Dr Baldwin's "noble" project'.[9]

Meanwhile, after a series of experiments at Cornell University funded by the CIA, two neurologists came to the conclusion that the most effective torture employed by the KGB was simply to force a victim to stand for days, while their legs swelled, their skin erupted in lesions and they began to hallucinate, a technique known today by the euphemism 'stress position'.[10] Others at Cornell disagreed, arguing that sensory deprivation was far more promising, as it appeared to break prisoners down in a way that left them malleable and anxious to talk. Lawrence Hinkle, a psychiatrist at Cornell and a regular recipient of CIA funding, argued that it had a further attraction: the interrogator 'can delude himself that he is using no force or coercion'.[11]

In 1956, one of Hebb's colleagues at McGill, Ewen Cameron, was approached by the CIA after an agency psychologist read that he too was conducting sensory deprivation experiments, accompanied by electro-convulsive therapy, on patients at the university's psychiatric treatment centre, the Allan Memorial Institute. Cameron accepted CIA funding for a series of experiments as part of a secret and highly illegal research project codenamed Project MK-Ultra, a successor to Project Bluebird. Over the next six years, approximately 100 people who were admitted to the Allan Memorial Institute with moderate mental health problems became unwitting guineas pigs in a series of extreme behavioural experiments, under the guise of treatment for schizophrenia.

In a three-stage experiment that Cameron called depatterning, patients would be placed in a drug-induced coma for up to two months, followed by a further month of regular ECT, and then be forced to listen to looped tape recordings for up to twenty-one days. The Allan Memorial Institute experiments were just a small part of MK-Ultra, designated by the CIA as MK-Ultra Subproject 68. Like the rest of the project, however, they were seeking to develop a means of brainwashing in order to extract information from resistant subjects.

Within ten years of the end of the Korean War the scientific literature being used to aid interrogation had grown enormously, with one bibliography prepared for the US Air Force citing 102 unclassified reports and papers in the English language alone, among them Robert Jay Lifton's 'Thought Reform of the Chinese Intellectuals', Hans Eysenck's 'The Dynamics of Anxiety and Hysteria' and a paper entitled 'Belated Reactions in Former Concentration Camp Inmates'.[12]

When some of the details of MK-Ultra were brought to

public attention during a series of US Congressional hearings in the late 1970s, it emerged that one of Cameron's victims, who was known only as Mary C, had been held in a sensory deprivation chamber for thirty-five days, an extraordinarily cruel length of time given what was known about the experiences of Hebb's students after twenty-four hours. In 1980, a number of the former guinea pigs sued both the CIA and the Canadian government: two of them remained so severely damaged by the experiments that they suffered severe prosopagnosia and were unable to recognise faces or basic everyday objects.[13]

If the human mind had become one of the Cold War's battlegrounds, the victims at the Allan Memorial Institute were the cannon fodder.

The growing realisation among scientists on both sides of the Atlantic during the 1950s that isolation and sensory deprivation could be used to break down an individual's resistance to interrogation would have come as no surprise to Harold Dearden, the resident psychiatrist at MI5's Camp 020. Although scientific understanding of human psychology was relatively rudimentary in 1940, Dearden grasped the use to which isolation could be put when attempting to break down a spy or a suspected fifth columnist. From the outset, isolation was a key part of the regime that he devised for use by 'Tin Eye' Stephens and he told at least one inmate that the prolonged periods of isolation were intended to make them eager to talk.

As a result of the work of Dearden and others, the British military and intelligence agencies were familiar with the use of sensory deprivation long before Henry Tizard's encounter with Donald Hebb and the CIA. In 1956, the experimentation conducted after the Montreal meeting resulted in the formation of a body called the Medical Intelligence Working Party, which worked closely with the Intelligence Corps and presented a secret report to the Ministry of Defence. The report, on aids to interrogation, was entitled 'States of Isolation'. All records of these experiments have either been destroyed or remain hidden away in closed government archives, however, and the MOD maintains that it can find no trace of the report.

Alongside their own experiments, and receiving updates from McGill and the CIA, the British were also keeping a close watch on scientists in the UK who were interested in sensory deprivation. During the 1950s Stanley Smith, a psychiatrist at the Moor Hospital in Lancaster, studied 'perceptual isolation' in an attempt to better understand mental health problems among people losing their hearing. He arranged for three sound-proofed cells to be built, and his subjects wore thick gloves and socks as well as goggles. Smith spent thirty-six hours in one of the chambers himself – 'I found it very unpleasant indeed' – along with twenty volunteers, who reported anxiety, tension, panic attacks and, in seven cases, 'body-image disturbance' which resulted in them believing their heads had left their necks, or that their arms were bigger than the rest of their bodies.

After Smith reported his findings in *The Lancet* in 1959 he received a telephone call from the War Office. 'They didn't ask for any help. They just said: "Have you been doing anything else?" They were rather taken aback when I told them about hearing loss and that sort of sensory loss.'[14]

Some of the experiments were less fruitful. As well as drawing upon their wartime experiences and the experiments in sensory deprivation that were being conducted on both sides of the Atlantic, the British made some rather unsatisfactory forays into pharmacology and the manipulation of sleep.

They had been interested in the use of so-called 'truth drugs', such as sodium thiopental and sodium amytal, throughout the 1940s and 1950s. In 1948, 'Tin Eye' Stephens told his court martial that MI6 had urged their use on the inmates of Camp 020, but he had refused.[15] Similarly, the War Office asked MI5 to use barbiturates to 'pick the brains' of Rudolf Hess, Hitler's deputy, after he flew to Scotland in 1941.[16] One declassified CIA report of June 1948 refers to a 'United States–Britain combined operation' to use drugs like sodium amytal. Such use was 'strictly unauthorised and no account of it was made in writing', the report said.[17]

During the twelve-year conflict against Communist insurgents in Malaya that began in 1948, the British Special Branch conducted highly secretive drug experiments on unwilling prisoners. Dick Craig, who ran Special Branch before joining MI6 at the end of the conflict, wrote later that 'the employment of excessive strong-arm measures to extract information was common, and much use was made of the highly vaunted truth drug'. Eventually, he added, such measures were largely abandoned as counterproductive, as the British attempted to win over the civilian population.[18]

The British also took an interest in hypnopaedia, or sleep-learning, believing that the Soviets had developed a technique for indoctrinating people by playing them messages while they slept. A declassified Ministry of Defence report shows that its scientists believed that a slowing down of the cerebral cortex during sleep left parts of the brain susceptible to 'outside stimulation . . . suggested thoughts and words'. Eventually, the British concluded that while hypnopaedia might have uses in indoctrination it was of no use in interrogation.[19]

Like the CIA, the Ministry of Defence experimented with the use of LSD to assist interrogation and a number of experiments were conducted on servicemen who were given increasing doses of the drug, alongside others given sodium amytal. Eventually the MOD concluded that 'ethical considerations apart, the effects of LSD was so unpredictable and varied so much from individual to individual that it was not practicable to use as an aid to interrogation'.[20]

★

Founded in 1799 with the noble aim of promoting 'the application of science to the common purposes of life', the Royal Institution of Great Britain is the oldest and perhaps most venerable scientific research body in the world. Ten chemical elements have been discovered there and fourteen of its scientists have won Nobel Prizes. Its raison d'être has always been nothing more or less than the advancement and betterment of mankind.

The scientists who gathered to hear the weekly evening lecture on 26 February 1960 were astonished, therefore, to hear an eminent psychiatrist hold forth on the lessons he had learned while serving as a wartime torturer, an occupation that had, as he explained, given him the chance to deliberately drive people mad.

The speaker was Alexander Kennedy, the psychiatrist who had conducted a number of drug experiments on unwilling prisoners while serving at CSDIC's prison in Cairo, and who had gone on to become scientific adviser to the Intelligence Division in post-war Germany. In 1960, he was professor of psychological medicine at the University of Edinburgh, a Fellow of the Royal College of Physicians and an Associate Fellow of the British Psychological Society. He was eager to explain to his fellow scientists how the 'unique opportunities' offered by the war had enabled him to discover how to destroy an individual's sense of personal identity, creating almost a 'tabula rasa . . . a palimpsest upon which new and artificial values can readily be inscribed by an interrogator'.[21]

Kennedy, then aged fifty-one, explained to his audience that what they were about to hear was based upon his knowledge of the psychological effects of sensory deprivation; his understanding of 'the induction of artificial neuroses'; and the psychological study of 'human beings under acute stress'. He said he was also familiar with the methods employed by experienced interrogators, from the days of the Spanish Inquisition to the modern military's practice of 'detailed interrogation'.

First, he said, it was essential that the subject be thoroughly disoriented through the use of sensory deprivation, 'confusing stimuli' and the creation of doubt over the values that the interrogator considered to be right or wrong. Then he or she must be subjected to 'synthetic conflict and tension', which should 'build up anxiety to the limits of tolerance', until the subject's desperation to escape becomes what Kennedy described as pathological. At this point, he said, the interrogator holds out the prospect of relief.

Expanding on these three essentials, Kennedy said that the subject should be kept in a dark room, the walls of which should not reflect sound, and should be brought food at random intervals by silent, uniformed guards. Sensory deprivation reduces consciousness, Kennedy explained, and 'when the level of consciousness is low, fatigue or very small amounts of drugs will produce hallucinatory experiences especially if ambiguous sounds and unstructured visual stimuli are presented to the subject'.

In a quite extraordinary aside, Kennedy told the audience that the effects of this regime were strikingly similar to the distress he had noticed in the elderly psychiatric patients he had treated in the north-east of England during the immediate post-war years, after he had arranged for their beds to be moved so that they faced in an unexpected direction and after they had 'lost their spectacles'.

During 'detailed interrogation', he went on, 'deep sleep may be prevented by stimulation, by refusing to let the subject remain in a comfortable position or close his eyes, or by the use of such drugs as thyroxine or amphetamine'. By testing pulse rate or skin resistance during this process, it was possible to determine when the subject was becoming most anxious. By introducing specific musical notes at this point, or revolving discs with patterned colours, it should be possible to reproduce the physical effects of anxiety at will.

The lessons to be learned from this, Kennedy told his listeners, were that 'the manipulation of anxiety' may be more fruitful for the psychologist than any insight into its cause. 'It may be that the lessons of a barbaric assault on the mind may lead us to re-examine some of the established tenets of psychotherapy, and so assist in the resolution of neurosis for more civilised ends.'

Kennedy did not disclose whether he was still working for the intelligence services or the British military. But he did let slip during his lecture that although one purpose of his wartime interrogations had been the extraction of information, this was not his main object. Rather, the 'highly specialised form of stress' to which he had subjected individuals during detailed interrogation had 'as its object the transfer of loyalties'. If a man who fell into his hands at the CSDIC interrogation centre at Ma'adi could be induced 'sincerely to change his loyalties', he could then be used 'to give false information to his sponsors'.[22] As Cyril Cunningham, the resident psychologist at the Air Ministry's shadowy A19 department would come to realise, torture was frequently inflicted on prisoners to turn them into double agents.

This almost certainly explains the torture of Elie Haggar, the young spy whose interrogation by Kennedy was witnessed by Dick White. Haggar was an Egyptian chemistry student at Lyons University who had been sent back to the Middle East after being recruited by the Abwehr. His arrest in 1943 had been carried out with the utmost secrecy, not least because his father was head of the Egyptian police.[23] Kennedy's service record contains the slightly cryptic observation that he possessed 'unique experience of the work of the secret organisations on the personnel side, with particular reference to the selection of agents and dealing with rejects'. As at Camp 020 and Bad Nenndorf, British intelligence officers at Cairo were using torture to turn agents such as Haggar into double agents, and to ensure that they never seriously contemplated a treble-cross.

Unsurprisingly, Kennedy's disclosures caused uproar. Two days after his lecture, the *Observer* published a lengthy report under the headline 'Spies Brainwashed in Britain'. The following week the *Daily Mail* picked up the scent, with a front-page splash headlined 'Brainwash Shocks'. The *Mail* examined the activities of something called the Psychological Warfare Unit, based at the Intelligence Corps' headquarters at Maresfield in Sussex. The Ministry of Defence confirmed to the newspaper that servicemen undergoing resistance-to-interrogation training at Maresfield were locked in stocks for long periods, forced to sit for long periods on a small one-legged stool, and locked in narrow boxes and doused in water. It was not true, the MOD insisted, that they were also stripped naked and forced to stand for long periods while chained to nearby objects. 'Men are made to stand and sometimes chained,' a spokesman said, 'but usually with underclothes on.'[24]

The following day, the Prime Minister, Harold Macmillan, sent a terse note to the Secretary of State for War, Christopher Soames. 'I would be glad if you could circulate a paper on brainwashing to the Cabinet. What is the Psychological Warfare Unit? I really think your colleagues would be interested to hear all about this.'[25]

Questions were asked in the Commons. 'To what extent have techniques of brainwashing been developed by the security organisations of Her Majesty's government?' demanded Barbara Castle. Macmillan replied that 'the techniques to which these questions refer have never been used by any organisation responsible to Her Majesty's government'. The following day, Macmillan's briefing from the War Office was amended to include the qualification 'so far as the War Office knows'. When issuing subsequent denials, Soames was careful to say that such techniques had not been used in this country, no doubt having been made aware that they had been employed at Ma'adi.[26]

Some time later, Francis Noel-Baker, a Labour MP who had

served alongside Kennedy at Ma'adi, wrote to Macmillan: 'It is within my personal knowledge – and that of people with whom I served during the war – that a technique of brainwashing certainly was used by Major Kennedy (as he then was) at the Combined Services Detailed Interrogation Centre outside Cairo and elsewhere, during the last war. Unfortunately, similar techniques were also employed during the Emergency in Cyprus. I should appreciate your assurance that formal instructions have been given forbidding these practices.' Noel-Baker was informed that the British military only trained personnel in the means to resist brainwashing, and were not taught to inflict it.[27]

The *Mail* kept digging, however, and soon heard whispers about German prisoners having been tortured at the London Cage during and after the Second World War. The newspaper submitted eleven written questions to the War Office, asking about sleep deprivation, hooding, beatings, something called 'keep on the move treatment' and mock executions. Its reporters also put it to the War Office that four inmates had committed suicide at the Cage. Soames fired off a letter to Macmillan conceding that 'apparently some German prisoners of war were ill-treated' at the Cage, adding, in a desperate attempt to reassure the Prime Minister: 'This, of course, is not brainwashing.'

Declassified Ministry of Defence papers show that a senior MOD official had a word with the *Mail*'s editor, Bill Hardcastle, and the Cage story was quietly spiked.[28]

By 1961, a decade after the Montreal meeting, a number of scientists believed that they had found the perfect torture regime: a system of interrogation that would produce 'truth in the shortest possible time', as 'Tin Eye' Stephens would have put it, that guaranteed an agent would become a double agent and that left few marks. In July 1963, the CIA codified the system in a remarkable document known as the *Kubark Counterintelligence*

Interrogation Manual, which remained classified for more than thirty years.[29]

Kubark was the CIA's cryptonym for itself and the purpose of the 128-page manual, as its introduction explained, was 'to help readers avoid the characteristic mistakes of poor interrogators' when extracting information from 'resistant sources'.

In a chapter entitled 'Deprivation of Sensory Stimuli', the manual cites the work conducted by Donald Hebb at McGill University and John Lilly at the National Institute of Health in Maryland, which demonstrated that 'the deprivation of sensory stimuli induces stress; the stress becomes unbearable for most subjects'. Thought must be given to the location where the prisoner is to be detained:

> The more completely the place of confinement eliminates sensory stimuli, the more rapidly and deeply will the interrogatee be affected. Results produced only after weeks or months of imprisonment in an ordinary cell can be duplicated in hours or days in a cell which has no light (or weak artificial light which never varies), which is sound-proofed, in which odours are eliminated, etc. An environment still more subject to control, such as water-tank or iron lung, is even more effective.

Drugs and hypnosis have limited uses, according to the manual. However, in a chapter entitled 'Threats and Fear', the trainee interrogator is informed that 'the threat of coercion usually weakens or destroys resistance more effectively than coercion itself. The threat to inflict pain, for example, can trigger fears more damaging than the immediate sensation of pain.'

A chapter entitled simply 'Pain' quotes Lawrence Hinkle, the psychiatrist at Cornell, who had observed that while all men have a similar pain threshold they react very differently to the experience of it, and warned that 'intense pain is quite likely to produce false confessions, concocted as a means of escaping from distress'. Not that pain was to be discounted by the authors of the manual; rather, it should be applied sooner rather than later. 'If an interrogatee is caused to suffer pain rather late in the interrogation process and after other tactics have failed, he is almost certain to conclude that the interrogator is becoming desperate. He may then decide that if he can just hold out against this final assault, he will win the struggle and his freedom. And he is likely to be right.'

The manual then offers the view that 'whereas pain inflicted on a person from outside himself may actually focus or intensify his will to resist, his resistance is likelier to be sapped by pain which he seems to inflict upon himself'.

Quoting from a study of the torture of American airmen during the Korean War published six years earlier in the *Bulletin of the New York Academy of Medicine*, the manual states:

> in the simple torture situation the contest is one between the individual and his tormentor (. . . and he can frequently endure). When the individual is told to stand to attention for long periods, an intervening factor is introduced. The immediate source of the pain is not the interrogator but the victim himself. The motivational strength of the individual is likely to exhaust itself in this internal encounter . . .

The *Kubark Counterintelligence Interrogation Manual* was reflecting conclusions that had been reached not just by the US, but also by Canada and the UK.

In November 1971, Brigadier Richard Mansfield Bremner, commandant of the British Army's Intelligence Corps, sat down at his desk at Templer Barracks in Ashford, to the south-east of London, and began writing a brief history of the development of UK military interrogation methods since the Second World War.

Bremner's aim was to justify those methods on the basis of the intelligence that the techniques had squeezed out of people. What he wrote was so disturbing, however, that senior MOD officials stamped the words 'UK Eyes Only' at the top and bottom of each page of his report and decreed that it should remain classified for at least 100 years. In the event, it was included in a batch of MOD papers that were declared fit for public consumption after just thirty years and dispatched, along with hundreds of other documents, to the country's National Archives.[30]

Bremner's report showed that the British military had forgotten none of the secrets of Camp 020, or Bad Nenndorf and the mysterious interrogation centre at Plön. It had absorbed everything that there was to learn from the dilution technique of Kenya, from Omorphita interrogation centre in Cyprus and from Fort Morbut at Aden. And it had distilled the most useful lessons of the pioneering work of Harold Dearden and Alexander Kennedy and the ground-breaking science of Hebb, Hinkle and Cameron. Finally, the army, navy and air force had taken on board the grim utilitarianism of the *Kubark Counterintelligence Interrogation Manual*.

The British had devised a method of torture that combined isolation, sensory deprivation, seemingly self-inflicted pain, exhaustion and humiliation. It was a method that was simple to teach, inexpensive to apply and required no drugs or devices. It could be employed close to the front line during times of war or in discreet urban interrogation centres in times of peace. It was guaranteed to leave no marks that would result in either official embarrassment or the risk of war crimes prosecutions. It would, however, cause intense pain and terror, plus lasting psychological damage.

The method was based on the combination of five stresses,

known within the Intelligence Corps as the 'Five Techniques'. They were starvation, or what Bremner termed 'sparse diet'; sleep deprivation; hooding; the use of an incessant hissing sound known as white noise; and 'wall-standing'. This last was a stress position in which the victim would be forced to stand with his or her legs spread wide apart, leaning forward with arms spread wide and high, with much of their weight supported against a wall on outstretched fingers.

Before being forced into this position, the victims would be stripped, subjected to a medical examination to ensure that they would survive what was to follow, then dressed in an outsized, shapeless, buttonless boiler suit that resembled the clown-like clothing that the prisoners at Bad Nenndorf were obliged to wear. The hoods were made of denim, although a couple of sandbags could be used if necessary. The white noise was produced by compressed air from a generator.

The hooding and noise quickly produced the psychosis that was first seen at McGill University. Wall-standing produced the self-inflicted pain recommended by Kubark. It was so painful, however, that the Five Techniques were always supported by a sixth, unspoken, technique: anyone who refused to maintain the stress position would be very severely beaten.

Nothing about the Techniques was written down, Bremner reported, no doubt as a result of extreme misgivings about the morality and legality of their use. Instead, the method was passed on by successive generations of Intelligence Corps interrogators by word of mouth.

'From 1945 to 1956, the interrogation skills acquired during World War II were kept alive by a Territorial Army unit known as IS9,' Bremner wrote. In 1956, the Interrogation Branch was formed at the Corps' then headquarters at Maresfield, with representatives from the RAF and Royal Navy as well as the army running interrogation courses for army officers and NCOs.

Initially, the courses were 'directed at the interrogation of prisoners of war and refugees', but they were later modified to include interrogation of suspected spies and insurgents. In the mid-1960s the Interrogation Branch was renamed the Joint Services Interrogation Wing and was absorbed into the grandly named School of Service Intelligence, based at Ashford in Kent.

In 1945, Bremner wrote, 'interrogations took place to clear up a number of problems left over from World War II. The subjects were mainly prisoners of war, refugees and alleged war criminals. Police Special Branches were not involved.' In the three insurgencies of the immediate post-war years – Palestine, Malaya* and Kenya – 'interrogation techniques were used and used with success', but few records remained.

Bremner believed it was worth noting that in Kenya 'it is known that a system was evolved in which Mau Mau terrorists were persuaded, in a matter of hours, to change their allegiance and lead raids against their comrades'. In Cyprus during the 1950s, Bremner said, combined military and police 'screening teams' worked across the island and a 'full scale interrogation centre was also set up'.

The military and Special Branch officers teamed up again in 1960 and 1961, in British Cameroons in West Africa, a state that is today divided between Nigeria and Cameroon. 'This operation was mounted when members of a subversive group from the neighbouring Cameroon Republic were arrested on British-controlled territory, which they were using as a base.' Two army officers, one warrant officer and four NCOs converted an annexe of a hotel into an interrogation centre and set to work: 'Of 20 high-grade suspects, 15 co-operated fully. Information elicited included full details of rebel training camps in Morocco and other north-west African countries – even to

---

* Long after the conflict in Malaya, the leader of the Communist guerrillas, Chin Peng, claimed in his memoirs that interrogation of his captured troops, including women, had been so severe that on occasion some committed suicide, or possibly died under torture.

course syllabi. The heavy involvement of Communist China in African affairs was confirmed for the first time.'

In February 1963, a dozen interrogators, including an RAF officer, set up three centres in Brunei during the suppression of an insurgency by the Indonesian-backed North Kalimantan National Army. 'This was a large scale operation which involved, initially, 2000 prisoners,' according to the Bremner Report, and some of the Five Techniques were employed.

In June that year, an interrogator was flown to Swaziland after 1,500 men at an asbestos mine went on strike, demanding a basic wage of £1 a day. Swaziland was another protectorate and hundreds of British troops were being flown in to break the strike. 'It was thought that labour problems at the local asbestos mine were created by subversive organisation,' Bremner wrote. The lone Intelligence Corps warrant officer went to work with local Special Branch officers. 'In the event, no subversive organisation was found. Thus was a valuable negative result achieved, in that it quickly established that local grievances were the cause of unrest and no subversive organisation was involved.' The interrogations, Bremner added, helped to 'clear up' the strike.

The report touches upon some of the interrogations carried out in Aden: it was said to be 'recognised to be the main source of intelligence'. Four of the Five Techniques were also employed in the South American colony of British Guiana during riots which erupted in July 1964. A pair of army interrogators set up an interrogation centre and trained Special Branch officers in the use of hooding, sleep deprivation, starvation and wall-standing; the use of white noise had not yet been developed. The rioting had been triggered not only by racial tension and economic grievances, but, historians now agree, by repeated British intervention, at the instigation of the United States, to undermine the government of the popular but left-leaning premier, Cheddi Jagan.[31] Bremner recounted that after a number of people had been interrogated, the Intelligence Corps concluded that they had been involved in 'purely criminal activities'.

Next stop was Borneo, for a two-year operation beginning in 1963 during the *Konfrontasi*, the undeclared war between Malaysia and Indonesia. The Malaysians were supported by Australian and New Zealand forces as well as the British, who established a second interrogation centre on the Malaysian peninsula itself, according to the Bremner Report. The 'subjects' included both civilians and members of the Indonesian armed forces: 'Detailed Order of Battle information on the regular Indonesian forces was produced in quantity.'

The use of white noise was first employed in 1970 during counter-insurgency operations in Oman, following the adaptation of a generator to produce compressed air, hissing at around eighty-five decibels.

By the time Bremner wrote his report, the Joint Services Interrogation Wing was helping to train interrogators from the United States, Jordan, Germany and Norway in the Five Techniques – 'our very simple system is admired' – while Hong Kong police, some detectives from Scotland Yard's Special Branch and some MI5 officers also received training. With an irony that appears to have passed Brigadier Bremner by, his report explains that the interrogation school also trained members of the British armed forces to resist interrogation, by showing them what they might expect 'at the hands of an unscrupulous enemy'.

For most of this period the Intelligence Corps' secret torture unit took its orders direct from the War Office and was subject to little, if any, outside interference. Military scientists and physicians were occasionally consulted, in 1956 and again in 1965, when the MOD established a body called the Working Party on Research into Interrogation Aids.[32] There is no evidence of any military lawyers examining the work of the

Interrogation Wing, however: they appear to have given the organisation a very wide berth.

Before long, a decision would be taken to employ the Five Techniques closer to home, and this time on British subjects.

5

The Five Techniques: Northern Ireland, 1971–2

'The techniques which the Committee examined will not be used in future as an aid to interrogation. The statement that I have made covers all future circumstances.'
Edward Heath, Prime Minister,
2 March 1972

In the early hours of 6 February 1971, a group of gunners from the British Army's Royal Artillery Regiment waited anxiously at the junction of New Lodge Road and Lepper Street in north Belfast for the order to baton-charge a 100-strong mob of youths throwing bricks and petrol bombs in their direction. Among the soldiers was Robert Curtis, aged twenty, who had just received a letter from his wife, Joan, informing him that he was about to become a father.

A short burst of shots was heard from a high-rise block nearby and Curtis fell to the ground. One round had hit him in the shoulder and entered his heart. There was so little blood that one of his mates put a lit cigarette between his lips, not realising he was already dead.[1] Curtis was the first British soldier to die in Ireland since the 1920s. As a direct response, the Unionist Prime Minister of Northern Ireland, Sir James Chichester-Clark, announced: 'Northern Ireland is at war with the Irish Republican Army Provisionals.'

Two other people died that night: an IRA volunteer called

James Saunders and a Catholic civilian, Bernard Watt, both shot dead by the army. Three days later two BBC technicians and three labourers who were driving to a transmitter on a County Tyrone hillside were killed when their vehicle was blown apart by an IRA bomb. By the end of the month a second soldier, two officers of the Royal Ulster Constabulary and a civilian had been killed. Shortly afterwards, Billy Reid, the IRA man who had killed Gunner Curtis, was himself shot dead.

After eighteen months of escalating political and sectarian violence, the situation in Northern Ireland was spiralling out of control at a bewildering pace.

The Northern Ireland government became convinced that the only solution to the growing lawlessness was internment without trial. Internment had worked during the abortive IRA campaign of the late 1950s and the hope was that it would provide a breathing space for some political progress. The Cabinet in London saw it as preferable to direct rule. The British Army was against internment, with the General Officer Commanding Northern Ireland, General Sir Harry Tuzo, making clear that he considered it militarily unnecessary. But Edward Heath, the Prime Minister, was in favour: it was a chance, as he put it, 'to bypass the wall of silence by swooping on terrorist suspects without warning'.

For Dick White, it was an opportunity to discover more about the IRA. And for the Intelligence Corps, it was another chance to experiment with the Five Techniques.

By this time, Dick White was Sir Dick, the country's most senior intelligence officer. He had been appointed director general of MI5 in 1953 and immediately set about reorganising the agency along civil service lines. Three years later he was abruptly moved to the very different world of MI6, and was to remain chief of that agency for the next twelve years. On retirement from MI6 he had been persuaded to accept the newly created post of coordinator of intelligence at the Cabinet Office.

White travelled to Belfast that March, and on his return there were discussions between the Cabinet Office, the MOD and senior figures in the intelligence community. A decision was taken that a small number of those who were to be interned would be selected for interrogation. For White, whose earliest experiences with MI5 had included Camp 020 and the successes of the Double Cross system, it was an axiom, reinforced by a lifetime's work, that interrogation held the solution to the growing confusion and disorder in Northern Ireland. Ministers were informed that a number of individuals were to be subjected to interrogation in depth and that they would be 'liable to be subjected to a measure of fatigue, isolation and noise'. They were not told of the precise methods to be employed.[2]

The RUC's Special Branch was advised to make a formal request for interrogation training and in April the Joint Services Interrogation Wing flew six officers and eight NCOs to Northern Ireland. All three branches of the armed forces were represented. Ten Special Branch detectives were selected for training and a purpose-built interrogation centre was constructed inside a fenced compound at a former Second World War airfield at Ballykelly, fifteen miles east of Derry. Hundreds of people were to be rounded up for internment during what would be codenamed Operation Demetrius, but just a handful were selected for the Five Techniques, in a connected operation codenamed Operation Calaba. A number of senior RUC officers expressed reservations about what was being planned, but their objections appear to have been brushed aside. They were assured that no police officer would be held responsible if the use of the Five Techniques was ever criticised.[3]

Operation Calaba was to have calamitous results. Far from providing the intelligence that would enable the police and the army to dismantle the IRA, the use of torture enraged the Nationalist population and encouraged countless young men and women to take up arms against the British. The methods that had been so successful at Camp 020 and which were then employed during counter-insurgency operations across the globe would fan the flames of a tragic conflict in Northern Ireland. It would burn for a further thirty years.

When the soldiers came for Patrick McNally, banging on the door of his home in Armagh at 4.30 a.m., there was an almost-civil exchange on his doorstep. 'I said: "Is it internment?" One of them said: "Yes."' McNally dressed quickly and went with the troops to the grounds of a local hospital, where he and a few other men were loaded into a truck and driven away to an army barracks.

It was 9 August 1971, a warm, overcast day, and as it dragged on, Patrick McNally realised that other men in the hut where he was held were being taken away for questioning and that some were not returning. Eventually, by the morning of 10 August, there were just four men remaining. He and the other three internees were forced to perform sit-ups and press-ups throughout much of that day and the following night. Suddenly the next morning, around fifteen soldiers and a dozen police officers burst into the hut, handcuffed all four men and, without warning or explanation, placed hoods over their heads. They were bundled into a vehicle and then into a helicopter. As McNally recalled:

> Not a word was spoken the whole time. About an hour, or between half an hour and an hour in the helicopter. Then out of the helicopter, into another vehicle, all the time very roughly handled ...
>
> We had a medical examination, stripped naked, still with the hood on. A short examination. No words spoken. Then into the boiler suit, about three sizes too big for me, open down the middle. Then taken out and

stood against the wall, inside a building somewhere. At this time, in the beginning, I think we were lined together because you could feel people standing beside you.

After a while I began to move and became restless. That was the first contact I had with anybody; my arms were falling down; they would raise them up and bang them against the wall. You were never allowed to keep your head down, just a few minutes and then it was pulled back.

The noise was there at the start, but it didn't annoy me much. I was expecting it to be turned off. Only after a few hours that I began to think more about it. In the beginning it didn't seem loud but after a while it seemed the only thing that mattered, nothing seemed to matter only the noise.

After a while your hands and arms were numb. I imagined I was on a round wall, kept thinking it was a massive big pillar, kept thinking there was a roundness on the wall. After, I don't know how long, I think I fainted, was lifted up again. It just seemed an endless time against the wall. I know I had collapsed a few times. If you made any movement, if your hand crumbled, they would bang your hand against the wall, give you the odd dig in your ribs to remember you to stand right ... After a few more hours of that I was thinking I would never come out of it.[4]

In London, Edward Heath and members of his Cabinet had hoped internment would come without warning, but in Northern Ireland nobody was surprised. The army had been planning for it since April and throughout the summer people had watched the construction of a large new prison, to hold the bulk of the internees, at a disused RAF base at Long Kesh, nine miles outside Belfast.

At the outset of Operation Demetrius the army hoped to detain 464 men on a list drawn up by the Special Branch of the RUC. But with internment so widely expected, few leading members of the Provisional IRA were sleeping at home and only 337 men on the list could be found. The list was entirely inadequate – 'hopelessly out of date' in Heath's view.[5] Among those detained were wrong family members, peaceful civil rights campaigners and men who had been active in the IRA fifty years earlier. One was seventy-eight years old.

Conspicuous by their almost complete absence from the list were Protestants. As the Irish writer Tim Pat Coogan put it: 'What [the list] did not include was a single Loyalist. Although the Ulster Volunteer Force had begun the killing and bombing, this organisation was left untouched, as were other violent Loyalist satellite organizations.'[6] It was another eighteen months before the first Loyalists were interned and during the four years that internment lasted, of the 1,981 people detained, only 107 were Protestant.

After being taken to police barracks and then on to army camps, most of the internees were subjected to systematic rough handling. Many say they were forced to run, barefoot, over 'obstacle courses' strewn with broken glass. They were commanded to squat while awaiting interrogation or forced to carry out physical exercises. They were subdued through assaults and threats. What food was available was poor, and the troops and police officers ensured that sleep was fitful at best by banging their batons on the walls of the huts where the internees were housed.

For the majority of those seized that day, that was as far as the ill-treatment went. The list of suspects was so inaccurate that 104 of the men were released within days. But twelve of those detained had been selected as subjects for the Five Techniques.

The intention was to extract the sort of high-quality intelligence about the IRA, its members and its order of battle, that had been so lacking when the initial internment list had been drawn up. For this reason, there was a geographical element to the selection of the men: four of the twelve were from Belfast, four from Counties Down and Armagh, and four from Londonderry and Tyrone.

Not all were members of the IRA. Paddy Joe McClean, a thirty-eight-year-old Republican and remedial-school teacher, was told during interrogation that he had been selected because they had 'wanted someone from the Omagh area'. Because he was a well-known civil rights leader it was assumed that many IRA men must have confided in him.[7]

Furthermore, a number of men detained on the first day of Operation Demetrius who were widely known to be senior members of either the Provisional or the Official IRA were not selected for the Five Techniques because they were not considered healthy enough. Those who were selected were mostly young and all looked extremely fit – fit enough to survive what lay ahead.

All twelve men were first put through a process intended to frighten and confuse. Joe Clarke, a motor-racing mechanic from west Belfast, and at nineteen the youngest, said later:

> After being hooded I was led to the helicopter and I was thrown bodily in. On being put into the 'copter, the handcuffs were removed and were applied to the back of the hood to tighten it around the head. The helicopter took off and a journey which I would estimate to have taken about an hour began. We were taken from the 'copter and led into a building and eventually into a room where I was made to stand in a search position against a wall – fully stretched, hands as far apart as humanly possible and feet as far from the wall as possible. Back rigid and head held up. Not allowed to relax any

of the joints at all. If [there was] any relaxation of limbs
– arms, elbow joints, legs, knee joints – someone came
along and grabbed the limb in a rough manner and put it
back into position.[8]

McClean was told he was going to be dropped from the
helicopter:

A hood was pulled over my head and I was handcuffed
and subjected to verbal and personal abuse, which
included the threat of being dropped from a helicopter
which was in the air, being kicked and struck about
the body with batons on the way. After what seemed
about one hour in the helicopter I was thrown from it
and kicked and batoned into what I took to be a lorry.
The lorry was driven only a couple of hundred yards
to a building. On arriving there I was given a thorough
examination by a doctor. After this all my clothes were
taken from me and I was given a boiler suit to wear
which had no buttons and which was several sizes too
big. During all this time the hood was still over my head
and the handcuffs were removed only at the time of the
medical examination.[9]

This was just the start. So far, the men who had been selected
for the Five Techniques had simply been subjected to a conditioning process, similar to that taught to British troops in an
attempt to prepare them for the shock of capture in the event of
a conventional war, and to train them to promote and preserve
the shock of capture experienced by enemy prisoners.

After being examined by a doctor and handed his oversized
boiler suit, McClean was put against the wall. Like the other
men, a number was written on the back of each of his hands with
a marker pen. He was Number One. Hooded, hot, bewildered

and in increasing pain, he says he felt immense pressure inside his skull. He remained against the wall for what seemed an age. 'My brain seemed ready to burst. What was going to happen to me? Was I alone? Are they coming to kill me? I wished to God they would, to end it.' Whenever he attempted to move, he was struck on his hands, ribs, kidneys or kneecaps. 'Certain periods are blank – fatigue, mental and physical, overwhelmed me. I collapsed several times, only to be beaten and pulled to my feet again. Food, water and the opportunity to relieve my bowels were denied me. I collapsed again . . .'[10]

McClean believed that he was subjected to the Five Techniques for two days and nights. He was probably not far wrong: the British government later disclosed that the twelve victims, and two others subjected to the same interrogation regime later in the year, had been kept against the wall for between nine and forty-three hours.

After around twelve to fourteen hours at the wall, another of the men, Pat Shivers, began to experience signs of the sort of psychosis earlier reported by Donald Hebb at McGill University and Stanley Smith at the Moor Hospital in Lancaster. He passed out several times and was beaten and slapped back into position. 'One time I felt, or imagined, I had died.'

Eventually, Shivers was taken for away for interrogation. Men behind him removed the hood from his head and he found himself standing in a room before a Special Branch detective, who was sitting behind a desk with a glass of water. Shivers was invited to take a drink.

The detective began asking questions, but Shivers was barely able to speak and slightly hysterical. 'He got angry and told me to speak up. Began asking questions about IRA activity and arms dumps around Toome. I did not know what he was talking about. After about half an hour he said: "I am going to send you in there again," which he did.' Shivers was taken for more 'conditioning', during which he was struck about the face, neck and knees. He was then put against the wall and collapsed once more.

> By this time I was at the end of my tether, my whole body, my arms, legs started to tremble uncontrollably. I passed out again. After this, the doctor wrapped me up in blankets and carried me out to what appeared to be a small surgery. I lay there shivering and shaking. He took my pulse, felt behind my ankles, got excited and took some blood pressure twice. He put something in my mouth, I thought it was a drug and spat it out. The second time he said: 'Keep that in your mouth as I am only taking your temperature.' He spoke with an English accent. The bag was still half over my head: I couldn't see him.

Shivers was given a hot drink – 'they held my mouth and forced it in' – and allowed to lie down to rest.

Patrick McNally was interrogated several times in-between long periods against the wall:

> One time I took the hood off when I was standing against the wall. There was a light in the place, but I couldn't see well, [there] just seemed to be a dim orange light from the roof. I saw two men, both stripped to the waist. One of them said in an English voice: 'Do you want to see anybody?' I answered: 'No.' Immediately they put the hood on again. I got a few thumpings. They were wearing what seemed to be the bottom of a tracksuit or gym suit. Looked to be blue trousers. As the hood was being put on again I could see the white gym shoes. They were very fit and strong-looking.

He said the interrogations were carried out by three different men. One appeared relaxed and 'never cut up rough' during questioning, another shouted, slapped the table and pushed him around, and a third would put his arm around his shoulders in a show of kindness, and never ask the same question twice. 'If you said no to anything, he would make you feel he believed you.'[11]

None of the detainees knew where they were. Some were told that they were in England, others Scotland; a few were led to believe that they were 'somewhere on the Continent'. For decades afterwards the conventional wisdom in Northern Ireland was that the 'Hooded Men', as they came to be known, had been held in Palace Barracks at Holywood outside Belfast. Their true place of detention, Ballykelly airfield, was concealed from two subsequent official British inquiries and from the European Court of Human Rights, and kept secret for decades.

Like the other men, McNally suffered hallucinations while at the wall. After his final interrogation he was fed, washed, told to sign a form that he could not see and given a final medical examination. He was then photographed, first alongside one of his interrogators and afterwards alone. As he was driven off to jail, still hooded, his guards treated him gently – 'sort of guiding you instead of pushing you into the vehicle, your foot was lifted up and set into it'. During the helicopter ride that followed his guards repeatedly touched and patted him, offering comfort and reassurance.[12]

The men were taken to Crumlin Road Jail in Belfast, where they discovered that seven more inmates were being lined up for the Five Techniques. The guards told these men – Numbers 13 to 19 – that they were about to receive 'the horror treatment', although in the event this did not happen. Those who had been through the treatment told their fellow internees what had happened and their experiences were written down by other prisoners in the hope that their accounts could be smuggled out of the jail. One, Jim Auld, recalls his statement being taken by a Belfast pharmacist who had been interned, who advised him that the account was so disturbing that it would not be believed. Auld eventually agreed to 'water it down' a little.[13]

Members of the Roman Catholic clergy had already expressed their anger over the violence that accompanied many of the arrests on the first day of internment: several people had been shot dead during the operation. When the twelve men's statements reached them, the clergymen were outraged, and among those who protested directly to Edward Heath was Archbishop William Conway, the Primate of All Ireland.[14]

Details of the men's statements began to appear in the press on both side of the Irish border. The British media looked the other way, however. As the *Sunday Times* later noted: 'Most British newspapers found the mounting allegations so incendiary that they ignored them, or confined their concern to the political violence that occurred during the forty-eight hours of 9–10 August.'[15]

Despite this, a number of MPs demanded the recall of Parliament from its summer recess. Heath resisted, but on 31 August, Reginald Maudling, the Home Secretary, announced that he was appointing a committee to investigate allegations of 'physical brutality' – a euphemism for torture. Maudling appointed Sir Edmund Compton, the parliamentary ombudsman, to conduct the inquiry, along with Edgar Fay, QC, a circuit judge, and Dr Ronald Gibson, a senior officer of the British Medical Association.

The three convened in secret. Only one complainant appeared before them, and this man's lawyer was not permitted to cross-examine witnesses or have access to transcripts of the evidence. On the other hand, Compton and his colleagues listened to ninety-five soldiers, twenty-six police witnesses, eleven prison officers and five regimental medical officers.

In October, while the committee was sitting, the *Sunday Times* became the first British newspaper to report on the use of the Five Techniques in detail, in a front-page article headlined 'How Ulster Detainees are Made to Talk'. Pat Shivers was quoted at length about the way he repeatedly lost consciousness after being hooded and forced into a stress position against a wall for several days. The Ministry of Defence responded by hastily arranging briefings for journalists, informing them that the IRA was beating up its own volunteers so their injuries could be presented as evidence of army or police brutality.[16]

While hearing evidence, Compton and his colleagues settled into a hotel in County Antrim. The RUC's Special Branch and officers and men of the Joint Services Interrogation Wing appear to have been undeterred by the committee's presence in the province, however. In mid-October two further subjects were picked up and prepared for the Five Techniques.

One of these men, twenty-three-year-old Liam Shannon from Belfast, was a member of the Provisional IRA; the second, Liam Rodgers, from County Down, appears to have been selected because the army believed him to have been a member of the Official IRA.

Like the other men, Rodgers was examined by a doctor before being subjected to the Five Techniques. Unlike the others, he was held in a room that was extremely cold, from which he would be taken out from time to time and forced to run, still hooded, apparently to revive his circulation.[17]

Shannon later described how, over the course of nine days, he was beaten repeatedly while being held at several different RUC stations and army barracks. On one occasion, he says, a firearm was discharged behind his head while he was standing facing a wall: 'I could hear the shot thud into a wall.' While being transferred to one army barracks, the Saracen armoured personnel carrier in which he was being held, face down, came to a halt on the staunchly Loyalist Shankhill Road. 'The soldiers threw open to doors and shouted: "We've got an IRA man in here." I could just hear what sounded like a crowd groaning as one. I felt a couple of blows on my legs, and the soldiers laughed, shut the door again and drove on.'

Finally, Shannon arrived at a place where he was stripped naked and examined by a 'very English' doctor. He told this man that he had an ulcer and back problems, and subsequently learned that police seized his medical records from his family doctor. 'I believe they were trying to see how far they could take us, what we could withstand.'

Shannon had the number 21 written on the back of his hands before being put into an outsized boiler suit – 'it was clearly a way of degrading you' – hooded and forced against the wall. 'Sometimes I would flail around trying to hit them, but I just hit the wall. The hood was tied to the epaulettes on the boiler suit so that I couldn't take it off. After a while of this, hooded at the wall, I completely lost it. I went out of my head.'[18]

When Compton presented his report to Parliament in November, he itemised each of the abuses under a separate heading, such as 'noise', 'sleep', etc., but ignored the cumulative effects that the Five Techniques were intended to create. He also failed to acknowledge the psychological impact of the abuses, concentrating only upon their physical impact. One example of his laconic approach is his recording that 'it was confirmed that it was the general policy to deprive the men of opportunity to sleep during the early days of the operation'.

In addition to not being concerned with the suffering of the men, Compton chose not to concern himself with the law, focusing instead on the question of what constituted 'physical brutality'. His report concluded that the Five Techniques did constitute 'physical ill-treatment', but that they fell short of the 'physical brutality' that Maudling had asked him to investigate. In two key paragraphs he concluded:

It will be noticed that while we are asked to investigate allegations of physical brutality, our conclusions are in terms of physical ill-treatment. Where we have concluded that physical ill-treatment took place, we are not making a finding of brutality on the part of those who handled these complainants. We consider that brutality is an inhuman or savage form of cruelty, and that cruelty implies a disposition to inflict suffering, coupled with indifference to, or pleasure in, the victim's pain. We do not think that happened here.[19]

The accounts of the victims told an entirely different story, of course. But Compton was saying that any act that is considered to be necessary could not amount to 'physical brutality', or torture. His report attracted widespread ridicule in Northern Ireland, not least among Catholics, who regarded it as a whitewash. However, the report did concede that there had been ill-treatment. This provoked a heated debate in the Commons and there were calls from Amnesty International for an inquiry into 'serious and apparently substantiated allegations of ill-treatment of internees in Northern Ireland'. Heath, meanwhile, damned Compton's efforts as 'one of the most unbalanced, ill-judged reports' he had ever read, adding: 'The number of incidents involved in the arrest of 300 odd men were small and, in the conditions of war against the IRA, trivial. They seem to have gone to endless lengths to show that anyone not given 3-star hotel facilities suffered hardship and ill-treatment. Again, nowhere is this set in the context of war against the IRA.'

In particular, Heath believed that too little weight had been given to the intelligence value of the interrogations, which the army maintained had included the identification of 700 members of the Provisional and Official IRA, details of organisation, communications and supply routes, the location of safe houses and information about future operations.

What Compton's report did establish were the details of the arrest and interrogation procedures. Critically, he also exposed the fact that the Five Techniques were authorised, in the sense that they were standard service policy. They were governed by a directive that had been approved by the Joint Intelligence Committee: the Joint Directive on Military Interrogation in Internal Security Operations Overseas. This document described torture as 'professionally unrewarding', but said that interrogation called for a 'psychological attack' on the subject, and specifically provided for isolation and sleep deprivation. It had first been issued in 1965 and was amended two years later after Roderic Bowen's investigation into the torture at Fort Morbut in Aden.[20] For all his apparent eagerness to exonerate the army, Compton showed that the ill-treatment of selected prisoners had been an integral part of British military doctrine for years.

Despite the growing outrage within Roman Catholic communities in Northern Ireland and across the Republic, the depth of the alarm at the increasing lawlessness in the province was such that many in Parliament and the media remained supportive of the abusive interrogation regime. The liberal *Guardian* newspaper, for example, published a leading article in praise of the new torture techniques. 'Some of the methods used in detention and interrogation centres . . . have been shown to be intolerable: others thoughtlessly harsh,' the newspaper conceded. 'But . . . a vigorous and tough interrogation of suspects must go on. Discomfort of the kind revealed in this report, leaving no physical damage, cannot be weighed against the number of human lives which will be lost if the security forces do not get a continuing flow of intelligence.'[21]

Support from such unexpected quarters notwithstanding, there was sufficient public and Parliamentary disquiet for Maudling to be obliged to defend the Techniques in the Commons. He did so on the basis that successive governments had used them and that they worked. 'The purpose of this interrogation was to obtain vital information about the terrorist forces and their stocks of arms and explosives,' he told MPs. 'The principles applied in the interrogation of suspects in Northern Ireland and the methods employed are the same as those which have been used in other struggles against armed terrorists in which Britain has been involved in recent years.' Maudling added, however, that the government accepted 'it would be right now to review' the interrogation methods being employed in the province.[22]

He announced that a second inquiry would be held. A commission of three privy councillors, headed by Lord Parker, the Lord Chief Justice of England, would examine 'whether, and if so in what respects, the procedures currently authorised for the interrogation of persons suspected of terrorism and for their custody while subject to interrogation require amendment'.

Compton had accepted that 'physical ill-treatment' had occurred. Now Parker was being asked to consider whether that ill-treatment should be allowed to continue. Nobody was being asked to consider whether disciplinary action should be taken against those involved. There was no question of criminal charges.

Parker's committee sat in secret from early December 1971 until January 1972, hearing evidence from thirty-three witnesses, many of them from the armed forces. Dick White was called twice. The committee was given some sort of demonstration of the Five Techniques. At the end of their deliberations, the three members of the committee were unable to agree whether the ill-treatment should be permitted to continue or not, and two separate reports were submitted to the Prime Minister.

The Majority Report, written by Parker and John Boyd-Carpenter, Conservative MP for Kingston-upon-Thames, revealed something of the history of the Five Techniques and what they termed 'the art of interrogation in depth'. They explained how the Techniques had been passed from generation to generation within the Intelligence Corps by word of mouth, with no standing orders or training manuals ever prepared. 'Accordingly their exact application in real life situations depends on the training already received by those who employ them. Such techniques can easily be used to excess, and specially so when their use is entrusted to personnel not completely trained in their use.'[23]

The Majority Report said that the committee had heard evidence that the 'mental disorientation' caused by the Techniques was expected to disappear within hours although 'some mental effects may persist for up to two months'. It is not clear how this conclusion was reached, as the report also noted: 'One of the difficulties is that there is no reliable information in regard to mental effects, particularly long-term mental effects.'[24] They were satisfied, however, that the use of sensory deprivation, 'subject to the proper safeguards', would be in conformity with the Directive on Military Interrogation issued by the Joint Intelligence Committee.

Parker and Boyd-Carpenter – whose son, an army officer, was serving in Northern Ireland at the time – insisted that they did 'not subscribe to the principle that the ends justifies the means'. But six paragraphs of their report did just that, highlighting the claim that the interrogations had led to the discovery of arms caches, safe houses and communications routes, and to the identification of 'a further 700 members of both IRA factions'.

Remarkably, although the Majority Report accepted that 'the use of some if not all the techniques in question would constitute criminal assaults', it did not call for them to be discontinued. It was all a matter of the degree to which the Techniques were applied, Parker and Boyd-Carpenter concluded, as well as the medical history of each subject: the Techniques 'might amount to no more than an inconvenience for a fit man'. They recommended that as long as the army had the express authority of a government minister, and provided that an officer and a doctor with some psychiatric training were present, the use of the Five Techniques should continue.[25]

The Minority Report was submitted by Lord Gardiner, who had served as Lord Chancellor in the previous Labour government. Gardiner had become a pacifist after serving on the western front during the First World War and had been prominent in the campaign to abolish the death penalty in the UK. It had been to Gardiner that Peter Benenson, the founder of Amnesty International, had written to express his disgust on realising, five years earlier, that the British abuses of prisoners in Aden were worse than any other he had ever investigated.

Gardiner seized the opportunity to mount an assault on both the immorality and the illegality of the Five Techniques. He began by expressing his dismay at Compton's definition of physical brutality:

> Lest by silence I should be thought to have accepted this remarkable definition, I must say that I cannot agree with it. Under this definition, which some of our witnesses thought came from the Inquisition, if an interrogator believed, to his great regret, that it was necessary for him to cut off the fingers of a detainee one by one to get the required information out of him for the sole purpose of saving life, this would not be cruel and, because not cruel, not brutal.[26]

He also pointed to the clear illegality of the Techniques:

> Forcibly to hood a man's head and keep him hooded against his will and handcuff him if he tries to remove it, as in one of the cases in question, is an assault and both a tort and a crime. So is wall-standing of the kind referred to. Deprivation of diet is also illegal unless duly awarded

as a punishment under prison rules. So is enforced deprivation of sleep.

He was scathing about the failure of the Joint Intelligence Committee and the military to take account of their obligations under international law when approving the Directive on Military Interrogation:

> As we have been told by those responsible that the army never considered whether the procedures were legal or illegal, and as some colour is lent to this perhaps surprising assertion by the fact that the only law mentioned in the Directive was the wrong Geneva Convention, it may be that some consideration should now be given to this point.

Gardiner went on to raise the possibility that the Five Techniques infringed Article 5 of the Universal Declaration of Human Rights; Articles 7 and 10 of the International Covenant on Civil and Political Rights; Article 3 of each of the four Geneva Conventions; and Article 3 of the European Convention on Human Rights. He added, however: 'As the procedures were admittedly illegal by the domestic law and no Minister had power to alter the law, it is not necessary, for the purpose of the point I am discussing, to decide whether or not they were also illegal by international law.'

He warned that the psychosis induced by sensory deprivation could prove permanent, and that as 'neither troops nor civilians had ever been subjected to such cumulative techniques as were used in Northern Ireland . . . it was impossible scientifically to prove that they would, or that they would not, have lasting effect'.

Nor was it clear to Gardiner that intelligence could not have been gleaned without resorting to the Five Techniques.

Some of the fourteen men were 'co-operative from the start', he reported. With so many people being detained during Operation Demetrius, some increase in the flow of information was inevitable. Moreover, it was to be expected that the torturers themselves would seek to justify their work: 'It is natural that those applying the procedures should consider that they would not have obtained so much information, or not obtained it so quickly, by other means.'

As to the question of the Techniques' future use, Gardiner reiterated that they were illegal, 'and as no Minister can alter the law, their use cannot be continued without legislation'. As a result, Gardiner said, the real question the committee needed to consider was whether it should recommend that Parliament pass a law allowing the police to ill-treat suspects to extract information during an emergency. To do so would not only be immoral, he said, it would also be difficult, if not impossible, for legislators to set any logical restriction upon the degree of ill-treatment that could be brought to bear:

> If it is to be made legal to employ methods not now legal against a man whom the police believe to have, but who may not have, information which the police desire to obtain, I, like many of our witnesses, have searched for, but have been unable to find, either in logic or in morals, any limit to the degree of ill-treatment to be legalised. The only logical limit to the degree of ill-treatment to be legalised would appear to be whatever degree of ill-treatment proves to be necessary to get the information out of him, which would include, if necessary, extreme torture.[27]

The only way around this conundrum, he said, would be to enact legislation permitting government ministers to decide 'the limits of permissible degrees of ill-treatment'. And that, he warned, would have an 'effect on the reputation of our own country' as well as representing a departure 'from world standards which we have helped to create'. Gardiner appeared to be daring Heath and other members of the government to contradict him.

Finally, Gardiner saw correctly that the army was attempting to import into Northern Ireland the torture techniques that it had employed with impunity during post-war counter-insurgency operations across the globe. But he too fell for the old canard: that the British had not resorted to torture during the Second World War:

> The blame for this sorry story, if blame there be, must lie with those who, many years ago, decided that in emergency conditions in Colonial-type situations we should abandon our legal, well-tried and highly successful wartime interrogation methods and replace them by procedures which were secret, illegal, not morally justifiable and alien to the traditions of what I believe still to be the greatest democracy in the world.

When the two contradictory reports landed on Heath's desk, he probably saw them as a godsend. He could agree whole-heartedly with the sentiments of the Majority Report, and hail the intelligence breakthrough that had been achieved through the use of the Five Techniques, and then accept in full the conclusions of the Minority Report. This is exactly what he did, on 2 March 1972, as both reports were being published. He told the Commons:

> The government, having reviewed the whole matter with great care and with reference to any future operations, have decided that the techniques which the Committee examined will not be used in future as an aid to interrogation. The statement that I have made covers

all future circumstances. If a Government did decide – on whatever grounds I would not like to foresee – that additional techniques were required for interrogation, then I think that . . . they would probably have to come to the House and ask for the powers to do it.

Heath's decision appeared to be something of a tribute to the moral and legal authority of Lord Gardiner. It may also have been intended to ensure the continuing support of the Labour opposition for the government's Northern Ireland strategy.

More than forty years later, it would become apparent that the government's promise was not all it seemed.

Several of the men subjected to the Five Techniques were interned for a number of years after their ordeal ended. On release, most were interviewed and examined over a period of five years by Professor Robert Daly, a lecturer in psychiatry at University College, Cork, who had an interest in the effects of sensory deprivation.

In a report published in 1975, Daly said that personality tests showed that, compared to the British norm, the men were 'more affected by feelings and emotionally less stable and easily upset; shy, timid; suspicious, more apprehensive and self reproaching; worrying and troubled . . . more tense, frustrated, driven and overwrought'.

Some of the men also suffered a degree of lasting physical damage. One of those examined was Sean McKenna, who, at the age of forty-two, had been the oldest of the victims. In February 1975, Daly found that McKenna 'had a feeling of impending fatal illness (a "brain tumour" or a "heart attack"), and had gross symptoms of anxiety'. Four months later McKenna suffered a heart attack and died.

Almost forty years after being subjected to the Five Techniques, when in his sixties, Liam Shannon was still complaining of nightmares and flashbacks, would panic whenever anything covered his face and was suffering gastrointestinal disorders that he said dated from his mistreatment.[28]

If the use of the Five Techniques had a destructive impact upon the bodies and personalities of the fourteen men, its effect upon the Troubles was no less catastrophic. The imposition of internment without trial – and the growing realisation among the Roman Catholic and Nationalist minority in Northern Ireland that the army and RUC were severely mistreating many of those interned – led to an immediate upsurge in violence.

There was severe rioting in towns and cities across the province in the three days that followed the launch of Operation Demetrius in August 1971. Up to 7,000 people were left without anywhere to live as their homes were burned to the ground and twenty-one people died. During the eight months of the year before internment there had been thirty deaths resulting from political and sectarian violence. In the five months after the launch of Operation Demetrius there were 143 deaths, including forty-six members of the security forces. There had been 304 bomb blasts across the province in the first six months of 1971. In the fourteen weeks that followed the introduction of internment there were 616.[29] The Provisional IRA, in particular, enjoyed a flood of new recruits.[30] And according to Lord Saville's marathon inquiry into the killing of fourteen demonstrators by British troops in Derry in January 1972, the violent clashes that preceded the massacre had, in part, been fuelled by the use of the Five Techniques.[31]

It is even possible that the use of the Five Techniques is one of the reasons that the cycle of violence lingers on in Northern Ireland in the twenty-first century. In May 2009, two young British soldiers were gunned down as they collected takeaway pizzas at the gates of Massereene Barracks in County Antrim. The Real IRA admitted responsibility for the killings and two months later police charged Pat Shivers's son with the murders. In January 2012, Brian Shivers, then aged forty-six, was convicted and jailed for life. He had been was six years old when the army had called at his home to take away his father. According to a number of Republican sources in Northern Ireland, Pat Shivers had been nothing more than a civil rights activist when he was selected for torture.

The realisation that not only had internees been ill-treated but the ill-treatment had been authorised led the Irish government to announce in November 1971 that it was bringing a case against the British government for breaches of the European Convention on Human Rights. Over the next six months, representatives of the sixteen European states that had ratified the convention heard evidence from 119 witnesses, and it quickly became clear that they wished not just to establish the truth surrounding the allegations but also to identify the senior officials responsible.

The British, not surprisingly, were less than helpful. The Ministry of Defence refused to allow any of its witnesses to attend the hearings in Strasbourg, claiming that the building in which they were taking place was insecure. The Norwegian Commissioner eventually offered a disused military airfield near Stavanger in Norway, where the British witnesses, identified only by ciphers, gave evidence from behind a screen.

Some witnesses refused to give their name to Norwegian customs officers on arrival in the country and some, confusingly, were given several different ciphers. It transpired, for example, that one RUC Special Branch interrogator known as PO17B was also the witness known as PO12B. It then emerged that he was the man introduced to the commission as PO13G as well.[32]

The European Commission of Human Rights delivered its verdict in January 1976. It noted that the facts were not in dispute: the British government had made no attempt to deny that the men had been treated in the manner they described. In their defence, the British denied that the Techniques amounted to torture, or to inhuman or degrading treatment. The commission dismissed this defence, saying : 'The Five Techniques applied together were designed to put severe mental and physical stress, causing severe suffering, on a person in order to obtain information from him.' The use of the Techniques in combination 'directly affects the personality physically and mentally', and it was this combined use that put the British authorities in breach of Article 3 of the Convention, which prohibits torture.

In Northern Ireland, the commission went on, the British had been engaged in practices that must be considered a form 'not only of inhuman and degrading treatment, but also of torture'. And the British methods, although undoubtedly modern, were no different, morally or legally, to those techniques of torment that had been employed by torturers for centuries.[33] Finally, the commission added, the fact that guerrilla warfare resulted in emergency conditions was no excuse for governments to resort to torture.

The day before the commission's findings were to be published, Merlyn Rees, the Northern Ireland Secretary, invited a number of newspaper and television editors to his office to enjoy drinks and discuss what was about to emerge. Almost all the UK media subsequently took their cue from Rees, criticising not the UK government for stooping to torture but the Irish government for having the temerity to complain about it. 'Angry Rees Attack as Dublin Charge of Torture is Upheld,' reported *The Times*. 'Rees Angry as Eire Presses Torture Issue,' said the *Daily Telegraph*. The *Daily Mail* headlined its leading article 'The Fatal Flaw of the Irish' and declared that Rees 'has every right to feel exasperated' by the Dublin government. The British media appeared to have lost sight of who was torturing whom.

The British government appealed against the commission's

findings and in January 1978 the European Court of Human Rights concluded, by thirteen votes to four, that the use of the Five Techniques fell short of the aggravated form of cruel and inhuman treatment that could be described as torture. However, the court ruled that the UK government was in breach of Article 3 nevertheless, because the Five Techniques amounted to 'inhuman and degrading treatment'.[34]

When Edward Heath told the Commons in March 1972 that the Five Techniques were to be banned, and that that pledge 'covers all future circumstances', he was not promising an end to rigorous interrogations by the British military. On the contrary, he said: 'I must make it plain that interrogation in depth will continue but that these techniques will not be used. It is important that interrogation should continue.'

More than thirty years later, declassified British government documents showed that both British intelligence officials and the military had been eager to present the Five Techniques to the Parker inquiry in a manner that offered the best chance of their being retained. The question of how to achieve this became the subject of considerable debate within the MOD and other government departments during late 1971 and early 1972.[35] It was during this internal debate that the Bremner Report had been written, detailing the development of the Five Techniques in counter-insurgency operations since the Second World War.

In November 1971, Sir James Dunnett, the permanent under-secretary at the Ministry of Defence, had a number of meetings to discuss the issue with the secretary of the Joint Intelligence Committee and Dick White.[36] They agreed that the deprivation of sleep was too useful to be abandoned. They also decided that white noise, hooding and wall-standing should be presented as measures designed to offer security not only to the guards but to the prisoners themselves. At one meeting it was even suggested that they should tell Parker that 'most of the detainees wanted to keep their hoods on in the cells quite voluntarily' to conceal their identities from other prisoners.[37]

This small group of securocrats struggled for several weeks to work out a way of retaining interrogation techniques that the military regarded as invaluable but a growing number of voices in Parliament, the judiciary and the media were condemning as abhorrent, and that were about to be declared in breach of international humanitarian law. They needed to find a way to square the circle.

By early 1972, a way through had been found. A remarkable sleight of hand was to be performed that would allow the government to both publicly renounce the Five Techniques and secretly retain them. These methods of torture would be banned – yet, at the same time, they would not.

On 29 June 1972, the Joint Intelligence Committee sent its revised interrogation guidelines, Directive on Interrogation by the Armed Forces in Internal Security Operations, to the MOD, the Home Office and MI6. At the Home Office, Maudling's private secretary said that 'MI5 will pay full regard to the Directive insofar as interrogations are conducted by them or on their behalf', while Alec Douglas-Home, the Foreign Secretary, pledged that 'the Directive will also be observed in the conduct of any interrogations which may be conducted on or behalf of MI6 in British territory'.[38]

The directive stated that detainees, in peacetime and during war, were 'not to be subjected to torture or cruel, inhuman or degrading treatment'. To this end, 'techniques such as the following are prohibited: any form of blindfold or hood; the forcing of a subject to stand or adopt any position of stress for long period to induce physical exhaustion; the use of noise-producing equipment; deliberate deprivation of sleep; the use of restricted diet'.[39]

The previous month, however, the JIC had decided that there should be two parts to the directive. In a memo written at the

MOD by the assistant under-secretary to the General Staff, it was explained that Part I would be published, if the government came under pressure to do so. Part I would contain no reference whatsoever to Part II, however, and Part II would never be published. Moreover, Part II would be considered to exist only in draft form, which would, the official noted, 'of course, enable us to say that no further instruction about detailed methods of interrogation had so far been approved'.[40]

Part I of the directive would do nothing more than 'lay down general guidelines about the treatment of those who are being interrogated'; it would not 'deal with the detailed methods of questioning to be adopted'.

Part II, which would 'deal with the actual conduct of interrogation', would then be quietly and informally passed to the Joint Services Interrogation Wing at Ashford.

And this is indeed what happened. Six weeks after Part I was formally promulgated to the military, the police and various government departments, Sir Cecil Blacker, vice-chief of the General Staff, sent a copy of Part II to Brigadier Richard Bremner, the Intelligence Corps Commandant. 'You will note that you are the only addressee outside the Ministry of Defence,' Blacker told Bremner in a covering letter. He added that the provisions of the document 'are to be observed in all future training in interrogation by the armed forces in internal security operations, and are to be reflected in all training instructions issued by the Intelligence Centre'.[41]

Thirty-six years later, in February 2008, when the MOD declassified most of its documents relating to the use of the Five Techniques, it was still refusing to release the highly classified Part II guidance that had been sent to Bremner. This document, it said, was too 'sensitive' to be covered by the Freedom of Information Act and its release would not even be considered for another ten years. Eventually the MOD was forced to hand the document over to a public inquiry into the death of Baha

Mousa, an Iraqi hotel receptionist who died in British Army custody in September 2003.

The Part II directive addressed just one of the Five Techniques, the deprivation of food and drink: 'Subjects must be given sustenance not less than that consistent with an adequate prison diet.' What this meant was not defined. However, the 'draft' directive implicitly allowed for sleep deprivation: 'It is not possible to lay down rules for the length of time for which an individual may be interrogated. Much will depend on the urgency with which information is required.' Ominously, in view of the army's use of generators to produce white noise, it adds: 'A stand-by generator will be required.' On the two final techniques, hooding and the use of stress positions, Part II of the directive is silent. The implications of the reference to the generator, the open-ended interrogation sessions and the failure to mention stress positions or hooding were not spelt out, but they would not have been lost on Brigadier Bremner, who had been informed that what he was reading dealt with 'the actual conduct of interrogation'.

Five years after Heath made his pledge, Sam Silkin, the UK Attorney General, appeared before the European Court of Human Rights to repeat the British government's promise: 'The Five Techniques will not in any circumstance be reintroduced as an aid to interrogation.'[42]

The existence of Part II of the directive was concealed from both the court, which gave the British credit for having issued Part I, and the European Commission of Human Rights.

The JIC, a body that worked within the Cabinet Office, at the very heart of government, had approved this sleight of hand. And Prime Minister Edward Heath was well aware of the ploy. One memo written by him in June 1972 warned that 'we cannot completely exclude the possibility that pressure to publish [the Directive] might at some time become irresistible, or that the Directive might come under scrutiny by some form of inquiry. Before it has been promulgated I should like to be sure that it has been considered from that point of view.'[43]

Meanwhile, the Irish Troubles raged on. At the beginning of 1972, the IRA had confidently proclaimed that outright victory was within sight, and the death toll seemed to be rising daily. Amid an atmosphere of growing fear and panic, an ever greater emphasis was placed upon the urgency and importance of gathering intelligence, which continued to put those responsible for extracting it under pressure to achieve results.

6

Plenty of Slap and Tickle:
Northern Ireland, 1972–91

*'The fabrication of malicious complaints provides terrorists
with a large number of benefits. Their campaign is a sign
of police success, not police misconduct.'*
Kenneth Newman, RUC Chief Constable,
24 June 1977

Immediately after Edward Heath's government announced the
ban on the Five Techniques in March 1972, a series of directives
were sent to the army and the police spelling out the implications
of the new ruling. The army was told 'no form of coercion is to
be inflicted on persons being interrogated. Persons who refuse
to answer questions are not to be threatened, insulted or exposed
to other forms of ill-treatment.' The directive sent to the RUC
said that although 'it is recognised that persons arrested or
detained in internal security operations are likely to be valuable
sources of intelligence and that interrogation is the only way of
gaining it urgently', they must not be mistreated. But while the
five specific techniques employed by the Intelligence Corps and
the RUC at Ballykelly were said to have been prohibited, other
techniques that could persuade a prisoner to talk were not. And
some army and police interrogators appear to have decided that
the directives required an imaginative response.

*

John Moore was arrested at his home shortly before the ban was announced and driven the short distance to Girdwood Barracks, an army base in north Belfast, for questioning about a gun attack on an army patrol. He says that after being beaten and stripped to his underpants he was repeatedly asked where he had hidden the firearm. As he later recalled:

> They marched me next door: there were surgeons there, and an operating table. They had big green cloaks and masks, round hats. They sat me down on a chair beside the table. On the table was a small bottle, and two syringes with needles. Somebody came from behind and put on a blindfold. Then I heard someone saying he was going to give me an injection on the arm. He gave me an injection, then he tied something around it, then he did something to my fingers, fiddling about with them. Then he says: 'Are you going to tell us what you did with the gun?' I repeated the same answer; I never had a gun. Then I felt this feeling in my arm, electric shocks, two given to start off with: not painful, just uncomfortable. Then every time they asked a question, it only kept increasing. My mouth dried up. I couldn't talk. They brought over a plastic cup of water and gave it to me to drink. I said: 'All right, I'll tell you what you want to know; I'll tell you who fired the rifle.'[1]

At around the same time as John Moore's interrogation, Joe Docherty was also taken to Girdwood. He had been arrested on the morning of his seventeenth birthday – 'they could hold me longer once I turned seventeen' – and described being subjected to sleep and sensory deprivation while hearing screams nearby. 'The soldiers who picked me up warned me I was going to get a rough time of it. They were all right, like, they were trying to help: they told me to try to keep my head up. When I got to

Girdwood I was forced to sit in a small white cubicle and stare at a perforated white board a few inches from my face. I was beaten and slapped about by the RUC if I tried to move, and had my testicles squeezed from time to time. And all the time I could hear screaming and squealing from the other fellows.

'That went on for almost three days. Then I was put in an all-white cell with a chair in the centre of the room. Soldiers came and brought in a cot bed and I was allowed to sleep. Then I would be shaken awake and told that I had been asleep for hours. This happened several times.' In-between 'rest' periods Docherty would be interrogated. 'When I was taken away from Girdwood to be interned, I thought I had been there for about eight days, but it was only three. I later realised I was only being allowed to sleep for ten minutes at a time.'[2]

Patrick Fitzsimmons, another north Belfast man, reported similar treatment at Girdwood. He described being blindfolded by men dressed as surgeons before receiving an injection in his arm. 'I thought they were taking my blood pressure: a band was wrapped round my arm. Then I felt an electric shock. It got higher and higher and I felt it going through my legs and the rest of my body. I was holding onto the arm of the chair. Another person lifted my arm off the chair. The shocks went all through my body, down through my feet and all. Then I heard a voice: "I think he has had enough." '[3]

By the end of October, eight months after Edward Heath had proclaimed the ban on the Five Techniques, more than twenty men were complaining that they had been subjected to electric shocks during interrogation at Girdwood. According to some accounts, Archbishop William Conway, the Primate of All Ireland, lodged fresh complaints with Downing Street, and the Irish foreign ministry is also said to have raised the matter. The electric shock treatment quietly came to an end.

During this period two Roman Catholic priests, Denis Faul and Raymond Murray, began documenting allegations of abuse made by men who had passed through Girdwood and Holywood Barracks in east Belfast. Among the twenty-five separate techniques that they identified were beating, burning, stretching, 'hand squeezing of the testicles', blindfolding, 'insertion of instruments in the anal passage', firing blank rounds at prisoners and playing Russian roulette with them. Some soldiers were also using the technique now known as waterboarding, as revealed during the trial of one of their victims.

In October that year, soldiers of the 1st Battalion the Parachute Regiment arrested Liam Holden, a nineteen-year-old chef, in the early hours at his parents' home in the Catholic Ballymurphy area of west Belfast. The soldiers took him to a primary school in a nearby Protestant enclave, where some members of the regiment had been housed alongside the young pupils. He was questioned in a temporary building in the corner of the playground that was occupied by the battalion's intelligence section. Holden was taken from the school and driven to Castlereagh, the RUC's interrogation facility in east Belfast, shortly before the first children began to appear at the gates with their mothers. By this time he was ready to sign a confession in which he said he had been responsible for the killing of Frank Bell, an eighteen-year-old private from the Parachute Regiment who had become the hundredth soldier to die in Northern Ireland that year when he was shot by a sniper in Ballymurphy a month earlier.

When Holden came to trial in April 1973 he described being beaten by soldiers, burned with a cigarette lighter, hooded and threatened with execution. He had been pushed to the ground and held down by around six men. A towel was folded and placed over his face and water was slowly poured from a bucket onto his face. 'It nearly put me unconscious,' Holden told the jury. 'It nearly drowned me and stopped me from breathing. This went on for a minute.' A short while later he was subjected to the same treatment again.[4]

Doubtless the jury was less than impressed by a defendant who insisted he had confessed to murder because a little water had been poured onto his face. Although this technique had been used in Cyprus, it was, after all, another three decades before accounts began to emerge of the CIA's use of waterboarding during the 'war on terror' and before the full horror of that technique of torture began to be understood. Holden was found guilty of murder and sentenced to hang: the last person to be sentenced to death in the UK. His sentence was later commuted to life imprisonment and capital punishment was abolished in Northern Ireland a few months later. Holden served seventeen years in jail and was still protesting his innocence in 2012, when the Court of Appeal in Belfast re-examined his case.

Although disturbing, such episodes of mistreatment appeared random, even haphazard in their nature and occurrence. It seemed that a handful of soldiers and RUC detectives were simply seeing what they could get away with and that their superiors were turning a blind eye. But what came next in Northern Ireland was a far more sophisticated application of state-sponsored violence, one with clarity and a real sense of direction.

Suspected terrorists were to be beaten not just to extract intelligence but to ensure that they were convicted of serious criminal offences and then removed from society, and this was to be done in a fashion that bore some semblance of justice. Police officers would play their part, of course, but so too would lawyers, judges, civil servants, journalists and, on occasion, physicians. New legislation would be needed: a statute featuring sufficient ambiguity for the interrogators to believe that they were being tacitly encouraged by Parliament. Torture was about to be normalised and a small number of key figures, men of vision and real resolve, would be needed to drive the policy through.

One man who had given considerable thought to the need

to remove from society those who posed a threat to the state was Frank Kitson, who had been honing his views on counter-insurgency strategy and tactics, within the law, for more than a decade. Back in the autumn of 1969, Kitson, then a forty-two-year-old lieutenant colonel in the British Army, was given an unusual mission. He was told that for the next year he was to take up residence at University College, Oxford, where he would conduct an examination into the defence of the realm.

The other students at University College at that time included a shaggy-bearded Bill Clinton, who was studying philosophy, politics and economics, and, as one wit later put it, not inhaling, not getting drafted and not getting a degree. Many other students were also steeped in the radicalism and anti-war sentiment of the times. Not so Kitson. A veteran of the war against the Mau Mau in Kenya and Communists in Malaya, Kitson's orders were that he should reflect upon his experiences and then scan the horizon, examining what needed to be done 'to make the army ready to deal with subversion, insurrection and peace-keeping operations during the second half of the 1970s'.[5]

When Kitson's thesis was published in 1971, under the title *Low Intensity Operations: Subversion, Insurgency and Peacekeeping*, it made an immediate impact among those struggling to cope with the mounting violence and lawlessness in Northern Ireland. It also enhanced Kitson's stellar reputation in the British Army: in little more than a decade he would be appointed commander-in-chief of UK land forces. Among some on the Left, the book caused uproar for its suggestion that the military should use the civil administration to fight subversion, and that the rule of law might be subverted to the aims of the military.

Kitson wrote:

Firm policy rulings should be taken before operations against those practising subversion can start. An excellent example concerns the way in which the law should work. Broadly speaking there are two possible alternatives, the first one being that the law should be used as just another weapon in the government's arsenal, and in this case it becomes little more than a propaganda cover for the disposal of unwanted members of the public. For this to happen efficiently, the activities of the legal services have to be tied into the war effort in as discreet a way as possible.

The other alternative, Kitson said, with no obvious enthusiasm, 'is that the law should remain impartial and administer the laws of the country without any direction from the government'.[6]

From Oxford and by now a brigadier, Kitson went to Northern Ireland as commanding officer of 39 Infantry Brigade. By early 1972, as the IRA's campaign became more determined, many in the army and the RUC believed the 'extreme circumstances' of which Kitson wrote had arrived in the province.

By midsummer, all the major protagonists in the conflict realised that it was going to be a prolonged and bloody battle. During early July people were dying at the rate of three a day. Republicans killed Protestants, soldiers and police officers; Loyalists slaughtered Catholics; horror piled upon horror. In the early hours of 11 July, a gang of drunken Loyalists broke into the north Belfast home of a Catholic widow, raped her, then shot dead her mentally disabled fourteen-year-old son as he lay by her side. On 21 July, nine people died and 130 were injured when the IRA detonated twenty bombs in less than an hour across Belfast. On the last day of the month, a further nine people, including three children, were slaughtered and more than thirty injured when three car bombs exploded in the main street of the hitherto-peaceful County Londonderry village of Claudy. A local Roman Catholic priest had directed the attack.[7]

Meanwhile, not only was internment – detaining terrorism

suspects without trial – failing as a method of dealing with the violence but it was widely acknowledged to be counter-productive. It had triggered an upsurge in attacks and encouraged more young men and women to join the IRA. The new recruits included some who had been interned without trial despite having no previous connection with the violence. Internment was also undermining the UK's reputation overseas, particularly in the United States. But while the British government had always acknowledged that internment could not continue indefinitely, it was unclear how the existing judicial system in Northern Ireland could cope with the growing lawlessness at a time when witnesses faced intimidation and, in some instances, murder.

Amid the carnage of the summer of 1972 and with the embarrassment of the revelations about the Five Techniques still fresh in ministers' minds, Edward Heath and his Northern Ireland Secretary, William Whitelaw, needed to find a new way of taking off the streets those responsible for the violence and locking them away for long periods, when there was no evidence against them, only intelligence. They doubtless consulted Sir Dick White, who although semi-retired remained part-time security coordinator at the Cabinet Office. Between them, they concluded that the man most likely to provide a solution was a law lord, Lord Diplock.

Baron Diplock of Wansford was a man of formidable intel-lect, regarded by some as the greatest judicial architect of his generation. He was also seen by his enemies as one of the most reactionary judges of his day. Critically, perhaps, he was the same Kenneth Diplock who had served as secretary of Churchill's wartime Security Executive when it set up MI5's torture centre, Camp 020.

Diplock's brief was to consider 'what arrangements for the administration of justice in Northern Ireland could be made in order to deal more effectively with terrorist organisations by bringing to book, otherwise than by internment by the Executive, individuals involved in terrorist activities'. Within seven weeks he produced a report in December whose recommendations fundamentally changed the basis upon which suspects were treated and reopened the door for the possibility of torture.

At a stroke, the Diplock Report swept away trial by jury, with all its traditional safeguards. Instead, cases involving terrorism suspects should be heard by a single judge. Diplock could not cite any examples of jury intimidation, but he could point to the recent murder of a potential witness and recommended that the courts should not be expected to rely on witnesses in future.

The report also recommended another, more radical change. A confession, Diplock noted, would be seen by many as 'the most cogent evidence that a person had done that which he is accused of doing'. The Court of Appeal in Belfast had ruled in May that year that confessions were not admissible if they were obtained in a centre established specifically to extract such statements.[8] Diplock clearly regarded this judgment as foolish. 'The whole technique of skilled interrogation is to build up an atmosphere in which the initial desire to remain silent is replaced by an urge to confide in the questioner,' he wrote.

Finally, confessions should be accepted as evidence, Diplock said, so long as the court was satisfied, on the balance of probability, that it had not been 'obtained by torture or inhuman or degrading treatment'.

The government accepted Diplock's recommendations, which formed the basis for the 1973 Emergency Provisions Act (EPA). Section 6 of the Act incorporated the new test of admissibility of confessions, although the standard of proof – 'beyond reasonable doubt' – was not defined or qualified. Nor were the words 'torture' and 'inhuman or degrading treatment'. Defence lawyers immediately saw that the EPA gave the RUC's interrogators enormous latitude, and argued that it should have prohibited 'the use or threat of physical violence' – words that had appeared in the Diplock Report but had vanished during the drafting of the emergency legislation.

RUC detectives also immediately saw the opportunities that the new law presented. They assumed that the vague wording of Section 6 was deliberate, that it was a signal that coerced confessions were now acceptable. 'After all, do repeated slaps around the face amount to torture?' one RUC interrogator asked many years later, while discussing the Act. 'What about an occasional kick in the balls?'[9]

Suspects would have no automatic right to see a lawyer before being released or charged. Finally, the EPA extended the period of time that police could hold a suspect from forty-eight to seventy-two hours. The following year, after the IRA bombed two pubs in Birmingham, killing nineteen people and injuring 182, the government introduced the Prevention of Terrorism Act, which gave police across the UK the power to hold suspects for five days. In Northern Ireland, however, RUC detectives usually found that the three days provided by the EPA gave them all the time they needed to extract a confession that would be accepted by the courts.

The judicial framework was now in place for a new phase in the war in Northern Ireland, one that would, in Kitson's words, allow for 'the disposal of unwanted members of the public'. The last internees were released in December 1975, and from then on, anyone sentenced by the new, juryless Diplock Courts was to be regarded as a common criminal. The fact that the new Act defined terrorism as 'the use of violence for political ends' was neither here nor there.

Primary responsibility for the defeat of the IRA was to be taken from the army and handed to the RUC, along with the locally recruited part-time soldiers of the Ulster Defence Regiment. This policy of normalisation was to be known as Primacy of the Police or Ulsterisation.

At the same time, effective interrogation was about to move to centre stage during police investigations. The next phase was to build the RUC's capacity to conduct large numbers of effective interrogations, and to ensure that the police had exactly the right leadership for the difficult years ahead.

At this time the Chief Constable of the RUC, Jamie Flanagan, was looking forward to retirement and the real power in the force lay in the hands of his English deputy, Kenneth Newman. Although a quiet and slightly studious individual, Newman had become a policeman for the most frivolous of reasons. In 1946, after serving as a teenage aircraftman in the Far East during the latter stages of the Second World War, he was demobbed and shipped back to Britain. One damp and overcast day he saw a recruitment poster for the Palestine Police Force. The poster depicted a man in shorts and a police hat, standing under a palm tree. Newman decided on the spot that he would rather be where the sun was shining, so he signed up. He was joining a force whose officers (including the notorious Douglas Duff) were not slow to employ physical force when they deemed it necessary.

In 1948, when the Palestine Police Force was disbanded, Newman returned to the UK and joined Scotland Yard, where, as he later put it, he 'ploughed solidly up the ranks'. By 1973, when he joined the RUC as Deputy Chief Constable, he was developing a reputation as one of the most talented British police commanders of his generation, and it was clear he was being lined up to be the next head of the force. Newman would drive forward the Ulsterisation process.

As he prepared for the top job, Newman developed a close friendship with Bill Mooney, the RUC's most senior detective. Mooney, a man whose 'eyes constantly danced with shrewdness', according to one former colleague, realised that the RUC was about to come under the command of a man every inch as foxy as himself. A number of their senior former colleagues recounted how these two men would sit up long into the night, drinking and discussing the way it would be once Newman was Chief Constable: the way they would employ the Emergency Provisions Act, with all its ambiguities, to take the war to the IRA.

In May 1975, twelve months before Newman's appointment as Chief Constable, Mooney pulled together a team of twenty-three detectives who would investigate only terrorist offences and who would do this by concentrating on interrogation. Initially known as the 'A Team', they were young men, most still in their twenties. The A Team's detective sergeants played a key role, keeping their constables on a tight leash during inter-rogations. If a suspect suffered too many visible injuries – or worse still, needed hospital treatment – any statement they signed could be worthless.

By the time Newman was appointed Chief Constable in May 1976, the level of violence was escalating to a new and frightening intensity. While fewer soldiers were being killed, the civilian casualty rate was growing steadily, partly because paramilitaries were bombing more bars. It was to be one of the bloodiest years of the Troubles, with 308 people losing their lives. Only 1972 had had a higher death toll.

Newman was facing carnage. Twenty-five people died during his first month in office. They included a Catholic milkman shot at point-blank range as he went about his round in west Belfast; two young men, one Catholic, one Protestant, killed by a bomb planted in a popular students' haunt in the city; a twenty-two-year-old Protestant Sunday School teacher, killed by a bomb on her train; and three Catholic men killed by a bomb in a pub in County Armagh. Five of those who died that month were Newman's own officers.

Newman wasted no time expanding his interrogation teams. The A Team became known as the Headquarters Regional

Crime Squad, and three more Regional Crime Squads were established across the province, at Derry, Armagh and Belfast, each comprising around twenty officers.

The previous month, following the unexpected resignation of Harold Wilson, James Callaghan had become prime minister and set about reshuffling his Cabinet. The new Northern Ireland Secretary was to be Roy Mason, an indomitable little Yorkshireman who had gone to work down a coal mine at the age of fourteen. In his previous ministerial role, as Defence Secretary, Mason had adopted a military approach to problem-solving. In contrast to his predecessor, Merlyn Rees, who had prided himself on his ability to listen and to seek compromise, Mason led by issuing orders.

The month after his appointment, Mason told the Labour Party annual conference that he believed Northern Ireland had had enough of new government policy papers and initiatives and now 'needed to be governed firmly and fairly'. Martin McGuinness, then the twenty-six-year-old head of operations for the IRA's northern command, had a far more succinct appraisal of the new man's approach. 'Roy Mason', he was quoted as saying years later, 'nearly kicked the shit out of us.'

The actual kicking, of course, was carried out by the men of Newman's newly created Regional Crime Squads, in the privacy of the twenty-one interview rooms at Castlereagh and the nine at Gough Barracks in Armagh. Mooney would be prowling around in the corridors outside, firing up his men. 'He would be saying: "What are you, men or mice? Get in there!"' one interrogator recalled many years later. 'If you didn't get a confession quickly he would see you in the corridor and say: "Have I got to get in there and do it myself?"'[10]

Suspects were not just kicked. They were punched, burned with cigarettes and lighters, dragged around interview rooms by their hair, forced to assume stress positions – including the wall-standing ostensibly banned in 1972 – and deprived of sleep.

Their wrists and elbows were twisted into excruciating positions and then held in those positions for hour after hour. Fingers were pushed under their ears. They would be forced to do sit-ups and press-ups. They would be stripped naked and choked. Plastic bags would be placed over their heads. They would be instructed to eat mucus from their interrogators' noses.

What happened to Bernard O'Connor, a music teacher from Enniskillen, was not untypical. He was arrested in January 1977 and taken to Castlereagh for questioning. There, detectives told him that he was a leading member of the IRA, a murderer and a terrorist, and that he was leading young boys astray. During the first day of interrogation, he says, he was forced to stand on tiptoes with his knees slightly bent and his arms stretched in front of him, while being slapped and punched in the stomach. He could hear shouting and screaming in the other interview rooms. Then he was forced to do sit-ups and press-ups, and at one point was choked. He says he was stripped naked and forced to place his soiled underpants over his head and run in circles around the room – an allegation that other suspects also made around that time.

O'Connor was examined by his own doctor in the presence of a Castlereagh medical officer. The doctor recorded that O'Connor had difficulty raising his arms, that his abdomen, kidneys and legs were tender, and that both ears and one eye were bruised. O'Connor, however, refused to make any complaint, fearing that to do so would make matters worse. He was interrogated twelve times, one session lasting seventeen hours. One interrogator brought him cough sweets and talked about God. Another pair of detectives gave him their names, showed him photographs of bomb victims and talked gently to him about how relieved he would feel after confessing. All the other sessions involved different forms of torture. After refusing to sign any statement throughout his three days at Castlereagh, O'Connor was released without charge.[11]

It was not only male suspects who were mistreated. After Patricia McGarry was arrested in July 1977, at the age of seventeen, the policeman who sat beside her in the Land Rover kept shouting in her ear: 'You're going to Castlereagh!' During her first interrogation, a detective who stood behind her both tugged and patted her hair. During the second session, the detectives began by patting her hair and gently coaxing her to confess, before starting to shout, swear and scream into her ears. One session featured a female interrogator, who forced McGarry to face the wall while she slapped and swore at her. During her final interrogation – her seventh – she says she was forced to stand with her back to a wall while two detectives appeared to attempt to dislocate her arms at the shoulders. 'I was roaring, crying, screeching.' One of the detectives wrote a statement and McGarry signed it. 'They wrote another statement and I signed that. Then another two.'[12]

Republicans and Catholics were not alone in being treated in this way. The first targets for the A Team had been members of the Loyalist Ulster Volunteer Force operating around east Antrim. At first, Loyalists who had passed through Castlereagh were reluctant to speak out about their experiences, preferring to suffer in silence rather than have their voices lend any support to the anti-RUC propaganda of the IRA. In October 1977, however, Unionist politicians released a number of statements taken from men who had been detained in the east Antrim raids, who complained that they had been slapped, punched and held over electric fires.

Newman may not have known the details of what was happening inside the interrogation rooms and, not surprisingly, insisted that nothing untoward was happening at Castlereagh, Gough or any other RUC station. Complaints from lawyers and members of the Police Authority were brushed aside. After a sixty-four-year-old man from Tyrone required hospital treatment following interrogation at Castlereagh, a delegation of Roman Catholic priests and Nationalist politicians demanded to see the Chief Constable. He sent his deputy, Jack Hermon, to meet them, then drafted a long statement in which he said complaints of mistreatment were part of a propaganda campaign. Prisoners, he said, had been wounding themselves with knives and forks, nails and cans of lemonade, and butting their heads against walls: 'The fabrication of malicious complaints provides terrorists with a large number of benefits. Their campaign is a sign of police success, not police misconduct.'[13]

Newman was able to rely on the backing of Unionist politicians and had the unwavering support of Airey Neave, the opposition Northern Ireland spokesman, as well as the Labour government. And he had little to fear from the British media. With some exceptions, most journalists tended to look the other way rather than investigate the growing number of allegations of brutality, or would report the RUC's claims that the complaints of interview room assaults led to the deaths of more police officers.

When an eighteen-year-old police officer, William Brown, was shot dead in Fermanagh eleven days after the BBC broadcast a documentary detailing some of the allegations emerging from Castlereagh, the police officers' union, the Police Federation, immediately blamed the programme-makers. 'Trial by TV: BBC Accused,' read the Daily Mirror's headline. The Daily Express went one better: 'Murder by TV'.[14]

At Westminster, MPs of all parties condemned any media attempt to investigate what was happening at Castlereagh, limited though those efforts were. Neave, who had served in the wartime military intelligence unit that controlled CSDIC after escaping from the infamous German POW camp at Colditz, angrily demanded 'a review of present attitudes to media freedom'.

For many years the men of the Regional Crime Squads refused to admit that they had employed anything other than peaceful and lawful methods to break the men and women they questioned.

A form of *omertà* governed everything they said about the matter in public and much of what they had to say in private. Some maintained that the IRA's propaganda about the horrors of Castlereagh had been so compelling that suspects were terrified when taken there and confessed in order to avoid a beating to which they would never have been subjected. One detective claimed to have extracted heartfelt confessions from hardened killers by quoting at length from the Pope's sermons.[15] More often than not, detectives insisted simply that their interviewees wanted to 'get it all off their chests'.

It was to be decades before there was even the slightest crack in the code of silence, but a handful did cooperate with me in the writing of this book. One former officer admitted that he had employed 'torture, inhuman and degrading treatment' – exactly what the law prohibited.[16] Another explained how interrogators became known for the use of specific techniques, such as hyperflexing – the twisting of joints as suffered by Patricia McGarry and others. Most interrogators did not describe what they were doing as torture, however. Instead, they called it 'slap and tickle'.[17]

Unlike the men of the Joint Services Interrogation Wing and the handful of Special Branch detectives who took part in Operation Calaba, the Castlereagh interrogators were not taught any torture techniques. 'We had no training in this sort of thing, but some teams were eventually seen as having a speciality,' one former interrogator explained. 'Eventually the arm twisters were rumbled. The doctors could see signs of swelling and tenderness. They were quietly told: "Stop – your system is showing through here."'[18] Punching in the centre of the stomach was a simple and much-favoured method, as the interrogators realised that fewer bruises tended to form around areas where soft tissue was not attached to bone.

The men of the Regional Crime Squads became convinced that their methods were working. And if the casualty rate in

Northern Ireland could be taken as an indicator of success, they were: in 1976 the death toll was 308; the following year it fell to 116 and in 1978 it was eighty-eight. It would never again be as high as it had been before the Regional Crime Squads were formed.

The satisfaction that was felt within the ranks of the RUC went all the way to the top. The squads were becoming so successful that Bill Mooney and other senior officers were content for them to carry on as they were. 'We were getting headlines every day about the number of people charged, about so-and-so getting thirty years,' a former interrogator recalls. 'Everything was wonderful, but there was no doubt that people were getting assaulted. There was plenty of slap and tickle.'

Any officers who had doubts about what they were doing, who feared that the violence at Castlereagh would engender more hatred of the RUC within the Nationalist community and possibly prolong rather than shorten the conflict, learned quickly to keep their own counsel. So too did those with doubts about the guilt of any of the prisoners. 'We would often pick up a large number of people for questioning about the same offence. There would be a conference each morning, and we would be reluctant to say that we thought so-and-so might not be involved, because another team might go in there and get a confession, and then you would be left looking pretty stupid.'[19]

Nevertheless, most of the former Castlereagh interrogators insist that they did not attempt to force confessions from men they thought were innocent. 'Going to jail for something you didn't do must be one of the worst fates a man could suffer,' said the former detective who admitting using torture, inhuman and degrading treatment to obtain confessions. Many also insisted that by the late 1970s, the quality of the intelligence that triggered arrests was so solid that they didn't just suspect their victims were guilty, they knew it.

★

One such case concerned Tommy McKearney, who had been named by sources as the commanding officer of the East Tyrone Brigade of the IRA. Those same sources indicated that he was the man behind the murder of Stanley Adams, one of seven Ulster Defence Regiment men killed during the autumn of 1976, most of them gunned down at their homes or places of work.[20]

Stanley Adams was the local postman in Altmore, County Tyrone. Altmore is a remote, slightly forlorn place; quiet, with wide skies and very few people. Its farms and moorland lie on high ground – in Gaelic, *allt mór* means great height – and the few trees that grow there are doubled over like old men, bent north-eastward by the wind. Adams knew each of the straight and narrow lanes that criss-crossed Altmore and the local people all knew him.

On the morning of 28 October 1976, he parked his van outside one of the area's more isolated farmhouses and delivered a single letter. As he strode back down the drive, two men darted silently from a nearby outhouse. Each of them produced a handgun and opened fire at point-blank range. Adams fell backwards onto the lawn. A third man, who had been holding hostage the woman owner of the house, emerged from the front door clutching the letter. All three ran to their car and sped away.

Twenty-nine years old, Adams was a single man, a Protestant from the nearby town of Pomeroy. He was also a part-time lance corporal in the British Army's local reserve force, the Ulster Defence Regiment. As such, he was deemed by the IRA to be a legitimate target. While on his post round, they told themselves, he could also be gathering intelligence. *The Times* reported his death in just three paragraphs at the foot of a report about a fire brigade strike in Belfast.

The RUC had no evidence against McKearney, just intelligence: the fruits of bribery or blackmail, of brief whispered conversations and bugged telephone calls – nothing that could be used in court.

When the police caught McKearney, they drove him to Castlereagh. McKearney fully expected to be mistreated when he got there, but even he was shocked at the patient, almost sophisticated way in which the rotating two-man teams of detectives went about their work.

McKearney was one of the few men who didn't break within the standard three days of questioning and for whom the RUC made use of the additional two days allowed them under the Prevention of Terrorism Act. Eventually, the detectives decided that they had enough from him. The intelligence had been correct and as a result of admissions he was said to have made at Castlereagh he was jailed for life, later accepting responsibility for the shooting. By the time he emerged from jail sixteen years later, he had renounced violence and left the IRA, and went on to become a peaceful and useful member of society.

So the torture worked? The McKearney case, and many others like it, showed that the use of torture in the RUC holding centres had short-term benefits and some longer-term utility.

Even some of those who suffered at the hands of their interrogators accept that the police were not trying simply to frame suspected paramilitaries. McKearney says: 'I think the RUC did attempt to match the person in the IRA who carried out the operation with the confession to taking part in that operation. I think they did try to do that. I suspect that genuine miscarriages of justice, where people were entirely innocent, were in a minority.'[21]

A common refrain among former RUC interrogators is that miscarriages of justice were probably no more prevalent in Northern Ireland at that time than they were across the rest of the UK. But miscarriages there were, and some people served lengthy prison sentences after confessing to crimes they did not commit.

Some Diplock Court judges were more assiduous than others in examining the circumstances in which the defendants before them had confessed. During the thirty-nine months from July 1976 to September 1979, 3,312 people appeared in court in Belfast accused of terrorist offences. The overwhelming majority were prosecuted on the basis of their confessions. The courts ruled that twenty-eight 'confessions' were inadmissible and in a further fifteen cases the Director of Public Prosecutions decided not to bring charges because he was not satisfied that the standards of Section 6 of the EPA – prohibiting the use of torture or inhuman or degrading treatment when obtaining confessions – had been met. During the same period, the DPP prosecuted fourteen police officers for assault. All of them were acquitted. No officer ever admitted an offence.

It was not until 1997 that the Criminal Cases Review Commission was established to investigate possible miscarriages of justice. Twenty-five years after the A Team first went to work, the CCRC began to examine a number of Diplock Court convictions, and many were found wanting. Among the people whose cases the commission referred to the Court of Appeal were several who had pleaded guilty on the advice of their lawyers after they had signed confessions that had been beaten out of them. In a series of judgments that offer tacit acknowledgement of the truth of what happened at Castlereagh, several convictions of those who had offered a guilty plea were overturned.

Among the more tragic cases was that of Robert Hindes and Hugh Hanna, two Protestant men who had been fourteen and sixteen when they were arrested in October 1976. Hindes had been arrested first and questioned about the murder six weeks earlier of Peter Johnston, a twenty-eight-year-old Catholic accountant who had been shot dead by Loyalist gunmen at his home in north Belfast. A few hours into his interrogation, Hindes confessed to the killing and named his accomplice as a boy called Hanna. At this point Hugh Hanna was also picked up. He also quickly confessed. At their trial, both boys pleaded guilty and each served a total of nine years behind bars.

When Hanna first asked the Criminal Cases Review Commission to take up his case in 1997 he was rejected on the grounds that he had not made any attempt to appeal against his conviction immediately after the trial. But Hanna's father wrote to the RUC, imploring the force to look again at the case. An assistant chief constable agreed to reinvestigate and later told the commission of his deep concerns.

The boys' confessions were made after sustained physical and psychological abuse and were fundamentally implausible. In their statements, they said they had forced open Johnston's front door a little after 11 p.m., gone upstairs and shot him from his bedroom door as he lay on his bed. But at the point at which their confession was obtained, the interrogators had not yet seen the pathologist's final report, which said Johnston had been beaten and had then been killed by a shot from a gun held close to his right eye. The time of death was put at around 3 a.m. Soldiers stationed nearby had reported hearing shots at that time, a fact that was withheld from the defence. In addition, there were suspicions that the killers had actually broken in through a first-floor window, rather than the front door.

The Court of Appeal also heard evidence that when Hindes 'confessed' that his accomplice was called Hanna, he had been referring to a different boy of the same name. The police had picked up Hugh Hanna by mistake.

In September 2005, both convictions were finally overturned. It was too late for Hanna, then aged forty-three. A few hours before the appeal hearing began, he had been found hanged at his home.

As the Regional Crime Squads' campaign continued through 1976, an increasingly gung-ho atmosphere gripped the regular Monday morning security meeting at the headquarters of the Northern Ireland administration at Stormont in East Belfast. The meeting was chaired by Mason and attended by the Chief

Constable, the head of the army in Northern Ireland and a handful of civil servants. The Secretary of State would be told, bluntly, that 'the bastards are on the run'. The statistics appeared to confirm that view. Charges against alleged members of the IRA had increased by 121 per cent by the end of the year. Complaints of assaults during interview had also more than doubled, from 180 to 384, but at the tail end of 1976 nobody at Stormont wished to think about that. And the following May, the interrogators' methods received a resounding endorsement during one of the landmark trials of the Troubles.

Linda Baggley had followed her father, William, an English accountant, into the RUC reserves after he was shot dead while patrolling Dungiven Road in the Waterside area of Derry. In May 1976, a little more than two years after her father's death, she herself had been on foot patrol with a colleague in Dungiven Road. As she approached the spot where her father had died, two IRA gunmen walked up behind and opened fire at point-blank range. Baggley was hit in the back of the neck and died in hospital ten days later. She was the first female police officer to be shot dead during the Troubles. She was nineteen years old.

Later that year four men and one woman from Derry were arrested, questioned and charged with a range of offences, including murder and membership of a banned organisation. At trial all but one alleged that they had been subjected to torture to induce them to make the admissions that were to be used in evidence against them. One of the defendants, a boy of sixteen, alleged that he had been punched in the stomach and kidney area more than fifty times, slapped and punched in the face, burned with a cigarette and forced to strip before being struck in the testicles.

The judge of the case, Lord Justice Ambrose McGonigal, was something of an enigma to many Republicans. A Catholic, he had been educated in the Republic by Jesuits. At the outbreak of the Second World War he had been commissioned into the

Royal Ulster Rifles, won a Military Cross for his bravery during raids on German forces on the Channel Islands and became a founding member of the Special Air Service.

McGonigal would show grudging respect for those IRA men who refused to recognise his court, regarding them as behaving like proper soldiers. Such was the IRA's hatred for him, however, that he is said to have taken to carrying a firearm beneath his robes.[22]

Ruling on the defendants' complaints of mistreatment, McGonigal pointed out that the wording of Section 6 of the EPA was borrowed from Article 3 of the European Convention on Human Rights, which prohibits torture. Accordingly, he said, he looked to the European Commission for a definition of the terms 'torture, inhuman and degrading treatment'. He said that the term inhuman treatment had recently been defined, in a case against the Greek government, as treatment that deliberately caused severe suffering, while torture was defined as a deliberate and aggravated form of inhuman treatment. Degrading treatment was that which grossly humiliated an individual.[23]

But, McGonigal added: 'The Commission distinguished in the Greek Case between acts prohibited by Article 3 and what it called "a certain roughness of treatment".' The commission considered that such roughness was tolerated by most detainees and even taken for granted. Because treatment was inhuman only if it resulted in severe suffering, McGonigal ruled, Section 6 of the EPA 'leaves it open to an interviewer to use a moderate degree of physical maltreatment for the purpose of inducing a person to make a statement'.[24] Moreover, he said, a statement made by an individual who had been subjected to torture, inhuman and degrading treatment may remain admissible, as long as the mistreatment had not been *for the purposes* (my italics) of inducing the statement.

Four of the defendants were convicted and sentenced to life imprisonment. Defence lawyers who were already disturbed at the latitude that Section 6 gave to RUC interrogators now feared that those officers were receiving clear signals from the courts that ill-treatment was permissible provided that it could not be said to have resulted in severe suffering. It was not long before members of the legal profession in Northern Ireland were referring to McGonigal's judgment as the Torturers' Charter.[25]

A few months later, in 1977, the interrogators at Castlereagh did call a brief halt to the mistreatment of suspects, but not in response to any judgments handed down by the courts. One of the officers had noticed a section of wall panelling had been damaged, possibly when a prisoner was pushed hard against it. Instead of pulling the panelling back into place, he ripped it out and, to his horror, saw that a microphone had been wired into the cavity behind it. He and his colleagues checked the other twenty interview rooms and discovered that every one had been bugged. The detectives suspected that the listening devices could only have been placed there by MI5, probably with the assistance of Special Branch detectives, and realised that it could not have been done without the connivance of some of the uniformed staff who supervised Castlereagh.

'There was uproar,' one former interrogator recalled. 'We all immediately went on strike. We made it clear to Mooney that we weren't questioning another suspect.' The implications for the interrogators were enormous. Not only had every crime committed by a police officer during the extraction of 'confessions' been captured on tape; so too had every offer of assistance made by an interviewee. Every person who had pointed a finger at a neighbour or a work colleague or a husband had been recorded.

The interrogators were incandescent. 'Mooney called a big meeting in the conference room to try to calm things down,' recalls one. 'There was a lot of anger. A lot of it was directed at Mooney. He didn't appear to know it had been happening, but he gave an unconditional guarantee that all the bugs would be removed and that it wouldn't happen again.'[26] Eventually, amid much grumbling and a considerable amount of paranoia, the interrogators agreed to end their strike and go back to work.

The bugs were indeed removed, but MI5 appears to have regarded this episode not so much as a setback as an opportunity to upgrade their eavesdropping facilities. Some years later, when a senior English detective, John Stevens, was asked to go to Northern Ireland to investigate the collusion of some elements of the security forces in a number of Loyalist killings – including the murder of solicitor Pat Finucane – he is said to have discovered that the bugs had been replaced. Stevens was eager to recover any transcripts of the recordings in order to establish whether members of the RUC ever told suspects that their solicitors were to be targeted for assassination. He never got his hands on the transcripts, but members of his team took senior RUC officers to one side and confided in them that they had been bugged throughout the Troubles.[27]

Although the discovery of the bugs represented only a temporary interruption to the business of interrogation, the system was coming under increasing scrutiny from some who worked closely with the police.

Whenever a suspect was taken to Castlereagh or Gough they were offered an examination by a medical officer. The purpose of the examination was to ensure that the suspect was fit enough to be interrogated and to record any visible injuries they had on arrival. Many people refused this on the grounds that there was nothing wrong with their health; some doctors were more persistent than others in explaining the advantage of being examined before the interrogation began.[28]

At the end of their time at Castlereagh, prisoners would be offered a second examination. Again, this was not compulsory, and almost half of the prisoners refused. After days of interrogation, many prisoners were anxious to get out of

Castlereagh as quickly as possible; some asked to be examined instead at Townhall Street police station in Belfast city centre, where they were taken to be charged before being brought to court. Some explained that their interrogators had warned them that they faced further beatings if they made any complaint. A few were so fearful of retribution that after being examined they asked that their medical records be destroyed.[29]

One man was determined that this must end. Robert Irwin, the secretary of the Association of Police Surgeons, was a Protestant who worked as a general practitioner in a Catholic district. He was also a forensic examiner who had seen the remains of countless bomb victims. As a result he had very strong views on the need for paramilitaries to be effectively investigated, prosecuted and sentenced to lengthy terms of imprisonment. However, he had no wish to see suspects suffering ill-treatment.

During the summer of 1977, Irwin had a number of meetings with members of the Police Authority, the body of local politicians to which the Chief Constable was accountable, and explained that he and his colleagues were concerned at the growing number of injuries they were seeing that could not be self-inflicted. Irwin had already made representations to the RUC without success. The Police Authority members agreed to meet with Newman, but were brushed off with the assertion that all the cases were *sub judice* and therefore could not be discussed. The police doctors then asked to meet with the Chief Constable. When Newman finally saw them, almost three months later, he agreed to set up a committee at which complaints could be raised.

The first prisoner Irwin saw after his meeting with the Chief Constable was Tommy McKearney, the man arrested for the shooting of the postman Stanley Adams. He had been brought to Townhall Street from Castlereagh, where he had refused to make any complaint. He was pale and nervous, he had bruises around his head, his forehead, neck, forearms and stomach were swollen and his fingers were trembling. Irwin was appalled by McKearney's condition.

More than three decades later, McKearney described what had happened to him:

> They used a variety of measures, but for the most part they concentrated on two types of physical abuse. One was exerting pain through putting pressure on my wrists, and I was forced to do physical exercises. It lasted on occasions for several hours on end. Two bulky detectives would be interrogating me. One powerfully built RUC detective would keep me pinned in a position while the other one would hold my elbow and then press back on my wrist. And that could last for an hour or possibly two hours. And it's excruciatingly painful, to the extent that I remember after three or four days I would simply go into unconsciousness because of the pain.
>
> The detectives would order me to do press-ups, sit-ups, or perhaps stand in the search position, spread-eagled against the wall. Because I was doing press-ups on what were, after a day or two, very damaged joints, it added to the pain. And if I refused to do that they would again press down on my wrists.

At one point, a plastic bin bag was placed over his head and torso, then held tight around his throat while he was beaten:

> So there was an element of pain, there was an element of stress, and there was an element of humiliation, where they would force you to do the exercises rather than endure the pain. For a man in his twenties, the idea that you would succumb to do press-ups for interrogators because you were scared to endure the pain, that's not only stressful, it's a humiliating thing. I would say

without fear of contradiction that I was tortured by
RUC detectives.[30]

Journalists began to hear that Irwin and a number of other
doctors were increasingly concerned about the methods being
used at Castlereagh and a few made renewed attempts to
investigate. Eventually, ITV's *This Week* made a documentary
that examined several cases. Shortly before the programme was
broadcast, a meeting at the Northern Ireland Office concluded
that the allegations should be dismissed as the complaints of a
small number of 'political doctors'; that Newman should demand
to see the programme in advance; and that he should issue a
statement which included the extraordinary claim that 'the
current trend of allegations against the police is an international
problem which stems largely from the growth of international
terrorism'.[31]

At this point, Amnesty International decided to mount its own
investigation. It dispatched to Belfast a delegation that included
a Dutch lawyer and two Danish doctors with experience of
examining Chilean torture victims. As well as meeting seventy-
eight complainants and their lawyers, the delegates saw police
doctors, the Chief Constable and his senior officers, and the
Director of Public Prosecutions. They were not given access
to the police doctors' reports, however. This was the most
damning evidence and Roy Mason was determined that they
should not see it.[32]

While the delegation was in Belfast the leaders of all the
Christian churches in Ireland, Catholic and Protestant, north
and south, issued a joint statement expressing concern about
what was happening at the interrogation centres and warning
that any failure by the police to protect people in custody
threatened to undermine free society.

For the duration of the Amnesty visit, and for a short while
afterwards, the torture at Castlereagh came to a halt. The

beatings, the police doctors realised, could be turned off like a tap. But they could also be turned back on again, for they were by now the default response of the RUC to any escalation in sectarian violence.

Early in 1978, the Provisional IRA launched a fresh offensive, including a wave of fire-bomb attacks. On 17 February, members of the IRA used a meat hook to hang a large incendiary device, incorporating four petrol containers, outside a window of the La Mon House country hotel east of Belfast. Inside were 300 people, many of them attending the annual dinner dance of the Irish Collie Club. The blast created a fireball that set many of the diners ablaze. Twelve people died and more than thirty were injured. All the victims were Protestants and the dead included three married couples. The IRA issued a statement which admitted that its nine-minute telephoned warning to the RUC had been too late and accepted the criticisms of the relatives and friends of those who were 'accidentally killed'.

Pope John Paul II described the attack as an inhuman deed. One Unionist politician called for Republican districts to be bombed from the air by the Royal Air Force. Mason told the House of Commons that he believed the IRA had intended the carnage and that its apology was false.

The beatings at Castlereagh began immediately to increase, both in number and in intensity, and this time the mistreatment spread to Gough holding centre in Armagh. Irwin started to complain to anyone who might listen to him, at the Northern Ireland Office, the Department of Health and the RUC. He told a number of civil servants that he was convinced the beatings were the result of a policy directed by the Chief Constable. During one meeting with Newman he suggested that closed-circuit television cameras be installed in the interview rooms. Newman commented that that would be expensive. Recalling the government's deep embarrassment at being hauled before the European Court of Human Rights over the Five Techniques,

Irwin's reply was: 'Not as expensive as having to go back to Strasbourg.'

But the beatings continued.

Amnesty published its report in June. Over seventy-two pages, it detailed the many techniques of torture employed at Castlereagh. It found that a number of the victims were suffering continuing gastric complaints and some appeared to have a degree of brain damage. Medium-term psychiatric consequences for many of the victims were anxiety, depression and insomnia. Some were suicidal and a number had developed serious psychotic disorders. Amnesty urged a change in the rules governing the admissibility of self-incriminating statements and said that the machinery for investigating complaints against police was inadequate. The organisation concluded: 'Maltreatment of suspected terrorists by the Royal Ulster Constabulary had taken place with sufficient frequency to warrant the establishment of a public inquiry to investigate it.'

By the time Amnesty's report had been published, Mason was well aware of the truth of what was happening at Castlereagh. British government papers declassified in 2008 showed that the Northern Ireland Secretary had been told that RUC interrogators who specialised in beating prisoners were working at Castlereagh. A senior civil servant had warned Mason that Dr Irwin – a 'completely credible witness' – believed the beatings were the result of a policy directed by Newman.[33] Moreover, the Northern Ireland Secretary was being warned in intelligence briefings that the complaints would 'undermine a recent trend towards a more understanding attitude in America towards HMG's position' and that even the Soviet government was questioning the UK's human rights record.[34]

Two days after the Amnesty report was published, Mason conceded the need for an inquiry. As with Roderic Bowen's inquiry in Aden twelve years earlier, however, it was not to be an inquiry into allegations of torture, but an examination of detention and interrogation procedures. It would be headed by a Crown Court judge, Harry Bennett, QC. Speaking in the Commons, Mason dismissed the complaints detailed by Amnesty as 'unsubstantiated allegations against unnamed police officers' and said that the inquiry was needed in order to 'discern the difference between truth and propaganda'.

Even then, the beatings at Castlereagh and Gough didn't stop. During the autumn of 1978, as Bennett was taking evidence in private from fifty-eight witnesses, mostly policemen, doctors and lawyers, the number of complaints rose steadily. Dr Robert Irwin had finally had enough and decided to go public, giving a television interview in which he said that in the last three years he had seen between 150 and 160 cases in which the injuries were not self-inflicted.

The Northern Ireland Office responded by orchestrating a campaign against Irwin. Journalists were quietly briefed that he was motivated by malice because he had suffered a demotion; that he was a drunk; that his judgement was affected by domestic problems. Worse, a number of journalists were told that he harboured a grudge against the RUC because its officers had failed to identify and arrest a British soldier who had attacked two members of his family in their home three years earlier. The fact was that Irwin was a good friend of the officers leading the hunt for the assailant. Nevertheless, this smear duly appeared in the *Daily Telegraph*, which published a front page in which Irwin, an 'RUC critic', denied he was motivated by bitterness.[35]

Judge Bennett's report was published on 16 March 1979, the same day as the *Telegraph* story. Mason told MPs that the judge had found evidence of prisoners inflicting injuries upon themselves and implied that he had found no evidence of ill-treatment by police. Such behaviour 'cannot' happen in Northern Ireland, Mason said, and by adopting the judge's recommendations, 'we shall kill and defeat the Provisionals' propaganda campaign of allegations of ill treatment in Northern Ireland'.

Publication of the 143-page report was delayed until a few minutes after Mason's statement, so MPs were unable to challenge the Secretary of State on what Bennett had actually concluded. In fact, the judge had found that a number of the prisoners' injuries could not be dismissed as self-inflicted on the grounds of the 'nature, severity, sites and numbers of separate injuries' on individual suspects. 'There can be no doubt', Bennett stated, that some injuries 'were not self-inflicted and were sustained during the period of detention at a police office.'

Bennett recommended that medical examinations of suspects be conducted every twenty-four hours, that detectives be rotated away from interrogation duties, that the DPP should explain to the Police Authority his decisions not to prosecute police officers and that solicitors should be granted access to clients after twenty-four hours in police custody. Critically, he recommended that CCTV cameras be installed inside interview rooms so that uniformed officers could monitor their plain-clothes colleagues.

In spite of Mason's attempts to misrepresent Bennett's findings, there was an angry reaction in Washington, where Congress embargoed the sale of 6,000 pistols that had been due to be sold to the RUC. It was the sort of sanction that the Carter administration reserved for repressive regimes which did not respect the human rights of their own citizens.

The Bennett Report was to have far-reaching repercussions at home. At the time of its publication the Labour government was limping along with the narrowest of parliamentary majorities and a vote of confidence was due to take place in the Commons twelve days after publication. Having done their sums, the party whips realised that the outcome could hinge on just one vote. One Labour MP, Sir Alf Broughton, was dying in a hospital in Yorkshire. So desperate were the Labour whips that they considered bringing him to the Commons on a stretcher, but the Prime Minister eventually dismissed the plan as obscene.

Mason's deputy, Don Concannon, pleaded without success for the support of Frank Maguire, the Independent MP for Tyrone and Fermanagh. Maguire, a Republican, said that he could not vote for a government that condoned torture.

When the day came, the deciding vote was cast by Gerry Fitt, the Social Democratic and Labour Party MP for West Belfast, who had always supported Labour in Commons votes. Not this time. In what he described as 'the unhappiest speech I have ever made in this House', Fitt said:

> I made up my mind the Friday before last when I read the Bennett Report on police brutality in Northern Ireland. That has not received sufficient attention in this House or in the country. The report clearly states that men were brutalised and ill treated in the holding centres in Northern Ireland. When the true story emerges of what has been happening in the interrogation centres, the people in the United Kingdom will receive it with shock, horror and resentment. That is why I take this stand.[36]

Fitt, like Maguire, abstained in the vote that followed, which the government lost by 311 votes to 310. An election was called and the Tories, led by Margaret Thatcher, won a landslide victory.

But even the publication of the Bennett Report did not halt the beatings at Castlereagh. Complaints continued to be lodged by doctors and prisoners alike. Finally, at the end of the year, Newman left the RUC and returned to England as commandant of the Police Staff College at Bramshill in Hampshire, the UK's leading training centre for senior officers. By now he was Sir Kenneth, having been knighted for services to policing.

Robert Irwin later bumped into Judge Harry Bennett on an Irish Sea ferry. The judge thanked the doctor for his evidence, which, he indicated, had enabled him to reach the conclusions that he had. Many years later Irwin found himself at a social event in London along with Kenneth Newman. Lady Newman approached him and asked if he would be prepared to speak with her husband. 'Of course I'll speak to him,' said Irwin. 'But don't expect me to shake his hand.'[37]

In the event, Irwin and the other police doctors did not succeed in halting the torture. Nor did Bennett, or the clergymen and women of Ireland, or the handful of journalists who were prepared to investigate. The brutality was eventually brought largely to an end by Newman's own deputy, Jack Hermon, who succeeded him as Chief Constable.

Hermon was a strict Presbyterian who had previously been head of community relations for the RUC. He had a lot of good Catholic friends, including Denis Faul, who, along with his fellow priest and civil rights campaigner Father Raymond Murray, had been assiduously documenting the violent excesses of the British state for the last decade. Hermon took up his appointment on 2 January 1980 and within hours the interrogators at Castlereagh detected a change in the wind. Hermon noted that the CCTV cameras recommended by Bennett had still not been installed in the interview rooms and ordered that they be promptly fitted. A while later, Bill Mooney, the head of CID, was absent from the Monday morning conference, the key meeting of the interrogators' week. 'He was in with Hermon,' a former interrogator recalls. 'Mooney came out of that meeting and told us: "From now on, you're not to lay a finger on anyone at Castlereagh."'[38]

Complaints that suspects were being abused at Castlereagh continued to be made on occasion during the 1980s, but with nothing like the same frequency as they had during the previous decade. The Chief Constable, it appeared, had his interrogators very firmly under control.

Hermon retired in June 1989 and was replaced by Hugh

Annesley, a Dubliner and a former Scotland Yard officer. While Annesley could never be accused of attempting to restore the torture regime at Castlereagh, he appears initially to have underestimated the effort that would be needed to prevent its spontaneous revival, and for a while in the early 1990s a considerable number of men and women, both Republican and Loyalist, began to make familiar complaints.

In May 1991, for example, Damien Austin, a seventeen-year-old from a well-known Republican family in west Belfast, was one of a number of youths held at Castlereagh for questioning about a rocket attack on an RUC Land Rover that had claimed the life of a sergeant, Stephen Gillespie, a father of two children, and had left two other officers injured.

Austin and the other youths were suspected of acting as lookouts for the IRA men who had fired two rockets at the vehicle. They all firmly deny this, although some of the youths eventually pleaded guilty to relatively minor offences. It was one of a series of rocket attacks, and no doubt there was considerable anger within the RUC about the loss of lives and the appalling injuries officers were suffering. 'I was slapped, I was punched, I was actually burned in the face with a cigarette,' says Austin. 'I had a lighter held to my testicles. It just went on and on, no solicitor for forty-eight hours. I was a seventeen-year-old boy, with two intermittent policemen coming in, constantly questioning, harassing, slapping, punching, that kind of thing.'[39]

When Austin was rearrested the following August, Amnesty International was so concerned for his safety that it issued an urgent action notice, urging its members to write to both Annesley and John Major, the Prime Minister, demanding an investigation. Austin sued the RUC, which settled out of court, paying several thousand pounds.

Later that year, after other people made similar allegations, the United Nations Committee Against Torture announced that it was to examine police procedures at Castlereagh and elsewhere, to determine whether they complied with the UN Convention Against Torture, which had been incorporated into UK law three years earlier.

The committee sharply criticised the British government's record in Northern Ireland and said that the video-recording of interviews and granting suspects access to lawyers were measures that were overdue. Peter Burns, the Canadian barrister who chaired the committee, said: 'If you separate Northern Ireland from the analysis, then quite clearly the government of the United Kingdom meets in virtually every respect the obligations imposed by the Convention. On the other hand, I am left with enormous reservations about Northern Ireland.'[40]

In response to the UN report, the British government appointed an independent commissioner to monitor Castlereagh, Gough and Strand Road, and although it continued to resist video-recording, the violence during interviews began to come to an end once more.

When the Committee Against Torture returned to Northern Ireland in 1995, during an IRA ceasefire, they found that the RUC's treatment of suspects had greatly improved. Burns described it as 'light years apart' from his last visit. People still complained of being verbally abused and slapped above the hairline, where marks would not show. 'That's quite different from the complaints we had last time about hooding, punching, holding in dark cells for long periods of time and the withholding of food,' Burns said.

During the late 1990s, the peace process in Northern Ireland saw the Emergency Provisions Act largely repealed and Castlereagh interrogation centre was closed down in 1999. The Diplock Courts were finally abolished in 2007, with juries reintroduced for all but exceptional cases.

The torture continues to leave its mark, of course. Among those unable to escape from that past are the interrogators themselves, some of whom appear traumatised by their memories of what they inflicted upon others. Some have concluded that what they did was a terrible mistake, one that exacerbated the causes of the conflict; others insist they resorted to violence only in desperation, in a bid to vanquish the far more extreme violence that was engulfing their society.

One man who had a particularly fearsome reputation in the 1970s – and who still has difficulty discussing the methods that he employed – says simply: 'We are where we are – and we're left popping our Prozac and taking our pills at night. We could have had easy lives, but instead we chose to do what we could to try to save the lives of others.'[41]

But former paramilitaries argue that rather than saving lives the use of torture in Northern Ireland actually aggravated and prolonged the terrible violence. Tommy McKearney says: 'Torturing prisoners will provide a very short-term gain. In the medium term it's of doubtful value. The IRA quickly moved people and weapons and cars, and abandoned safe houses, once they realised their people were being tortured.

'In the long term it is destructive to the aims of those who are using it, because it thoroughly alienates those against whom it is perpetrated, and not only those who are suffering. Bear in mind that their communities feel the pain as well, families, neighbours and friends. It drives people to even greater excesses than they might have originally contemplated.'

Furthermore, says McKearney, there are Irish children not yet born who will grow up hating the British and the police in Northern Ireland because of the suffering that was inflicted at Castlereagh and Gough and Strand Road. 'What torture does, undoubtedly in my opinion, is embed a reservoir of hatred and detestation, one that doesn't go away for years, doesn't go away for generations.'

7

Standing Shoulder to Shoulder on the Dark Side: Britain and the Rendition Programme after 9/11

> 'Unless we all start to believe in conspiracy theories
> and that the officials are lying, that I am lying, that
> behind this there is some kind of secret state which is in
> league with some dark forces in the United States . . .
> there simply is no truth in the claims that the United
> Kingdom has been involved in rendition, full stop.'
> Jack Straw, Foreign Secretary,
> 13 December 2005

The moment the first Boeing 767 crossed that perfect blue sky on that late summer morning and vanished into the side of the North Tower, the post-9/11 era had begun.

Around the world, first reactions were both identical and curiously at odds. President George W. Bush's initial thought was: 'It must have had the worst pilot in the world.'[1] As the second aircraft struck and the television pictures showed not only the enormity of the attack but the thousands upon thousands of individual tragedies that were unfolding, Bush told Vice-President Dick Cheney that the country was at war, adding: 'Someone's going to pay.'

George Tenet, the head of the CIA, knew immediately that al-Qaida was behind the attack, but was thrown into confusion by the second strike, and the third against the Pentagon. 'We had no idea what was real and what wasn't, but everyone was wondering, what next?' He ordered the evacuation of the agency's headquarters at Langley, Virginia, but his head of counterterrorism, Cofer Black, insisted an eight-strong emergency response team remain. 'They could die,' warned Tenet. 'Well, sir,' replied Black, 'they're just going to have to die.'[2]

In the UK, a number of senior intelligence officers concluded quickly that although the attacks were on a vast scale, and certainly horrific, they were not qualitatively different from other terrorist incidents. Some were fearful of the American reaction.

The British Prime Minister, Tony Blair, did not see it that way. He was sitting in his room at the Grand Hotel in Brighton, polishing the speech he was about to give to the Trades Union Congress. His communications director, Alastair Campbell, walked in, switched on the television and told him he should watch. As Blair recalled:

It was clear the casualties would be measured in thousands. It was the worst terrorist attack in human history. It was not America alone who was the target, but all of us who shared the same values. We had to stand together. It was war. It had to be fought and won. But it was a war unlike any other. This was not a battle for territory, not a battle between states; it was a battle for and about the ideas and values that would shape the twenty-first century.

All this came to me in those forty minutes between the first attack and my standing up in front of the audience to tell them that I would not deliver my speech but instead return immediately to London.[3]

All civilian flights to the US were grounded and the skies over New York and Washington were eerily quiet. The following day just one aircraft penetrated US airspace. It was an executive jet carrying Sir Richard Dearlove, the head of MI6, and Eliza Manningham-Buller, the deputy head of MI5, along with a handful of other senior British intelligence officials. Tenet later said that he had no idea how they had managed it, but he considered their arrival, and the messages of sympathy and solidarity that they bore, to be the most touching moment of his years in office.

Before long, that commitment of solidarity would draw the UK into all manner of hideous moral and legal compromises. Ultimately, it would involve the British government in torture once again, and once again the victims would include its own citizens.

Two days after the 9/11 attacks, during a meeting of Bush's closest advisers, Cofer Black declared the country's enemies must be left with 'flies walking across their eyeballs'. It was an image of death so striking that Black became known among the President's inner circle as 'the flies on the eyeballs guy'. Unlike its allies – the UK, France, Spain and Israel – the US had little experience of serious terrorist attacks on its own territory, nor any understanding of the need for a patient response. Bush was impressed by Black. Colin Powell, the Secretary of State, could see that the President wanted to kill somebody.[4] The problem, as successive attorneys general had warned one president after another, was that they did not enjoy unfettered powers of life and death over the nation's enemies. The CIA had been banned from carrying out assassinations since 1976.

The President turned to his Department of Defense and found that it had no cogent, off-the-shelf plan for responding to an attack of this nature on the United States. The CIA, on the other hand, did have something in its arsenal: it had the rendition programme.

Since 1987, the CIA had been quietly apprehending terrorists and 'rendering' them to the US for prosecution, without any regard for lawful extradition processes. In 1995, President Bill

Clinton – apparently with the full encouragement of his vice-president, Al Gore – agreed that a number of terrorists could be taken to a third country, including countries known to use torture, a process that would come to be known as extraordinary rendition.

Mike Scheuer, the CIA officer who started that programme, faced few objections from Clinton's national security advisers when he began taking prisoners to Egypt, where they could be interrogated under torture. 'They just didn't want to know what we were doing,' he says.[5]

Before 9/11, however, there were limits. In 1998, for example, the CIA had drawn up a plan to kidnap Osama bin Laden in Afghanistan and take him to Egypt. A shipping container was installed inside a Hercules aircraft and inside that was bolted a dentist's chair fitted with restraints. The CIA were all ready to go when, at the last moment, the FBI persuaded Clinton's attorney general, Janet Reno, that bin Laden's inevitable death at the hands of the Egyptians would be an act of murder and that US officials would be responsible. Reno vetoed the plan.[6]

By 13 September, with a still-unknown number of Americans dead and the President wanting action, all such legal squeamishness had vanished. President Bush and Dick Cheney both believed al-Qaida had succeeded because government lawyers had been expecting the CIA to do its job with one hand tied behind its back. Bush said as much to his attorney general, John Ashcroft, when he warned him: 'Don't ever let this happen again.' So when the head of the FBI, Robert Mueller, went to brief the President a few days after 9/11 and began to talk of the need to gather evidence for future prosecutions, he was promptly silenced by Ashcroft. Prosecutions were beside the point, Ashcroft said. All that mattered was stopping another attack.[7]

That night, Cofer Black locked himself away at his office at Langley and within five days had drawn up plans for the CIA's response. It would entail a vast expansion of the rendition pro-gramme. Hundreds of al-Qaida suspects would be tracked down and abducted from their homes and hiding places in eighty different countries. The agency would decide who was to be killed and who was to be kept alive in a network of secret prisons, outside the US, where they would be systematically tormented until every one of their secrets had been delivered up. The United States had been blindsided by al-Qaida on 9/11 and that situation would not be permitted to occur a second time.

Black's plan was presented to the President and his war cabinet in a series of meetings during the days after the attacks. On Monday 17 September, Bush signed off the paperwork: with a stroke of his pen the CIA was granted the power of life and death over al-Qaida suspects and could arrange for men to be detained and tortured indefinitely. All this, Bush later said, was to remain invisible.

A few hours afterwards there was a brief glimpse of the manner in which the United States would disregard the restraints of international law when responding to the attacks. Speaking at a press conference, Bush said: 'There's an old poster out West that says, "Wanted: Dead or Alive."' The President then checked himself before saying that those responsible for the murderous attacks should be brought to justice.

Cofer Black's master plan had already been presented to the CIA's closest overseas allies. The evening before Bush signed off, Black and a handful of other senior CIA officers went to the British embassy on Washington's Massachusetts Avenue, where they told senior British intelligence officers what was about to happen.

At the end of Black's three-hour presentation, his opposite number at MI6, Mark Allen, commented drily that it all sounded 'rather blood-curdling'. Allen also expressed concern that once the Americans had 'hammered the mercury in Afghanistan', al-Qaida would simply scatter across South Asia and the Middle East, destabilising entire regions. Black was dressed in the same suit he had been wearing five days earlier and was clearly exhausted, but he appeared to relish the vicious retaliation he had planned. He told Allen that all the CIA cared about at that moment was killing terrorists. One of the CIA officers at the meeting, Tyler Drumheller, could see that while the British appeared laid-back, 'it was clear they were worried, and not without reason'. According to one account, even Black joked that one day they might all be prosecuted.[8] But the CIA's closest ally had been put on notice: the British could never honestly claim that they did not know what was about to unfold.

Shortly afterwards Allen departed for London, where Blair and Foreign Secretary Jack Straw were waiting to be briefed on the Americans' plans.

At the end of September 2001, the United Nations Security Council passed Resolution 1373, which required member states to do more to assist the US and each other in eliminating international terrorism and called for a series of measures 'in conformity with the relevant provisions of national and international law'.

The need to maintain a lawful response to the horrors of the al-Qaida attacks was stressed again and again throughout the resolution, but it was already too late. By then, Dick Cheney had said publicly that the United States was going to 'work through sort of the dark side' and that 'it's going to be vital for us to use any means at our disposal, basically, to achieve our objective'.

On 2 October, members of NATO met at the organisation's headquarters at Brussels and agreed that they should invoke Article Five of the North Atlantic Treaty, under which an attack on one member is to be regarded as an attack on all. At a second meeting two days later, the US representatives presented a number of specific requests, all of which were granted in a series of agreement documents that the US had itself drafted. Eight of those requests have since been made public. They included enhanced intelligence sharing, taking 'necessary measures to increase security' and granting blanket over-flight clearances for the United States and other allies' aircraft for military flights engaged in counterterrorism operations. However, NATO has since admitted that a number of other requests were granted; all of them remain secret.[9]

By now, the US had a broad agreement from its key allies that it would conduct its 'war on terror' in line with Cofer Black's secret plan. What this would involve was spelled out in further detail at a subsequent meeting of the heads of the intelligence agencies of the US, UK, Canada, New Zealand and Australia. These men and women gather once every year to discuss signals intelligence-sharing arrangements, and after 9/11 it was New Zealand's turn to play host. The venue was a house on the edge of the small South Island resort town of Queenstown.

The threat posed by al-Qaida, Tenet is said to have told the gathered spy chiefs, 'is a challenge which redefines the way we work, the way we think, the way we act'. The CIA would accept no restraints and would in future work with the intelligence agencies of any nation. 'Without them, and their help, we have no fucking global effort,' the head of the CIA is said to have declared. 'We'd be walking through the Arab world wide open and half blind.' As far as the CIA was concerned, he said, 'the shackles, my friends, have been taken off'. And the CIA must not be alone in working closely with the intelligence agencies of the Arab world: 'We must work as one.'[10]

Cofer Black used similar terms during a subsequent Congressional inquiry into the 9/11 attacks when asked about the degree of freedom given to the CIA. 'All I want to say is that there was "before" 9/11 and "after" 9/11,' he said. 'After 9/11 the gloves come off.'

By November 2001, with the supercharged rendition

programme about to go live, Bush issued a barely concealed threat to those allies who failed to offer anything less than full cooperation. At a press conference before a White House dinner with President Chirac of France, Bush said: 'A coalition partner must do more than just express sympathy. A coalition partner must perform. It's going to be important for nations to know they will be held accountable for inactivity. Either you're with us or you're against us in the fight against terror.'

Chirac offered the view that it was Resolution 1373 that set out the obligations of member states. Bush, clearly unimpressed, decided the press conference was over. 'The soup's getting cold,' he said.

Exactly what was required of America's allies in the fight against terror soon began to emerge. On the evening of 18 December, Paul Forell, a uniformed officer of the Swedish Border Police, watched as two cars pulled up outside his office at Bromma airport in Stockholm. A group of plain-clothes officers of the Säkerhetspolisen, the security service, walked into the office and informed him that a deportation operation was under way. Ten minutes later two more men arrived. They gave Forell their first names and said they were from the US embassy. As they were speaking, a US-registered Gulfstream V jet touched down and began to taxi towards Forell's office. Some of the Säkerhetspolisen men went to greet it.[11]

They returned with eight people: six Americans and two Egyptians. One of the Americans was a doctor. All of them were dressed in black and wearing black masks with small eye-holes. The visitors went to the parked cars and brought from them two handcuffed men: terrorism suspects Mohammed al-Zery and Ahmed Agiza.

The two prisoners were stripped and searched carefully. Their clothes were cut into pieces and placed in bags. Their hair, mouths and ears were carefully examined. Sedatives were administered by anal suppositories and they were put into nappies. They were then dressed in overalls, handcuffed again and leg irons were locked around their ankles. Then they were photographed and hoods without eye-holes were placed over their heads. Throughout this process the men in masks talked rapidly to each other in low voices. The two prisoners were walked to the Gulfstream and strapped onto mattresses at the rear of the aircraft, which immediately took off for Cairo.

Forell had witnessed one of the first of Cofer Black's extraordinary rendition operations. Two men had been abducted from a European capital and taken to the Middle East to be interrogated.

Over the next few years, scenes like this would be repeated hundreds of times across the world. Men were rendered not only from the war zones of Afghanistan and Iraq but from Kenya, Pakistan, Indonesia, Somalia, Bosnia, Croatia, Albania, Gambia, Zambia, Thailand and the United States itself. The US was running a global kidnapping programme on the basis of Cofer Black's plan and the agreements reached at October's NATO meeting.

Some prisoners were dispatched to Middle Eastern countries, including Jordan and Syria, or to Afghanistan and Uzbekistan. An unknown number were sent to secret prisons that the CIA operated in Thailand, Poland, Lithuania and Romania. Wherever the prisoners ended up, however, they had one thing in common: they were going to be tortured.

On arrival in Egypt, al-Zery and Agiza were taken to the Tora Prison complex, fourteen miles south of Cairo, where they began immediately to suffer appalling abuse. Agiza subsequently appeared before an Egyptian court and was jailed for fifteen years. Almost two years after being rendered, al-Zery was released without charge after the Egyptian authorities accepted what he had always protested: that he had never advocated violence. He was then able to tell how he had been hooded continuously during his first two months of imprisonment and had suffered electric shocks on his genitals, nipples and ears. His first year of imprisonment was spent in a cell less than five feet square.

Immediately after the 9/11 attacks Tony Blair had taken a train from Brighton to London, where he issued a statement that pledged unswerving support for the US. He described terrorism as 'the new evil in our world', perpetrated by people with no regard for the sanctity of human life. There was now to be a battle between the free world and terrorism, he said. 'We therefore here in Britain stand shoulder to shoulder with our American friends in this hour of tragedy and we like them will not rest until this evil is driven from our world.'

Quietly, Britain pledged logistics support for the rendition programme, which resulted in the CIA's Gulfstream V and other jets becoming frequent visitors to British airports en route to the agency's secret prisons. Over the next four years, a twenty-six-strong flight of rendition aircraft operated by the CIA used UK airports at least 210 times. Dozens of other private executive jets that the agency chartered were also regular visitors to the UK. Nineteen British airports and RAF bases were used, including Heathrow, Birmingham, Luton, Bournemouth and Belfast. The agency's favourite destination was Prestwick in Scotland, which it used more than seventy-five times.[12] One CIA pilot described Prestwick as an ideal refuelling stop. 'It's an "ask no questions" type of place, and you don't need to give them any advance notice you're coming.'[13]

The US authorities also asked the UK government for permission to build a large prison on Diego Garcia, the British territory in the Indian Ocean that operates as a US military base. A Royal Marines officer made some preliminary plans, before the project was dropped, for logistical rather than legal reasons. Diego Garcia continued to be used as a stopover for rendition flights, however, and senior United Nations officials believe that a number of prisoners were held and interrogated there between 2002 and 2003.

The UK would do more than offer mere logistics support to the rendition programme, however. It would 'perform', in Bush's words, by becoming an enthusiastic participant in the rendition and torture programme. As in the summer of 1940, its first victims would be British. But as then and since, Britain would enshroud its use of torture with the greatest possible secrecy.

In October 2001, when the United States and its allies went to war in Afghanistan to topple the Taliban regime that had harboured al-Qaida, it was inevitable that a small number of those captured on the battlefield would be British.

For more than a decade, MI5 had been aware that British Muslims had been travelling to Pakistan and Afghanistan to receive training at camps run by al-Qaida or associated groups. Pakistan's main intelligence agency, the Directorate for Inter-Services Intelligence, or ISI, operated some of the camps, and graduates were encouraged to take up arms against Indian forces in Kashmir. Before al-Qaida began targeting the West in the late 1990s, MI5 saw these trips as evidence of little more than exuberant adventurism among a small section of young British Muslim males: a form of jihadi tourism that posed no threat to the UK. All that changed after 9/11, when both MI5 and MI6 became anxious to extract as much information as possible from any British prisoners in order to assess the al-Qaida threat.

It was not long before prisoners were being taken during battles in the north and south-east of Afghanistan. Many more foreign fighters were captured while attempting to slip across the border into Pakistan. Hundreds were handed over to US forces by Afghan and Pakistani bounty hunters, who received large bundles of dollars for every non-Afghan they captured.

Among the handful of British nationals seized in Afghanistan were Shafiq Rasul, Asif Iqbal and Rhuhel Ahmed. These men from the West Midlands, who became known as the Tipton Three, spent around a month in captivity in the north of the country before being flown to an interrogation centre at Kandahar airport. By this time, the Red Cross was already complaining to US authorities about the systematic mistreatment suffered by prisoners at Kandahar.[14] On arrival all three were severely beaten. According to Iqbal:

> An American came into the tent and shouted at me telling me I was al-Qaida. I said I was not involved in al-Qaida and did not support them. At this, he started to punch me violently and then, when he knocked me to the floor, started to kick me around my back and in my stomach. My face was swollen and cut as a result of this attack. The kicks to my back aggravated the injuries I had received from the soldier striking me with a rifle butt.[15]

Another of the Britons who ended up in the Kandahar interrogation centre was Jamal al-Harith. Born Ronald Fiddler in Manchester in 1966, al-Harith had converted to Islam in his twenties and had travelled widely in the Muslim world before arriving in Afghanistan. After 9/11 he had been imprisoned by the Taliban, who suspected him of being a British spy. At one point he and several other prisoners were forced to share their large cell with a horse that had offended a local Taliban leader in some ill-defined way. As bombs and missiles rained down on the city throughout October 2001, the unfortunate creature clattered around, terrifying its cellmates. A British journalist found al-Harith languishing in the prison in January 2002 and alerted British diplomats in Kabul, believing they would arrange his repatriation. Instead, they arranged for him to be detained by US forces, who took him straight to Kandahar.

A fifth Briton was Moazzam Begg, from Birmingham, who managed to escape from Afghanistan to Pakistan before being detained early in 2002. After being interrogated for several days by both British and American intelligence officers in a grand house in Islamabad, he begged one MI5 officer to get word to his family. 'I can't help you there,' was the response. 'I'm not a social worker.' Begg was dispatched, hooded and shackled, to Kandahar, where he was beaten, stripped, shaved and photographed. 'I was past a state of shock. I couldn't believe all this was happening to me. The noise was deafening: barking dogs, relentless verbal abuse, plane engines, electricity generators, and screams of pain from the other prisoners.'[16]

Back in London, government ministers and their intelligence advisers could not decide what to do with the young British Muslims being interrogated at Kandahar and at a second interrogation centre that US forces had established at Bagram airbase north of Kabul. One idea was to have them brought back the UK and prosecuted, possibly for treason. MI5 asked the Crown Prosecution Service whether they could 'interview' the prisoners first and were told they could, as this would not inhibit any subsequent prosecutions.

In Washington, meanwhile, members of Bush's war cabinet had decided that the expanded rendition programme should result in the majority of prisoners being interrogated by the US military rather than overseas intelligence agencies. 'The Department of Defense simply thought they could do it better than the Egyptians or whoever,' says Mike Scheuer. They needed somewhere to carry out these interrogations and chose the Guantánamo Bay naval base on Cuba as the site for Camp X-Ray, a new maximum-security prison designed to hold hundreds of prisoners. The land had been leased in 1903 and was, in theory, on Cuban territory, thus putting the prison and its inmates outside the reach and protection of the US legal system. On 6 January 2002, the first US combat engineers and contractors arrived at Guantánamo to begin construction. Three days later, senior lawyers at the US Justice Department drafted a memo that concluded that the Geneva Conventions did not apply to al-Qaida fighters or members of the Taliban.

Twenty-four hours after the drafting of this memo, on 10 January, British ministers had second thoughts about prosecuting British Muslims captured in Afghanistan. Government lawyers were warning that these men appeared not to have committed any offence under UK law and there was deep anxiety that the US government would be furious if they were brought back to the UK and subsequently released. Furthermore, police interviews in the UK would not be so effective as interrogations conducted overseas. So ministers decided, in the words of a secret Foreign Office memorandum, that their 'preferred option' was the rendition of British nationals to Guantánamo.[17]

Events moved rapidly. Later that day Jack Straw, the Foreign Secretary, issued a classified telegram to the British embassy in Washington and embassies across the Middle East. No objection should be raised to the transfer of the British nationals to Guantánamo, he ordered, as this was 'the best way to meet our counter-terrorism objectives'. He added, however, that their removal from Afghanistan should be delayed long enough to allow questioning by a 'specialist team' of MI5 interrogators.

The first team of MI5 interrogators had arrived in Afghanistan the previous day, joining a number of MI6 officers who had entered the country at the end of 2001. The first interrogation was conducted at Bagram just as Straw was sending his telegram.

The makeshift prison at Bagram was located in a disused factory built during the Soviet occupation. There were discarded pieces of machinery scattered around the shop floor and notices in Russian hung on the walls. Concertina wire divided the building into pens. The interrogations took place in several offices on a first-floor landing.

By the time MI6 and MI5 officers first entered the prison there were eighty-odd prisoners there, mostly Afghans and Arab fighters. A handful were British and it was immediately obvious they were being mistreated. Some of the prisoners were chained upright inside the pens, with hoods over their heads. Others were being beaten. One of the officers alerted his superiors that the first prisoner he questioned had been abused by the US military before the session began and the complaint was passed rapidly back to London.

The next day both MI6 and MI5 sent written guidance to all of their officers in Afghanistan. Covering two pages, these instructions had been prepared earlier in anticipation of such a complaint and were very carefully crafted.

This was the first sign that in the 'war on terror' – the battle over 'the ideas and values that would shape the twenty-first century', as Tony Blair put it – Britain and the US would stand shoulder to shoulder. Even when working the dark side. The guidance said:

> You have commented on their treatment. It appears from your description that they may not be being treated in accordance with the appropriate standards. Given that they are not within our custody or control, the law does not require you to intervene to prevent this. That said, HMG's stated commitment to human rights makes it important that the Americans understand that we cannot be party to such ill treatment nor can we be seen to condone it. In no case should they be coerced during or in conjunction with an SIS* interview of them. If circumstances allow, you should consider drawing this to the attention of a suitably senior US official locally. It is important that you do not engage in any activity

---

* The Secret Intelligence Service, or MI6.

yourself that involves inhumane or degrading treatment of prisoners.[18]

So MI5 and MI6 officers should not be seen to condone torture and must certainly not torture any prisoners themselves. But, crucially, they could continue to question people whom they knew were being tortured.

The door that could have been shut upon the use of torture during British operations against Islamist terrorism had been left open just a crack. A crack was all that was needed. Over the years to come, all manner of horrors would slip quietly through.

If the interrogations at Kandahar were brutal, those at Bagram were pitiless. At least two Afghans died under interrogation after being chained from the ceiling of their cells for several days while being beaten about the legs. Post-mortem examinations showed that their injuries were so severe that, had they survived, their legs would have had to be amputated.

There are allegations that British intelligence officers witnessed the abuse at Bagram and even took part on occasion, despite the warning that they must not be seen to condone it. Shaker Aamer, a Saudi who lived in London before travelling to Afghanistan, has given a statement to one of his lawyers in which he says British intelligence officers were present while Americans beat him and smashed his head against a wall. Hassan Zamiri, an Algerian married to a Canadian, has made a similar statement alleging that British intelligence officers interrogated him while he was being beaten and, on one occasion, waterboarded, and that one, an Englishman who called himself Paul, took part in the beatings. Moazzam Begg says he spoke not only to British intelligence officers at Bagram, but to visiting British soldiers.

Judging by the accounts that some of the inmates gave when they were finally set free, there is reason to believe that those conducting the interrogations were not just seeking intelligence.

They were, as Cyril Cunningham, the in-house psychologist as the UK's secretive Cold War organisation A19, had put it, involved in the 'selection, control and operation of secret agents and informers': the Bagram interrogators were hoping to turn some of the inmates – and doubtless, in some cases, they succeeded.

MI5 and MI6 officers conducted around 100 interrogations in Afghanistan over the next three years and the reports they subsequently sent to their superiors in London left no room for doubt about what was happening. After the interrogation in July 2002 of Omar Deghayes, a Libyan who had been living as a refugee in Britain, one of his questioners sent a detailed report back to MI5 headquarters. The report, which was disclosed during court proceedings brought by Deghayes eight years later, said: 'The interview commenced at 1345 GMT and finished at 1600 GMT. Deghayes was brought to the interview room manacled and hooded. When the hood was removed, Deghayes looked pale and shaky. We asked if he was ill and he replied that he was suffering from malaria.'

After offering Deghayes water and asking him whether he felt well enough to continue, the officers introduced themselves as Paul and Martin. They warned Deghayes that he was facing a long period of incarceration in US hands and that they would not consider helping him unless he told them everything they wanted to know. Deghayes was mumbling and incoherent at times. When he answered questions about links with jihadist organisations in Libya, the officers told him he was lying.

After another interrogation a week later, an MI5 officer reported back to London that Deghayes was thinner but alert. Deghayes said he was suffering internal bleeding:

> He said the medical staff thought he was malingering and challenged us to explain how anyone could feign internal bleeding. Deghayes then launched into an

extended complaint about why he was being held. No evidence had been presented yet he was still in custody. He was also being treated badly, with head-braces and lock-down positions being the order of the day. He was treated better by the Pakistanis; what kind of world was it where the Americans were more barbaric than the Pakistanis? We listened but did not comment.

MI5 decided that Deghayes should be sent to Guantánamo. 'If he sticks to his story and just gives a few more details, we propose disengaging and allowing events here to take their course,' the officer wrote in his report to London. Deghayes was to spend more than five years at Guantánamo, where the abuse continued. At one point he was beaten so severely that he was blinded in one eye.

It is clear from the very small number of British government documents so far made public that ministers were informed about what was happening at the new US prisons within days of the decision being taken to consign British Muslims to Camp X-Ray.

On 14 January 2002, four days after Straw sent his secret rendition telegram, a senior official attached to the Cabinet Office sent a six-page memo to David Manning, Blair's foreign policy adviser, naming three British citizens held in Afghanistan and noting that they were 'possibly being tortured' at a jail in Kabul. By 18 January, at the latest, Blair had been made aware. The Prime Minister wrote by hand in the margins of one Foreign Office memo: 'The key is to find out how they are being treated. Though I was initially sceptical about claims of torture, we must make it clear to the US that any such action would be totally unacceptable.' Blair added a curious instruction to his officials: not to endeavour to stop the torture, but to 'v quickly establish that it isn't happening'.[19]

Despite the Prime Minister being made aware of the possible use of torture, the UK remained a committed partner in the rendition programme. All but two of the British citizens and residents who ended up in Guantánamo were sent there after Blair wrote his note. Documents later disclosed in court showed that after one British terrorism suspect, Martin Mubanga, was detained in Zambia, either Blair or someone close to him at Downing Street intervened to ensure that he could not escape rendition to Guantánamo. Mubanga denied any involvement in terrorism. Nevertheless, a reason for his rendition was set out in a note that Eliza Manningham-Buller of MI5 sent to John Gieve, the Permanent Secretary at the Home Office, which was also disclosed in court. 'We are . . . faced with the prospect . . . of the return of a British citizen to the UK about whom we have serious concerns, whom it may be difficult to prosecute and whose release could trigger hostile US reaction,' Manningham-Buller wrote.

Around the same time that British nationals were being packed off to Guantánamo, the euphemism 'handling' was being coined at the highest levels of British government to describe the manner in which the prisoners were being treated. Straw's secret telegram said it was for 'the US authorities to determine the detail of how these prisoners should be handled. They have told us they would be treated humanely.' Three months later, a senior Home Office official was noting, with evident relief, that on the matter of 'handling', there had been 'no press coverage here during the last four weeks'.

The British government still had the option of bringing the young British Muslims back to the UK for prosecution. At the end of February, according to the minutes of a meeting of British security officials, the US was telling the British government that it could have all of the British detainees if it wished. But the officials concluded that the UK 'should not be in any hurry' to take them. The representative from the Foreign Office was said to have remained quiet on this point, as his department had 'some obvious problems of public presentation'.[20]

Some senior Foreign Office officials had severe misgivings about the manner in which events were proceeding. In a meeting with John Gieve in mid-April, Sir Michael Jay, Gieve's opposite number at the Foreign Office, explained that his department wanted to press the Americans for legal access to the British at Guantánamo – 'and wanted to be seen to be doing it'. But, he explained, they had been overruled by Downing Street.[21]

When the first batch of prisoners were flown from Afghanistan to Guantánamo, a few hours after Straw sent his secret telegram, they were wearing nappies, orange jumpsuits, handcuffs and shackles. They were also wearing blacked-out goggles, earmuffs and thick gloves, to ensure they experienced the sort of sensory deprivation that had been found to be so devastating during the three-way Canadian, American and British experiments of the 1950s. Such was the level of anger after the 9/11 attacks that the US authorities felt no shame about the way they were treating their prisoners: pictures showing the men being dragged across the ground were taken by US Navy photographers and distributed to the world's media.

The US government was less candid about the principal purpose of Guantánamo, however. Defense Secretary Donald Rumsfeld said it was a place of detention where people who posed a threat could be kept from harming others. He even suggested that they were there for their own good, declaring a few days after Camp X-Ray opened for business that its inmates would be subjected to 'appropriate restraint' as there were concerns that some might attempt to kill themselves.

In truth, Guantánamo was always an interrogation centre, a place to which men could be consigned in order to squeeze from them every drop of intelligence that might possibly be of use. But while some of the inmates were undoubtedly dangerous terrorists – 'bad people', as Bush called them – others were anything but.

A number of US Department of Defense documents leaked several years later showed that men were sometimes rounded up and taken to Guantánamo because the information they possessed was considered useful, rather than because they were thought to be dangerous. Said Abassi Rochan, for example, a twenty-nine-year-old Afghan taxi driver, was taken to Guantánamo to exploit his local knowledge. His file stated that he was 'transferred to Guantánamo Bay detention facility because of his general knowledge of activities in the areas of Khowst and Kabul ... as a result of his frequent travels through the region as a taxi driver'.

The documents showed that Sami al-Hajj, a Sudanese cameraman for the al-Jazeera news network who had been detained on the Pakistan border while making his way into Afghanistan, was sent to Guantánamo 'to provide information on ... the al-Jazeera news network's training programme, telecommunications equipment, and news gathering operations in Chechnya, Kosovo and Afghanistan, including the network's acquisition of a video of UBL [Osama bin Laden] and a subsequent interview with UBL'.

The file of Jamal al-Harith, the man from Manchester who had been forced to share a Taliban prison cell with a horse, shows that he was sent to Guantánamo 'because he was expected to have knowledge of Taliban treatment of prisoners and interrogation tactics'. Eighteen months later, the camp authorities had satisfied themselves that he had no connection with the Taliban or al-Qaida, but decided against releasing him because his 'timeline has not been fully established' and because British diplomats who had seen him in Kandahar had found him to be 'cocky and evasive'.

In all, nine British nationals were sent to Guantánamo, along with at least nine former British residents. All were incarcerated for years, and from the moment they arrived they suffered beatings, threats, sleep deprivation and other torments. All were interrogated by MI5 officers and some also by MI6.

Shafiq Rasul, one of the Tipton Three, says: 'When we arrived at Camp X-Ray I was made to squat in the boiling heat outside for about six or seven hours altogether. I became desperate and eventually asked for some water. The soldiers realised I was English and a man from the Extreme Reaction Force came and started kicking me in the back and calling me a traitor.'[22]

Asif Iqbal says all his initial interrogations at Guantánamo were conducted by MI5 officers: 'In my first interview with the MI5 official, I was told that I should say that I had gone to Afghanistan for jihad. He said that I did not need to say I'd been a fighter because there are lots of ways that one can do jihad.'[23] When he and his friends denied this, they were told they would remain at Guantánamo for the rest of their lives.

Jamal al-Harith spent two years being kicked, punched, slapped, shackled in painful positions, subjected to extreme temperatures and deprived of sleep. He was refused adequate water supplies and fed on food with date markings ten or twelve years old. On one occasion, he says, he was chained and severely beaten for refusing an injection. He estimates that he was interrogated around eighty times, usually by Americans but sometimes by British intelligence officers.

Al-Harith was finally released after more than two years. Nine months later he issued a statement in which he explained that he was still in pain as a result of the beatings he received before interrogation. 'The irony is that when I was first told in Afghanistan that I would be in the custody of the Americans, I was relieved. I thought that I would then be properly dealt with and returned home without much delay.'[24]

MI5 and MI6 officers carried out around 100 interrogations at Guantánamo between early 2002 and the end of 2004.[25]

★

Even when British intelligence officers weren't present in the room, their input in the interrogation of prisoners with a British connection was often vital, as it was in the case of a twenty-three-year-old Ethiopian who had been living in London, Binyam Mohamed. Details of what happened to Mohamed would emerge piece by piece during civil proceedings that were subsequently brought on his behalf in the British courts. It was a textbook example of complicity in torture, one that would result in MI5 facing a criminal investigation for the first time in its history.

The story began in April 2002, when Abu Zubaydah, a Saudi militant suspected of being a senior al-Qaida figure, was interviewed by FBI agents who had helped nurse him back to health after he had been badly wounded during his capture in Pakistan. The FBI made no attempt to torture Zubaydah; on the contrary, they literally held his hand while he told them of two men who had been tasked with mounting an operation almost as ambitious as the attacks of 9/11: the detonation of a radiological dispersal device, or dirty bomb, in an American city. 'The idea that these terrorists don't talk?' one of his FBI interrogators, Ali Soufan, queried. 'If you approach them the right way, from my experience, sometimes you have a problem shutting them up.'[26]

One of the two men mentioned by Ali Soufan was quickly identified as 'Binyamin Mohamed', who had been detained at Karachi airport while attempting to board a flight to London with a doctored passport. Mohamed denies he is a terrorist and, despite having clear reason to regard him as suspicious, the US authorities would later admit that the dirty bomb plot never proceeded beyond some rudimentary Internet research. Given al-Qaida's proven ability to mount mass-casualty attacks, however, and the CIA's determination never to be blindsided again, the threat was taken seriously.

Mohamed was handed over to the ISI for brutal interrogation. The Pakistanis and Americans quickly established that Mohamed had been living in London before travelling to Afghanistan, and MI5 and Scotland Yard's Special Branch began questioning Mohamed's friends and associates in west London.

The following month, the CIA granted the British permission to question Mohamed. Prior to the first session the British were given a candid account of the way Mohamed was being treated. Eventually, the MI5 officer who conducted the interrogation would be required to appear in court, where, named only as Witness B, he would say that he believed his actions were in accordance with steps agreed by MI5's lawyers and the government. He did not, however, mention the interrogation policy that had been issued to MI5 and MI6 officers in Afghanistan the previous January.[27]

When the court discovered that MI5 and MI6 knew full well that Mohamed had been tortured before Witness B was sent to question him, the British government attempted to persuade the judges to omit this fact from their public judgments.

David Miliband, then Foreign Secretary, was particularly anxious to preserve the control principle in relation to intelligence, whereby material provided by one nation to another could not be released without the consent of the originating country. Under this heading, he argued that the public should not learn of seven key paragraphs from one court judgment that revealed that MI5 were aware that Mohamed had been 'intentionally subjected to continuous sleep deprivation' and that the effects of the sleep deprivation were 'carefully observed'; that Mohamed was told that he could be made to disappear; and that the interrogation and mistreatment were causing 'significant mental stress and suffering'.

When the seven paragraphs were eventually released on the orders of the Court of Appeal, Lord Neuberger, the Master of the Rolls, commented that 'some Security Service officials appear to have a dubious record relating to actual involvement, and frankness about any such involvement, with the mistreatment of Mr Mohamed'. He added that MI5 had wanted the evidence about this dubious record to be concealed.

As damning as Lord Neuberger's comments were, they could have been worse. The Foreign Office's lawyers had persuaded the judge to tone down his draft judgment, in which he said there was good reason to distrust any government statement based on information supplied by MI5, as the organisation had previous 'form' for behaving dishonestly over human rights issues.[28]

While Witness B said nothing in court about his prior knowledge of Mohamed's torture, he did let slip one intriguing fact. He explained that he served with a division of MI5 known as the 'international terrorism-related agent running section'. The court heard that this was the section routinely responsible for interviewing suspected terrorists.

The MI5 officers who were interrogating al-Qaida suspects – men who were being tortured in Afghanistan, Pakistan, Guantánamo and elsewhere around the world – were agent handlers. As at Camp 020, and at the Ma'adi interrogation centre near Cairo during the Second World War, it appeared that MI5 was seeking to recruit torture victims as double agents.

Mohamed was not tortured while Witness B was in the room: the officer's standing orders were that he could not be seen to condone torture. Instead, the young Ethiopian was questioned by the British over a cup of tea. There is some dispute about this cuppa. Mohamed says Witness B advised him to take some sugar with it, as he would need it where he was going next. Witness B denies this. What is not disputed is that shortly after this meeting, Mohamed was rendered to a secret prison near Rabat in Morocco, where the interrogation regime was even more cruel than anything devised by Pakistan's ISI.

First there was a fortnight of questioning and intimidation, a softening-up process conducted both by Moroccans and by a woman who called herself Sarah and claimed to be Canadian. Then the torture began.

Moroccan interrogators beat Mohamed for hours and subjected him to loud noise for days. Once a month, he says, his torturers used scalpels to make shallow, inch-long incisions on his chest and genitals. He was accused of being a senior al-Qaida terrorist. Mohamed says that he would say whatever he thought his captors wanted and he signed a statement about the dirty bomb plot.

It was clear that Mohamed was being interrogated, in part, on the basis of information supplied by the UK. He was shown photographs of people he knew from a mosque in Notting Hill in west London. At one point, he says, interrogators told him the GCSE grades he had achieved at a college in the area, asked about named staff at the housing association that owned his small flat and talked about the man who taught him kick-boxing. Scotland Yard Special Branch officers had been scouring his background for details, which were passed, via MI5, to the CIA and then to the men wielding the scalpels.

It was a two-way process. During the subsequent court case it would emerge that reports of what Mohamed was saying under torture flowed back to London. The Security Service's lawyers admitted that MI5 knew Mohamed was not in US custody during this period, but repeatedly denied knowing he was being held in Morocco. Then a number of documents disclosed during the case showed that Witness B had visited the Moroccan torture centre on three occasions while Mohamed was being tortured there. After the last visit, MI5 had sent the CIA a list of seventy questions that it wanted put to Mohamed.

Mohamed's torture in Morocco went on for eighteen months until a team of masked Americans came to take him away. One photographed his genitals, to establish that they had been mutilated when he was with the Moroccans, not in US custody. Then it was off to Afghanistan.

For five months Mohamed was detained in a darkened cell in a prison somewhere near Kabul. He says he was chained, subjected to loud music and questioned by Americans. Only after he was moved to Bagram was he exhibited to the Red Cross. Four months later he was flown to Guantánamo, where he says he was routinely humiliated and abused over the next four and a half years.

Mohamed became one of the best-known victims of rendition and torture after 9/11, and one of the most blatant examples of British complicity in US crimes. But he was far from alone.

In August 2002, with the first anniversary of the 9/11 attacks approaching, the interrogation teams at Guantánamo were facing urgent demands for more information. 'There was tremendous pressure to be seen to be getting something done,' recalled Michael Dunlavey, the reservist major general who headed the teams and reported directly to Rumsfeld and Bush.[29]

Throughout that month a series of brainstorming sessions were held at Guantánamo. In order to develop new techniques that could be inflicted on their inmates, a number of interrogators flew to Fort Bragg in North Carolina, home of US Special Forces, to study the Survival, Evasion, Resistance and Escape courses conducted there. Ironically, these were the courses designed to introduce US military personnel to the methods of torture they might suffer if they fell into the hands of a particularly barbaric enemy.

After watching the training sessions at Fort Bragg, the interrogators devised three categories of 'enhanced' interrogation techniques. Category I comprised shouting and deception. If that did not work, the interrogator could move to Category II, which allowed for hooding, light and auditory deprivation, the use of stress positions and up to thirty days of isolation. Category III allowed for 'mild, non-injurious physical contact', death threats, exposure to extreme cold and waterboarding.

Once the interrogators were in agreement on these new techniques, Dunlavey needed to find a military lawyer prepared to offer a legal opinion that they were not prohibited under international humanitarian law. He turned to Lieutenant Colonel Diane Beaver, a Staff Judge Advocate at Guantánamo. Beaver had no background in international law but Dunlavey was keen to obtain what he described as 'legal sign-off' for the Techniques: 'I wanted accountability, I wanted top cover.'[30]

Beaver knew exactly where to look for the legal authorities she required: the judgment of the European Court of Human Rights at Strasbourg on the use of the Five Techniques in Northern Ireland. At appeal, the court had concluded in January 1978 that their use amounted to inhuman and degrading treatment but fell short of 'the particular intensity and cruelty implied by the word torture'. Drawing upon this judgment, Beaver offered her opinion that the enhanced interrogation techniques that were wanted at Guantánamo were lawful.

At the same time that Beaver was working on her advice for the US military, a number of US government lawyers were casting around for legal justifications for the 'gloves off' methods being employed by the CIA. Alberto Gonzales, then the senior White House general counsel, received a memo authorised by Jay Bybee, his assistant attorney general, offering a possible distinction between 'torture', which US citizens were forbidden by law from inflicting on foreigners, and 'inhuman and degrading treatment', which Bybee insisted was something quite different. 'Physical pain amounting to torture must be equivalent in intensity to the pain accompanying serious physical injury, such as organ failure, impairment of bodily function, or even death,' Bybee wrote. 'The infliction of pain or suffering per se, whether it is physical or mental, is insufficient to amount to torture.'[31]

Bybee added that when the United States ratified the UN Convention Against Torture in the 1990s, it had added a rider that permitted US officials to employ all but the most brutal of mistreatment while operating overseas. In doing so, he said, the

US had relied on the legal precedent that the UK had established at Strasbourg.

The European Court's ruling on the Five Techniques had appeared, at the time, to represent at least a partial victory for the defence of human rights and dignity. A quarter of a century later, lawyers on the other side of the world who were attempting to forge a legal justification for torture had turned it into a complete defeat.

In December 2002, during a major speech at the Pentagon, Bush pledged that the United States would prosecute its 'war on terror' within the 'finest traditions of valour'. The same day, in an office not far away, Rumsfeld signed off on the enhanced interrogation techniques.

Within days the enhanced interrogation techniques were being employed at Guantánamo, where they became known as EITs. Before long they would migrate to Abu Ghraib Prison in Baghdad.

The CIA was already using the EITs, however. One of the first victims, as early as April 2002, was Abu Zubaydah, the man who had warned of the dirty bomb plot, after which responsibility for his interrogation had been taken away from the FBI and handed to the CIA.

The Red Cross later documented the techniques to which Zubaydah was subjected as a consequence of legal advice that relied upon the British government's appeal to Strasbourg. He was stripped, deprived of sleep, subjected to loud noise, repeatedly slammed against a plywood sheet that had been placed against a wall – probably to ensure that the assault could be described as 'mild, non-injurious physical contact' – and waterboarded. He was also locked for hours at a time in one of two specially constructed wooden boxes. While confined in the 'large' box, Zubaydah could stand upright but not move; in the smaller box he was forced to crouch.

Asked years later whether he had authorised the use of water-boarding, President Bush's response was unequivocal and unrepentant: 'Damn right!'[32]

In one month, August 2002, Zubaydah was waterboarded eighty-three times.

Jamal al-Harith and the Tipton Three were eventually released from Guantánamo after more than two years of interrogations by the US military and British intelligence officers. As they boarded an RAF Globemaster transport plane, a man called Martin from the Foreign Office was waiting for them. Martin had a request. 'Can you', he asked, 'make sure you say you were treated properly?'[33]

Martin's boss, Jack Straw, was particularly concerned that the wider world should never learn of the extent to which the British government had become involved in the torture of its own citizens.

At the time that Straw had sent his secret rendition telegram, he had apparently not anticipated that a number of the victims of Britain's support for the US 'war on terror' would subsequently sue his government and that the courts would order the disclosure of the telegram and other secret papers that documented the depth of the British government's involvement in rendition. Nor did he anticipate that his successor, David Miliband, would be forced to admit that the US had used the British territory of Diego Garcia during rendition operations.

In December 2005, almost four years after sending the tele-gram, the full truth about British complicity in rendition and torture was still a deeply buried official secret and Straw felt able to tell MPs on the Commons' Foreign Affairs Committee that the allegations starting to surface in the media were nothing more than conspiracy theories. 'Unless we all start to believe in conspiracy theories,' he told the committee, 'and that the officials are lying, that I am lying, that behind this there is some kind of secret state which is in league with some dark forces in the United States, and also let me say, we believe that Secretary [of State, Condoleezza] Rice is lying, there simply is no truth in the claims that the United Kingdom has been involved in rendition, full stop, because we have not been.'[34]

More than three years later, in July 2009, Straw was still expressing his 'abhorrence of rendition', which he said was nothing more or less than kidnap, and telling the Commons that he stood by his claim that allegations of UK involvement were a conspiracy theory.

Straw's statements were breathtaking. But they showed that the British government, unlike the US, would not exult in its treatment of detainees after 9/11. There would be no 'damn right!' admissions from the British. Ministers who wished to make use of torture would remain acutely aware that it was not only morally repugnant but illegal. It was to be a dirty little secret, known only to a select group of men and women. And if necessary, Britain's use of torture would be concealed through statements by senior political figures that were the direct opposite of the truth.

8

The Fruits of the Poisoned Tree:
Outsourcing Torture, 2002–11

'The Secret Intelligence Service and Security Service operate in a culture that respects human rights. Coercive interrogation techniques are alien to both services' general ethics, methodology and training.'

Cabinet Office Memorandum,
September 2004

With the Taliban toppled, Bin Laden in hiding and the United States and her allies on the front foot, the British government began preparing for the next phase of the 'war on terror'. For Tony Blair, it was to be an ideological battle upon which the future depended. For MI6, it was the war that flowed from America's decision to hammer the mercury and scatter poisonous fragments of al-Qaida across the region.

Most of those fragments tumbled over the border into Pakistan, a country with which the UK had close historic ties and which was visited by thousands of increasingly disaffected British Muslim youths every year.

As has been seen, during the first week of January 2002 a series of decisions were taken in rapid succession that that would determine the way in which MI5 and MI6 officers dealt with those taken prisoner during the 'war on terror'. But that week's decisions also influenced the handling of prisoners who were taken during the next stage of this prolonged war: the invasion of Iraq.

The British would not only provide logistics support to the rendition programme, consign British citizens to Guantánamo and interrogate people whom they knew were being tortured by their American allies. They also forged close friendships with some of the world's most notorious intelligence agencies, the organisations that would, in the words of George Tenet, save them from 'walking through the Arab world wide open and half blind'.

These relationships would ensure that while the UK's intelligence agencies were never seen to *condone* torture, they would become closely involved in its practice. And in time, these alliances would even offer the agencies the opportunity to mount their own secret rendition operations.

One half-forgotten episode gives an insight into the way these relationships were conducted and the manner in which they could be exploited to justify some of the more controversial strategic decisions being taken during the 'war on terror'.

In September 2002, police investigating a suspected terrorism fund-raising operation in London arrested an Algerian waiter called Mohammed Meguerba. After Meguerba was released – with police later claiming they didn't realise how dangerous he was – he returned to his homeland, where he was detained by the Algerian intelligence agency, the Département du Renseignement et de la Sécurité, one of the UK's new-found friends. Under interrogation by the DRS, Meguerba said he was involved in a plot to use recipes from the Internet to produce the toxin ricin. The victims were to be people in London.

The manner in which MI5 then arranged for Meguerba to be questioned was subsequently set out in a remarkably candid statement submitted by Eliza Manningham-Buller, by then the agency's director general. The statement was given during an unconnected court case concerning the attempted deportation of a terrorism suspect. Its purpose was to explain how MI5 interacted with overseas intelligence agencies known to use torture in an attempt to extract information from people who were being held by those agencies and, quite probably, being tortured.

Manningham-Buller explained that most intelligence from such agencies – or 'liaison partners', as they are known within the intelligence community – is passed first to MI6, but occasionally goes direct to MI5. Asking too many questions about the manner in which the information has been obtained can 'damage co-operation and the future flow of intelligence', she said, so such questions are best avoided. In any case, 'where the reporting is threat-related, the desire for context will usually be subservient to the need to take action to establish the facts'.[1]

Cases such as that of Meguerba highlighted the fact that 'detainee reporting can be accurate and may enable lives to be saved', Manningham-Buller said. The DRS had told the British on 31 December 2002 that Meguerba had said he was aware of a plan to mount a poison attack within the next few days, using substances that could be found at an address in London which didn't actually exist. 'Further information was sought from Algerian liaison,' Manningham-Buller's statement said.

On 2 January 2003, the Algerians offered a detailed description of the location at which Meguerba said the poison was stored. A flat in Wood Green, north London was identified. The following day Meguerba confirmed this to be the correct address and two days later it was raided by police. Several men were arrested and scientists from the Ministry of Defence conducted tests on a number of items inside.

The head of Scotland Yard's anti-terrorism branch, David Veness, and the government's Deputy Chief Medical Officer, Dr Pat Troop, issued a statement. 'A small amount of the material recovered from the Wood Green premises has tested positive for the presence of ricin poison,' they said.

Tony Blair appeared on television that evening warning that the 'find' was a stark illustration of the dangers of weapons of mass destruction and told a meeting of ambassadors in London that 'this danger is present and real and with us now and its potential is huge'. Within hours, advice on the symptoms of ricin poisoning was being issued by the Department of Health to hospitals and doctors' surgeries across the country.

Before long the ricin discovery was being used to justify the impending invasion of Iraq. In February 2003, Colin Powell, the US Secretary of State, told the United Nations Security Council that al-Qaida in northern Iraq was 'teaching its operatives how to produce ricin', while in March, after hostilities had begun, the chairman of the US Joint Chiefs of Staff, General Richard Myers, told CNN that US forces had destroyed an al-Qaida camp in Iraq where 'the deadly toxin uncovered during the police raid in Wood Green, north London' had been produced.

There was just one problem with all of this. No ricin had been found at the flat in Wood Green. None. Not a trace.

While there was evidence that a plot of some sort was being hatched on the premises, there is reason to suspect that it may have been encouraged by Meguerba in telephone calls he was ordered to make from his Algerian prison.[2] A handful of castor beans, which can produce ricin, had been discovered, but the government scientists' tests had found no trace of the poison.

This inconvenient fact remained concealed for two years, until the occupants of the flat went on trial and the government scientists who had examined the premises were called to give evidence. They admitted that every one of their tests had produced negative results. Eight people who had been accused of plotting a poison campaign were subsequently acquitted. The ninth, who was already serving a life sentence for murdering a police officer, was convicted of conspiracy to cause a public nuisance. The case prompted the BBC's legal affairs analyst to question whether criminal prosecutions were being 'shamelessly exploited for political purposes' to justify the invasion of Iraq or new restrictions on civil liberties.[3]

But what, meanwhile, had become of the man whose 'detainee reporting' had revealed the existence of the plot that put the UK on high alert for a terror attack, reminded the world of the dangers of weapons of mass destruction and offered a link between al-Qaida and Saddam Hussein's regime on the eve of the invasion of Iraq?

The British press had been told that Mohammed Meguerba was a 'super grass', the implication being that he was eager to assist the authorities. And yet, two years after the Wood Green raid, he was still languishing in an Algerian prison. In her statement, Manningham-Buller admitted that 'no inquiries were made of Algerian liaison about the precise circumstances that attended their questioning of Meguerba'. MI5 did not ask, in other words, whether he was being tortured.

In 2005, shortly after the 'ricin plot' trial had concluded in London, Meguerba appeared in court in Algiers, accused of membership of a terrorist organisation.

A reporter from *The Times* who was present recorded that Meguerba appeared frail. He also noticed that many of his teeth seemed to have been removed.[4]

Almost as soon as Iraq was invaded in March 2003, it was clear that the allied invasion had spurred the radicalisation of significant numbers of British Muslim youths. Later that year, MI5 and the police realised that some were planning attacks against their own country.

In March 2004, hundreds of police officers raided addresses across the south-east of England, arresting eighteen people. One man was detained in New York and another in Ottawa. Others were seized in Pakistan. Detectives announced that at a storage depot in west London they had recovered half a ton of ammonium nitrate. It could have been used to build an enormous bomb. The would-be bombers were associated with al-Qaida, the police said, and most were British.

The surveillance operation that preceded the arrests was the largest of its kind ever conducted in the UK and had gathered evidence that the men were plotting an attack on any one of a number of targets: a listening device recorded one gang member suggesting they bomb a popular nightclub in south London, on the grounds that nobody could 'turn round and say: "Oh, they were innocent", those slags dancing around'.

The police had moved in after some of the gang bought one-way tickets to Pakistan. In their haste, however, they were unable to locate and capture the individual said to be a key figure in the plot, the link-man between the gang in England and Abdul Hadi al-Iraqi, then the number three in al-Qaida. This man was Salahuddin Amin, aged twenty-nine, who had been born in London but was then living in Pakistan.

Both British and US government officials asked the Pakistani Inter-Services Intelligence agency to track down Amin. Eventually, after a number of his close associates were detained and tortured, Amin agreed to give himself up and met the ISI at the home of his uncle, a retired brigadier in the Pakistani Army. After tea and polite conversation he was taken to a secret ISI prison in the Saddar district of Rawalpindi. 'I knew I was going to be tortured,' he says. 'When you're a prisoner of the ISI, that's the very least you're going to get. But I hoped it might not be so bad, as I had given myself up.'[5]

Over the next few days, Amin was beaten, whipped, suspended from the ceiling by his arms and on one occasion threatened with an electric drill. He was also questioned repeatedly by two MI5 officers who called themselves Matt and Richard. Sometimes he was taken, blindfolded, to see them; on other occasions they would come to question him in the brightly lit and carpeted room where he was being tortured. While Amin sipped from a glass of water, they would ask him the same questions that he had already answered under torture. One of his torturers would be present, sitting behind the MI5 officers. Amin would then be asked a few more questions and these would form the basis of the next torture session.

Amin says he never once complained to 'Matt' or 'Richard' that he was being tortured. He saw little point: it had been made perfectly clear to him by the Pakistanis not only that the British knew he was being mistreated but that it was happening at their request.

Amin says he was questioned thirteen times by MI5 officers while he was in ISI custody. MI5 does not dispute this. However, it maintains that its officers did nothing illegal or wrong. After all, they could not be expected to know for certain what was happening when they were not in the room.

After ten months in the ISI prison Amin was deported to the UK, where he was tried and convicted along with four other members of the gang and jailed for life.

Two months after Amin was flown back to Britain, another young British Muslim was detained in Pakistan. Zeeshan Siddiqui, aged twenty-four, from west London, was considered a would-be terrorist, and one of his old college friends, Asif Hanif, had already killed himself and three other people in a suicide bomb attack on a bar in Tel Aviv.

Siddiqui later gave a statement to a lawyer in London, and an interview to the BBC, in which he said that after he was detained near Peshawar by another of Pakistan's intelligence agencies, the Intelligence Bureau, he was beaten and deprived of sleep, then strapped to a bed. He says he was tied to the bed for eleven days, during which time he was forcibly catheterised and had chemicals injected up his nose. Then, he says, he was questioned by four British intelligence officers:

They said to me: 'There are people from the British embassy who are designed to help people like you. We are not those people. At a later stage we will try and get those people to speak to you.' They told me they are from the intelligence. They said: 'Anything you can tell us today we can tell our Pakistani friends and they can help you.'[6]

The harrowing accounts of torture given by Amin and Siddiqui were later corroborated by Pakistani intelligence officials, who also confirmed that British intelligence officers were ultimately responsible.

The officials told Human Rights Watch, the New York-based NGO, that Amin was regarded as a 'high pressure' case and that both the UK and US governments' desire for information from him was 'insatiable'. One Pakistani official added: 'They were perfectly aware that we were using all means possible to extract information from him and were grateful that we were doing so.'[7]

Echoing George W. Bush's words, the Intelligence Bureau said they were under tremendous pressure to 'perform' in the 'war on terror', adding: 'We do what we are asked to do.' Despite the torture, they said that Siddiqui would not 'admit to anything useful', and it was decided to bring his case within the country's legal system. The moment Siddiqui appeared in court in Peshawar, he was seen to be in such a poor physical state that the magistrate ordered he be sent immediately to hospital.

British intelligence officers had not spelled out what they wanted the Pakistanis to do to Amin or Siddiqui. They did not need to: the Pakistani intelligence agencies' traditional way of extracting information was well known. And as Pervez Musharraf, the former president of Pakistan, said later, the British 'never once' asked that the Pakistanis desist from their usual interrogation methods: 'You have to get information. If you are extremely decent, we then don't get any information. We need to allow leeway to the intelligence operatives, the people who interrogate. Maybe [the British] wanted us to carry on whatever we were doing. It was a tacit approval of what we were doing.'[8]

By asking their Pakistani counterparts to detain a particular individual, by handing over lists of questions, by questioning them in-between Pakistani interrogations and by doing nothing to ensure that they were treated humanely in prisons where torture was known to occur, the British were consigning their targets to the most appalling abuse. But they were not in breach of the guidelines under which they operated. They could still argue that they had not been seen to condone torture.

In April 2004, a series of photographs depicting the abuse of prisoners by American guards at Abu Ghraib prison in Baghdad was leaked to the CBS television network. The pictures gave the world a shocking glimpse of the manner in which the US and her allies had been treating those who had been captured and interrogated during the 'war on terror'. They also reminded the leaders of those countries that in a world where everyone with a mobile telephone was equipped with a camera, the secrecy that had for centuries accompanied acts of torture, and allowed those acts to be denied, could no longer be assured.

With the assistance of government lawyers, MI5 and MI6 began revising the secret 2002 interrogation policy that governed the questioning of prisoners held overseas. They were anxious that no British official should be compromised by similar photographs. The policy was rewritten once in early 2004, when Salahuddin Amin and his cohorts were under surveillance and it was clear that the British would soon be asking the ISI to detain and question a number of suspects. It would be rewritten again in the summer of 2006, at a time when British police and MI5 were watching a group of jihadists apparently plotting to bring down ten airliners down over the Atlantic and when the

ISI would once again be asked to round up British suspects. At each stage of the revision process the document was so sensitive that successive ministers insisted that it should remain for ever secret. Once its existence became known, Tony Blair repeatedly evaded a series of questions about it, while David Blunkett, the former Home Secretary, suggested it was libellous even to ask him about the document. One Foreign Secretary, David Miliband, went so far as to insist that its publication would 'lend succour to our enemies'.[9]

There was good reason for such sensitivity. When the revised policy was eventually made public in August 2011, appearing in the *Guardian*, it could be seen to contain an acknowledgement that what MI5 and MI6 were doing was illegal. It also instructed senior officers to weigh the importance of the information they were seeking against the amount of pain that the prisoner was likely to suffer while it was being extracted. And it warned that the British public could be put at greater risk of terrorist attack if the contents of the policy were to become known, as it could lead to further radicalisation of Muslims.

The document does provide MI5 and MI6 officers with this injunction: 'The Agencies do not participate in, solicit, encourage or condone the use of torture or inhuman or degrading treatment. The Agencies will not carry out any action which it is known will result in torture or degrading treatment.' The ten-page document also contains clear advice on domestic criminal and civil law, as well as international humanitarian law.

However, five key paragraphs expressly permit MI5 and MI6 officers to conduct themselves in a way that could result in people being tortured. If, for example, the officer is dealing with 'a country known to use torture systematically' and despite taking steps to reduce the risk of torture 'foresees a real possibility that the consequences will include torture or mistreatment', he or she must refer the matter to a line manager. If the manager agrees with that assessment, a caveat must be added to any request for information, stating that the detainee must be questioned in accordance with international legal standards. Any assurances offered by the liaison partner must be assessed carefully. 'Once such apparently reliable assurances have been received, the intended action may be authorised and may proceed. It will be lawful.'[10]

In other words, MI5 and MI6 can ask known torturers to extract specific information from their prisoners as long as the torturers have promised they will not use their usual methods and such a promise is judged to be plausible.

Furthermore, the secret policy sets out circumstances in which British intelligence officers could be authorised to question a person held by known torturers, or hand over questions to be put to the detainee by known torturers, without such 'apparently reliable assurances' having been received. After taking advice from MI5 or MI6 lawyers, senior officers may 'balance the risk of mistreatment and the risk that the officer's actions could be judged to be unlawful against the need for the proposed action'. In deciding whether to give the green light, the likelihood that the prisoner will be tortured and 'the level of mistreatment anticipated' – the severity of the torture that the prisoner is likely to suffer – is to be balanced against 'the operational imperative for the proposed action'.

In other words, while maintaining that MI5 and MI6 do not 'participate in, solicit, encourage or condone the use of torture', those agencies will make use of torture if they believe the prisoner to possess information of sufficient importance.

The policy also hammers home the reasons why such operations need to be kept completely secret and the 'potential adverse effects on national security' of any disclosure. 'If the fact of the Agency seeking or accepting information in those circumstances were to be publicly revealed,' it cautions, 'it is possible that in some circumstances such a revelation could lead to further radicalisation, leading to an increase in the threat from terrorism.'

Finally, the policy explains that such a disclosure 'could result in damage to the reputation of the Agencies, leading to a reduction in the Agencies' ability to discharge their functions effectively'.

Of course, it was not just the reputations of MI5 and MI6 that needed to be protected. Decisions about operations that would end with people being tortured were to be taken at ministerial level and ministers were equally anxious not to be seen to have dirty hands.

The policy document sets out the need for intelligence officers to obtain political cover and for ministers to take responsibility for any crimes that may be committed by intelligence officers. 'In particularly difficult cases, senior management may need to refer the matter upwards, and in some cases it may be necessary to consult Ministers,' it says. 'This process is designed to ensure that appropriate visibility and consideration of the risk of unlawful actions takes place.'[11]

By mid-2007, this was happening regularly. After David Miliband was appointed Foreign Secretary in June that year, he would always be consulted by MI6 if it wished to conduct an operation that could result in a person being tortured.

As is clear from the secret policy, by the time any request reached a minister, the chances of the operation not resulting in torture would be slim. Intelligence officers in the field would have decided that if they asked for information to be extracted from a particular person, that person was likely to get hurt; the officers' line managers, their legal advisers and senior MI6 managers had all reached the same conclusion. And so they asked the minister.

Miliband is proud of the fact that, on occasion, he said no. On the other hand, according to a source with intimate knowledge of his deliberations, he often said yes. According to the same well-positioned source, Miliband's opposite numbers at the

Home Office, Jacqui Smith and then Alan Johnson, dealt in the same way with similar requests from MI5.[12]

Asked about the role they played in authorising such operations, Miliband and Smith issued statements saying they would never sanction torture, but declined to answer questions about the matter. Johnson remained silent.

British intelligence officers involved in torture operations enjoy not only political cover but also extensive legal cover, which is offered by an extraordinary section of a little-known piece of legislation.

Section 7 of the 1994 Intelligence Services Act is entitled Authorisation of Acts Outside the British Islands. It states: 'If, apart from this section, a person would be liable in the United Kingdom for any act done outside the British Islands, he shall not be so liable if the act is one which is authorised to be done by virtue of an authorisation given by the Secretary of State under this section.'

The act adds that 'liable in the United Kingdom' means liable under the criminal or civil law of any part of the United Kingdom. This means that UK criminal and civil law is disapplied from any British intelligence officer, or any other authorised person, who commits a crime – any crime whatsoever – as long as it is committed outside the UK and a Secretary of State has authorised that crime. This, as one or two sharp-eyed observers noted as the Act was passing into law, amounts to a licence to kill.

The government of the day made no attempt to deny this. Douglas Hogg, the Conservative Foreign Office minister responsible for steering the bill through Parliament, made clear at the committee stage that it covered the use of force and assassination. 'There clearly are circumstances . . . when lethal force would be justified,' he said. 'The Secretary of State would not, in ordinary circumstances, issue a clause 7 authorisation in respect of the use of force. I say "ordinary circumstances" because I can conceive of circumstances . . . when it would be right to do so. Examples would be serious emergencies or crises causing great damage to Great Britain or her citizens.'

The Act offers not only a licence to kill, of course, but a licence to torture, and to become complicit in torture by others. In the years after 9/11, according to some sources, the number of Section 7 authorisations signed off by ministers increased from a handful each year to several each week. There was a further increase after the July 2005 suicide bomb attacks in London. During 2009 alone, MI6 is reported to have asked Miliband on around 500 occasions for explicit authorisation to conduct operations that could otherwise have landed its officers in serious trouble.[13]

On 6 July 2005, Eliza Manningham-Buller met a group of MPs from the Labour whips' office to discuss the threat posed by al-Qaida. She assured them that there was no reason to believe an attack was imminent. The following morning, Sir Ian Blair, then Commissioner of the Metropolitan Police, told the BBC that his force was 'the envy of the policing world in relation to counterterrorism'.

A few minutes later the first of the bombs went off. Within an hour three more suicide bombers detonated explosive devices on London's tube and bus network, claiming the lives of fifty-two commuters and leaving 966 people injured, many of them permanently.

Two weeks later, as the country was beginning to overcome the initial shock, there were the attempted bombings of 21 July. In the mind of the public, the bombs that failed to explode triggered almost as much alarm as those that did, as they brought home the realisation that people could be vulnerable to a series of onslaughts. Within government and law-enforcement circles, the shock caused by the two incidents can only have been exacerbated by the belief, widely held during the early summer of 2005, that the threat of a terrorist attack had subsided.

Tony Blair called a press conference. 'Let no one be in doubt,' he said, 'the rules of the game have changed.'

That summer, a group of medical students at King's College in south London packed their bags and set off to join hospitals around the world for a period of training. Among them was a twenty-four-year-old who went to study at the Ziauddin Memorial Hospital in Karachi, the city where his mother had been born.

On the evening of 20 August, this student – let's call him Shahid – was dining with a number of colleagues at a restaurant in Karachi. Three men in plain clothes walked in and approached the group. They told Shahid that he was to leave with them. To ensure that there was no argument, one produced a handgun. Shahid accompanied the men from the restaurant and was bundled into a car. This was the last anyone would see of him for more than two months.

Shahid's friends in Karachi phoned his family in London, who contacted their constituency MP, John McDonnell, a long-standing family friend. McDonnell put in calls to Scotland Yard and the Foreign Office. The Foreign Office reported back that the Pakistani government said it knew nothing about the matter.

Shahid's father boarded a plane for Karachi, where he did everything he could to locate his son. He spoke to politicians, police officers and lawyers, and even to local gangsters. He called in old favours and forged new contacts. He cajoled and pleaded. Perhaps some money changed hands.

Weeks passed and there was no news of Shahid. The father was frantic with worry. He was a man in his sixties. The uncertainty and anxiety began to make him ill.

He called frequently into the offices of the British Deputy High Commission, located in a middle-class suburb of the city, to ask whether they had heard anything. Staff expressed their concern and sympathy, but appeared powerless to help.

At last, Shahid's father learned from an underworld source that his son was in the custody of the Intelligence Bureau. He went straight to the British Deputy High Commission with the news. To his dismay, the staff appeared uninterested. 'I asked them: "Aren't you going to pick up the phone and call the IB?" They simply replied: "No."'[14] The British diplomats he met were all perfectly courteous and expressed concern, but they appeared resolved to do absolutely nothing.

A little while later Shahid's father made contact, indirectly, with the Intelligence Bureau and a few days after that he received a call on his mobile phone, telling him to wait on a particular street corner. A van pulled up and the door slid open. Inside were a number of men in plain clothes and one man in police uniform. Shahid's father was instructed to get in and told he would be taken to his son.

As the van pulled away, the policeman asked whether he should put a hood over the old man's head. After some discussion, it was decided that this would not be necessary. Instead, Shahid's father was told to put his head down and not look out of the windows. As the van made its way through the crowded city streets, his fear steadily mounted.

Eventually the van swept into a high-walled compound and Shahid's father was taken across a courtyard, through a door and up some stairs. He was ushered into a room where four Intelligence Bureau officers were waiting for him. One apologised for holding his son for so long. Then he was introduced to the head of the agency, who said that his son had been detained by mistake. Finally, Shahid was brought into the room. He was shaking, dishevelled and clearly petrified.

In time, once they had left the Intelligence Bureau's torture centre behind them, Shahid would explain to his father how he had been beaten with staves, lashed with rubber whips and deprived of sleep. He had been forced to witness the torture of others. On one occasion, his captors burst into his cell shouting: 'You're a doctor, aren't you? Come with us!' He was dragged into a room where another prisoner lay close to death after a particularly severe beating. Shahid was ordered to save his life.

Every question had been about one subject and one subject only: the 7 July bombings in London. Towards the end of his two-month ordeal, Shahid had been taken to a room where two men were waiting for him. 'We're from the British government,' one said. They gave Shahid their first names and explained: 'There are people at the High Commission who are called consular officials, and it's their job to help British nationals who are in trouble, like you. You must understand that we are not those people. We're here to ask you some questions.'

They had proceeded to ask the same questions that Shahid had already been asked, and answered, while he was being tortured.

Shahid's opportunity to describe his experience would come later, however. For now, his father's only concern was to get him out of that building, out of Pakistan and home to London. He had decided that they would stay with his sister-in-law in Karachi that night and take the first flight to Heathrow next morning. One of the Intelligence Bureau officers offered to give them a lift.

Shahid and his father climbed back into the van. The gates swung open and they pulled out into the traffic. This time there was no instruction to keep their heads down and Shahid's father looked out of the window. There, across the road from the Intelligence Bureau building, the place where his son had been held and tortured for the last two months, stood the British Deputy High Commission: the offices of the British officials who had expressed such concern about the young man's disappearance, but who had appeared unable, or unwilling, to help.

★

Three years later, Waqar Kiani, a Pakistani journalist, was following up Shahid's story for the *Guardian*. Eventually, his inquiries took him to the Intelligence Bureau building across the road from the British Deputy High Commission in Karachi. Realising that he was being followed, Kiani returned to Islamabad. There, he found his apartment had been broken into and turned upside down. Some papers were missing.

A few hours later he was driving out of Islamabad when two vehicles, a Toyota jeep and a saloon car, ran him off the road. Men dragged him from his car, forced him into the jeep and tied a scarf around his eyes. Fifteen minutes later they reached a safe house, where Kiani was tied to a chair and a fierce red light was directed at his face.

Kiani was greeted by an interrogator who began to fire questions at him, while other men punched him in the stomach and kidneys and burned his arms with cigarettes. Kiani told them he was a journalist. 'We don't care about the *Guardian*, whatever that is,' one said. 'We are just doing our job.' It was made clear to Kiani that he should stop asking questions about the British. In particular, he should never again ask questions about Shahid.

The following morning, after being beaten and burned all night, Kiani was blindfolded again and bundled into the back of another vehicle. He could hear his captors discussing whether to kill him. 'Cut off his fingers,' said one, 'so he will not be able to write anything in future.' After being driven for three hours, Kiani was told that if he informed anyone of his experience his wife would be raped, the assault would be video-recorded and the video uploaded to the Internet. He was then pushed out of the vehicle and warned that if he looked back he would be shot.*

---

* Kiani waited three years before deciding it was safe for his ordeal to be reported, both in the *Guardian* and in an interview on Pakistani television. Five days later his car was pulled over by a police jeep and he was ordered out. Four policemen set about him with batons, fists and a rubber whip,

★

The following year, senior officials of the Intelligence Bureau told Human Rights Watch that their British counterparts had always known where Shahid was being held. One said: 'I do not know if the British knew we had given him a good thrashing and "the treatment". But they know perfectly well we do not garland terrorism suspects nor honour them. We would naturally be keen to produce results. Results are not produced by having chats with the suspect. We do what we do and it's not pretty.' Furthermore, he said, British officials at their offices across the road had been 'breathing down our necks for information' the entire time that Shahid was being tortured.[15]

Shahid resumed his studies a year after he was released, qualified as a doctor and found work at a large hospital on the south coast of England. He remains traumatised, however. He keeps his bedroom door locked and is paranoid about using telephones. And he is still terrified of MI5 and MI6, reasoning that if they could arrange for him to be detained and tortured once, they could do it again. His father lodged a complaint with the Foreign Office, but says he dropped the matter after Shahid was approached by MI5 officers, asking if there was anything they could do to help him pursue the matter.

Shahid was just one of many people picked up by Britain's 'liaison partners' in Pakistan in a frenzy of arrests and torture triggered by the London bombings. Within days, around 200 men had been seized in raids on mosques and madrassas in response to Blair's demand that the Pakistani authorities crack down on militant teaching in religious schools.

Among those arrested was Tahir Shah, aged thirty-eight, a British documentary film-maker and son of the renowned Sufi

telling him: 'You want to be a hero? We'll make you a hero.' He was beaten so severely that he needed hospital treatment. Three months later he fled the country.

writer and thinker Idries Shah. He was detained while filming in Peshawar on 18 July, hooded and shackled, and taken to an interrogation centre where he was forced into stress positions and deprived of sleep.

'When I was able to see, I got a peek into other rooms. I saw two crouching men with long black beards. A guard said they were Afghans who had been there for months. One was in a cell painted with black and white spirals to drive him mad.'

When Shah was taken for interrogation and the hood was removed, he found himself in what he describes as a fully equipped torture chamber: 'There was a rack for breaking feet, a bar for hanging a man upside down, rows of manacles, straps and batons, and pliers for extracting teeth. There were syringes with used needles, smelling salts, a medical drip and dried blood on the floor and walls.'

Shah realised that he was being held because he was a British Asian – his family's background is Indian and Afghan – and because he was suspected of being an Islamist terrorist. 'I eat bacon,' he told his interrogators. 'I drink wine. I don't even know the Muslim prayers.'[16]

That didn't help. It was another sixteen days before he was taken from the prison and put aboard a flight for the UK. On arrival at Heathrow he was questioned briefly by a man in plain clothes who did not identify himself. This man then returned the passport that had been taken from him by his interrogators in Pakistan.

It was not just in Pakistan that people were being rounded up and mistreated on the off chance that they might know something about the bombings. At the same time that Shah was being detained in Peshawar, two businessmen from West Yorkshire were being tortured in Dubai. Alam Ghafoor, aged thirty-four, and his business associate Mohammed Rafiq Siddique, aged thirty-eight, had flown to Dubai on 4 July. They were considering an investment in a property development enterprise. On 21 July, shortly after the second bombing attempts in London, they were dragged out of a restaurant by local intelligence officers and taken to an interrogation centre. For the next twelve days they were beaten, deprived of sleep and forced to stand in stress positions for hours at a time. They were told they would be killed and fed to dogs. Throughout this ordeal they were also told it was pointless to ask for assistance from the British embassy, as they had been detained and were being tortured at the request of the British.

Eventually, Ghafoor signed a confession admitting he was a friend of the bombers and had organised the London attacks. 'I wrote a false confession and put crazy things in it like "I have constant contact with Saddam Hussein and Osama bin Laden",' he said.[17]

Notwithstanding this confession, it was clear that the men were innocent. After they had been released without charge and permitted to leave the country, Ghafoor demanded that the Foreign Office hand over copies of all correspondence about his case that had passed between London and British diplomats in the United Arab Emirates. When he obtained the letters and emails, he noticed something peculiar. Some words had been blacked out by Foreign Office officials before they were handed over. While it was unclear what they were hiding, it was obvious that British consular officials in Dubai had not asked the UAE authorities for permission to see Ghafoor; they had been asking someone else, someone whose identity had been concealed.

In one email sent to London four days after the pair had been detained, a consular official wrote: 'Today I phoned [name withheld] trying to get permission to see them. First [name withheld] told me that there was no need because they would be deported soon. I asked if we could see them today or tomorrow. [Name withheld] told me that [name withheld] would check

with the UAE authorities . . . and would let me know. I didn't
hear from [name withheld] since then.'[18]

Ghafoor is convinced that the consular officials were asking
someone in MI6 for permission to see him.

At the end of 2005, the House of Lords handed down a judgment
that condemned and brought to a halt attempts to permit the use
of evidence extracted under torture in the English courts. It was
seen as a landmark judgment, one that significantly readjusted
the balance between measures intended to ensure collective
security and the fundamental rights of individuals. 'The Law
Lords were at their most majestic,' one commentator wrote,
'and their unequivocal condemnation of the use of evidence
obtained by torture reverberated around the world.'

The Lords' judgment followed an attempt by a lower court
to assert its right to consider evidence probably extracted under
torture. That assertion, by the Special Immigration Appeals
Commission, which hears appeals against decisions by the
Home Secretary to deport or exclude people from the UK on
national security grounds, had been supported by the Court of
Appeal, which ruled that the commission was a special court,
beyond the reach of the UN Convention Against Torture, and
that the law could not impose upon the Home Secretary 'a
duty of solemn inquiry as to the interrogation methods' used by
overseas intelligence agencies.

The Law Lords appeared to have halted such thinking in its
tracks.

'The English common law has regarded torture and its fruits
with abhorrence for over 500 years,' thundered the then senior
Law Lord, Lord Bingham. 'That abhorrence is now shared by
over 140 countries which have acceded to the Torture
Convention.' He was 'startled, even a little dismayed' at the
Court of Appeal's willingness to turn its back on both a deep-
rooted English tradition and an international obligation. Torture

evidence, he added, 'was offensive to ordinary standards of humanity and decency'.[19]

However, the Law Lords' judgment banned the use of torture evidence only in the courts. It did nothing to prevent government ministers or the country's intelligence agencies making use of it in other ways.

As Lord Brown added, later in the ninety-page judgment, it may well be that 'torture is an unqualified evil', but it may also yield information that can save lives. What then? 'Unswerving logic might suggest that no use whatever should be made of it. But there are powerful countervailing arguments too: torture cannot be undone and the greater public good thus lies in making some use at least of the information obtained.'

Brown insisted not only that the executive was entitled to make use of 'the fruit of the poisoned tree' but also that it had an obligation to do so: 'It has a prime responsibility to safeguard the security of the state and would be failing in its duty if it ignores whatever it may learn or fails to follow it up.'

So while the British courts would have nothing to do with evidence extracted under torture, those same courts had given free rein to the executive branch of government. It was a freedom that the executive would not hesitate to exercise.

In December 2005, around the same time that the Law Lords were handing down their landmark judgment, MI5 officers and police in the north of England were keeping a very close eye on two would-be terrorists, Rangzieb Ahmed and Mohammed Zillur Rahman. The two men appeared to be plotting a bomb attack somewhere in the UK. When they began making travel plans, senior MI5 officers decided to allow them to leave the country, while keeping them under surveillance, in order to learn more about their associates overseas.

For reasons that were not clear, Rahman, aged twenty-seven, from south Wales, flew to South Africa, where he disappeared from MI5's radar. Ahmed, a thirty-year-old from Rochdale in Greater Manchester, was followed to Dubai, where a listening device in a hotel room picked up his conversations about his plans and showed him to be a senior al-Qaida figure. He was then followed back to Manchester, where more information was gathered. Before long, the police and MI5 had sufficient evidence to put Ahmed away for life. And yet they held back.

In January 2006, Ahmed made plans to travel to Pakistan, but rather than tell the Crown Prosecution Service about him, the investigators decided it would be more interesting to see what happened if he was allowed to travel once more.

As soon as he was in the air, the Pakistani authorities were alerted that a dangerous terrorist was on his way. An MI6 officer wrote to the ISI warning that they knew Ahmed was planning an attack but were unclear where or when. It was suggested that the ISI might consider detaining him. Later, Manchester Crown Court would hear that when Ahmed was picked up, MI5 officers and detectives from the Greater Manchester Police drew up a list of questions to be put to him by the ISI. As the answers came back, according to senior sources in the Manchester police, more questions were handed over.

After thirteen months of torture and interrogation in unlawful Pakistani custody, during which time he received no consular assistance, Ahmed was deported to the UK, minus three of his fingernails. Upon arrival, he was arrested, driven to Manchester and charged with a series of terrorist offences. His defence team complained that the British complicity in his unlawful detention and torture was so great that he should not face prosecution. They lost this argument and also lost an appeal mounted on the same grounds.

During the legal argument that preceded his trial, Ahmed explained how he had been beaten and whipped at a secret ISI prison in Islamabad and prevented from sleeping for six days and nights. His account of what followed this softening-up process was so shocking that the prison officers who were guarding him sat with their heads in their hands.

'They pressed the bell and a guy came in. The interrogator said to him: "Can you bring the box?" They brought the box and put it on the table. It was made of metal. He opened it. He had pliers. Thick. Very, very thick. I was afraid and I was frightened. I didn't know what they were going to do. The officer said to the guards: "Put him on the floor." I laid down on the floor, face down. One grabbed my right leg, one my left, and one my right arm, and one from my left. I was handcuffed.

'One of the guys, he grabbed my hand like this. One of the officers had the pliers. He took my fingernail and put the pliers on my small finger on the side, and he started to pull it downwards. I was on the floor and he sitted down, like. He was asking me a question. He said: "Tell us who is waiting for you in Lahore." I was saying: "I will tell you everything." I was saying leave me, meaning leave me and I will tell you everything. He was saying to me: "No, first you tell, then we will leave you." It was very painful. I was crying and I was screaming. And I was saying to him: "Leave me, for God!" I was screaming, but they were not listening.

'He bended it right back. He didn't break it, but he pulled it from the skin. It was out from the skin. He didn't break it or anything, but he pulled it back. I was saying to him: "I will tell you who are waiting for me in Lahore." He was saying: "First you tell us and then we will let you go." He didn't stop. First he pulled it from this side, and afterwards he pulled it from this side, and after, at the end, he pulled it from the centre. It was completely removed.'[20]

Ahmed told the court that after the removal of the first nail, from the small finger of his left hand, he was allowed to sit down. A man wearing Western clothes came and gave him a painkilling injection in his arm before cleaning and bandaging the wound. That night he was allowed to sleep for the first time and for twenty-four hours he was left alone.

The following day he was taken back to the torture chamber to be asked a series of questions about two of the July 2005 London suicide bombers, Shehzad Tanweer and Mohammad Sidique Khan. While he was being asked these questions, the nail was slowly removed from his ring finger. Then the doctor appeared, he was given the painkilling injection and his new wound was dressed, and he was permitted forty-eight hours' rest.

Then it was the nail from his middle finger, while being asked questions about a plot against the United States. Each removal was followed by an injection and bandages.

At some point after this, Ahmed was handcuffed and hooded and taken from the prison to see two British intelligence officers in a carpeted office, with a sofa and desk, and drawn blinds. Ahmed says that one of the officers was from MI5 and the other from MI6: 'One of them, he's mixed race. Five foot six. Thirty, thirty-three. One was white. Shorter. Thirty, I think. The mixed-race guy was sitting on my left, the other on my front. The guy who was sitting on my left, he said to me: "We are not from the British consulate, we are from the British government and we want to ask you a few questions."'[21]

Ahmed says the two men could clearly see his bandaged fingers. After questioning him at length, they left and he never saw them again. Instead, they handed him over to American interrogators, who questioned him six days a week for several weeks – 'They had Sundays off.'

Before Ahmed's trial, the prosecution tried unsuccessfully to claim that his fingernails had been missing before he travelled to Pakistan, despite scientific evidence and medical records that showed this to be impossible. The prosecution also insisted that much of the legal argument before the trial should be held in camera.

Thanks to the secrecy of the court proceedings, the public was not meant to learn about the manner in which British intelligence officers and police managed the events that led to Ahmed's detention and torture by a notorious Pakistani agency. In the event they were disclosed, under the protection of parliamentary privilege, by the Conservative MP David Davis. 'I cannot imagine a more obvious case of the outsourcing of torture,' Davis told the House of Commons. 'The authorities know full well that this story is an evidential showcase for the policy of complicity in torture.'[22]

By 2006, the torture of terrorism suspects risked more than causing immense damage to the reputations of MI5 and MI6, and the nation as a whole. It was beginning to jeopardise the chances of bringing successful prosecutions.

After Ahmed's interrogation, it was clear that more care needed to be taken over British jihadists detained in Pakistan. Never again should one return home bearing visible signs of torture.

By this time, however, another British man, Rashid Rauf, had been in ISI custody for more than a year, having been arrested for his role in an al-Qaida plot to bomb airliners over the Atlantic. Police in the UK had made it clear that they wanted him deported and charged back in Britain. But Rauf, aged twenty-five and from Birmingham, had been severely tortured. According to his lawyer, Hashmat Ali Habib, he had been forced to spent long periods in a cell that was not much larger than a coffin.[23] He had also been questioned by British and American intelligence officers. He could not be deported to Britain because his back and torso had been left badly scarred. A senior British intelligence officer later admitted to Human Rights Watch that the mistreatment of Rauf had been a 'disaster' that made any 'successful prosecution in Britain most unlikely'.

In December 2007, three months after Ahmed was deported to the UK with three fingernails missing, the Pakistani government announced that Rauf – said to be a key figure in al-Qaida's most ambitious plot against the West since 9/11 – had escaped after being permitted to pray, alone, at a mosque on the outskirts of Rawalpindi.

Unsurprisingly, few in Pakistan believed the official account of Rauf's disappearance. A number of his associates predicted that it would be announced that he had been killed in a drone strike in some remote area of the country. This is exactly what happened eleven months later. No body was ever produced and Rauf's family is convinced he was murdered by the ISI in order to conceal evidence that he was tortured.

And yet the outsourcing of interrogation continued and the hand of British intelligence could be detected in other countries where British Muslims with terrorist connections were being picked up and tortured.

In the summer of 2008, while planning a trip to Egypt with a friend, Azhar Khan, a computer programmer from Berkshire, asked the Foreign Office for advice. He was a close associate of several members of the gang that had planned the mass murder of 'those slags dancing around' in a south London nightclub. He had been one of those arrested in the raids of March 2004, but had been released without charge. Khan was assured that he had no reason to be concerned about travelling to Egypt.

On arrival at Cairo airport he was immediately separated from his companion and taken to a prison, where he was stripped, hooded and shackled. For the next six days he was forced to stand in a room in which a number of people were being tortured. Every now and again he too would be called forward to be beaten and whipped. Sometimes his torturers would slip up behind him and give him an electric shock. One of the other victims in the torture chamber spoke English with a British accent.

Khan's Egyptian torturers asked him about a number of

discrepancies between the statement he had made when arrested in London four years earlier and comments he subsequently made while visiting his friends in high-security prisons in the UK. He was also asked detailed questions about his associates in the UK, leading some to suspect that the purpose of his torture was not so much to extract information as to intimidate a wide group of people.

After a week, Khan was released and allowed to fly home. Months later he was still receiving counselling, as well as treatment for stomach ulcers that had developed during the week that he was incarcerated.[24] Years later, he was said still to be suffering depression.

Several men were also detained and tortured in Bangladesh, where both MI5 and MI6 enjoyed close contacts with the Directorate General of Forces Intelligence, or DGFI, the country's main intelligence agency, and another Bangladeshi agency, the Rapid Action Battalion, or RAB. These agencies' routine use of torture is no secret, having been well documented not only by human rights groups but also by the Home Office. Despite this reputation, a decision was taken in March 2008 that the then Home Secretary, Jacqui Smith, should fly to Dhaka to lead counterterrorism talks with Bangladeshi government and intelligence officials. A senior counterterrorism official with the DGFI who was present at one key meeting says Smith asked that a number of individuals be investigated.[25]

Around a dozen people were subsequently detained and questioned. One man, Faisal Mostafa, a chemist from Manchester who had twice been tried and acquitted of terrorism offences in the UK, was taken to an interrogation centre in a northern suburb of Dhaka, where his hands were cuffed to bars above his head. He spent six days in this position before being unshackled, beaten on his feet, subjected to electric shocks, suspended upside down and beaten again.

Throughout the period of Mostafa's interrogation, Britain and Bangladesh were in constant touch. Matiur Rahman, RAB's deputy chief of operations, said: 'The British were interested in him for some time on the assumption he was part of an international network. We had bilateral cooperation. There was talk and information sharing between intelligence. They gave information to us and we gave information to them.'[26]

The information that was being passed from the Bangladeshis to the British was being extracted in the most barbaric fashion. At one point Mostafa was strapped to a chair and blindfolded before being interrogated about his co-defendants from his trials in the UK, about the Muslim Parliament, a debating forum in London, about a mosque in London's East End and about the British Islamist group al-Muhajiroun. While he was being asked these questions, a drill was slowly driven into his right shoulder and hip. He still has the holes to show for it.

Jacqui Smith has refused to answer questions about any authorisations she gave to MI5 to exchange information about Faisal Mostafa and others. She has also refused to say whether she accepts that individuals were placed at risk of suffering severe human rights abuses when she asked the Bangladeshi intelligence agencies to investigate them.

After her role in the matter received some media attention she wrote a letter to the press in which she said: 'It is categorically untrue that I asked the Bangladeshi authorities to investigate individuals in the knowledge or suspicion that they would be tortured.'[27]

By late 2008, the cloak of secrecy that allowed Britain's intelligence agencies to be so closely involved in the torture of terrorism suspects was looking threadbare. So flimsy was it that a number of lawyers, journalists and backbench MPs had peered through and were protesting at what they saw.

Media reports were also examining Britain's logistics support for rendition flights, the role that the UK had played in the interrogation and torture of Binyam Mohamed and the growing number of allegations of British complicity in torture in Pakistan.

Some at MI5 responded by whispering that the torture victims were liars or lunatics; others confirmed the facts but maintained that what they were doing was not illegal and was necessary to protect British interests and save British lives. One senior anti-terrorism detective responded to my questions with threats; another admitted privately that the allegations were true.

Ministers, meanwhile, responded with blanket denials, always using the same mantra: 'We do not participate in, solicit, encourage or condone the use of torture.' They were quoting directly from the secret interrogation policy, though they were careful not to disclose the existence of that document, nor mention anything else within it.

By February 2009, Martin Scheinin, the United Nations Special Rapporteur on human rights and counterterrorism, had seen enough. He reported that UK intelligence officers had 'interviewed detainees who were held incommunicado by the Pakistani ISI in so-called safe houses, where they were being tortured'. This, he said, had legal as well as moral implications: 'The active participation by a state through the sending of interrogators or questions, or even the mere presence of intelligence personnel at an interview with a person who is being held in places where he is tortured or subject to other inhuman treatment, can be reasonably understood as implicitly condoning torture.' Moreover, he added, the UK was among a number of countries attempting to conceal their 'illegal acts' from the courts and oversight bodies, in order to 'protect itself from criticism, embarrassment and – most importantly – liability'.[28]

Following the publication of his report, Scheinin said that not only was Britain deeply involved in the US rendition programme but its intelligence officers in Pakistan had 'directly participated in interrogations ... where torture was applied'.[29]

The same month, Parliament's Joint Committee on Human Rights opened its own inquiry into allegations of UK complicity in torture. In August 2009, it concluded that the British state would be complicit in torture if it asked a foreign intelligence service known for its systemic use of torture to detain and question a terrorism suspect; helped the overseas agency to capture the suspect; handed over questions 'to be put to a detainee who has been, is being, or is likely to be tortured'; sent interrogators to question a detainee known to have been tortured; or was in systematic receipt of information known or thought likely to have been obtained from detainees subjected to torture.[30] This, of course, is exactly what MI5 and MI6 had been doing in Afghanistan, Guantánamo Bay, Pakistan, Bangladesh, Morocco, Egypt and any number of other countries.

The committee asked Foreign Secretary David Miliband and Home Secretary Jacqui Smith to appear before it to give evidence. Both refused, prompting the committee to accuse the government of hiding behind a 'wall of secrecy'. The committee concluded that an independent inquiry was overdue.

Later that year, Human Rights Watch published a report on British intelligence operations in Pakistan that condemned Britain's role in the torture of terror suspects as cruel, counter-productive and in clear breach of international law. 'The British government effectively condone torture by putting questions to detainees in ISI custody and by visiting detainees who had obviously been tortured without halting cooperating in those cases,' the report said. Furthermore, it added, 'the conduct of the ISI has interfered with attempts to prosecute these individuals in British courts'.

By now, the British establishment was waking up to what had been happening and it was clearly uncomfortable. In a letter to *The Times*, thirteen peers complained that while the government denied condoning torture, 'the conflict between evidence and official denials is stark, and is undermining trust in our stated commitment to human rights'. An independent inquiry was needed, they said. The signatories included Margaret Thatcher's chancellor, Lord Howe, the former head of the armed forces, Lord Guthrie, and the former UK ambassador to the United Nations, Lord Hannay.

But while there was growing unease at the United Nations, at Westminster and in the media, the body that was supposed to provide democratic oversight of the intelligence services saw no evil, heard no evil and did nothing.

The Intelligence and Security Committee, or ISC, is a body of MPs and peers appointed by the prime minister rather than Parliament and is chaired by former ministers who have worked closely with the agencies in the past. Almost invariably the chairmen and women are politicians with some expectation of re-entering government. The committee was established by the same piece of legislation that provided the intelligence agencies with the 'licence to kill' of Section 7 authorisations. It sits only in secret, staff are provided by the Cabinet Office – a department that works closely with MI5 and MI6 – and before its reports are published they are censored in consultation with those agencies.

The ISC showed little interest in any forensic examination of Britain's relationship with overseas intelligence agencies after 9/11. And it appeared not to have noticed any of the events that had led to condemnation by the United Nations Special Rapporteur on human rights, the Master of the Rolls, Parliament's human rights committee and the world's major human rights organisations.

In 2008, the chair of the ISC was Margaret Beckett, who had been Foreign Secretary at the time that the secret interrogation policy had been rewritten in 2006. She refused to conduct an inquiry into the mounting allegations of complicity in torture. Her successor, Kim Howells, who had been a Foreign Office minister with responsibility for counterterrorism during some of the period when British Muslims were complaining of torture, appeared to see himself not so much an overseer of the agencies as a cheerleader, going out of his way to condemn the Master of the Rolls for his comment about MI5's 'dubious record' over Binyam Mohamed's mistreatment.

The ISC allowed the wool to be pulled over its eyes when it published a report in 2007 on the involvement of MI5 and MI6 in rendition, saying the agencies' only failing had been that they were 'slow to detect the emerging pattern' of rendition by the United States.[31] In coming to this conclusion, the committee accepted MI6's claim that it had believed the CIA's three-hour presentation on its global kidnap and torture programme, given at the British embassy in Washington five days after 9/11, to be nothing more than 'tough talk'.

In July 2009, as a result of the Binyam Mohamed court case, the Attorney General, Baroness Scotland, felt compelled to call in Scotland Yard to conduct an investigation. By then the Home Secretary was Alan Johnson. With scant regard to his responsibilities for policing and law and order, Johnson promptly gave an interview in which he said that the police investigation threatened to put the nation's security at risk. It was the first sign of the opposition that the police could expect to encounter among those serving the secret state.

Two Scotland Yard inquiries were mounted. Operation Hinton examined MI5's involvement with the interrogation of Mohamed, while Operation Iden looked at events at Bagram shortly after 9/11, where MI6 officers interrogated a number of suspects. Both investigations attempted to trace responsibility for Britain's involvement in torture beyond the role played by relatively junior officers, examining the actions of line managers and MI5 legal advisers, and beyond to senior officers, the Cabinet Office, permanent under-secretaries, ministers and secretaries of state.

After more than two years, police and prosecutors concluded that they had insufficient evidence to press charges. The Hinton team could not prove that MI5 officers must have known what was happening to Mohamed. Detectives on the Operation Iden team could not make contact with the key torture victims from Bagram.

The police were not the only people making inquiries. Within two months of the May 2010 general election, under pressure from his Liberal Democrat coalition partners, as well as some of his own backbenchers, the new prime minister, David Cameron, announced the establishment of a judge-led inquiry into the UK's involvement in torture and rendition. 'The reputation of our security services has been overshadowed by allegations about their involvement in the treatment of detainees held by other countries,' he said. As a consequence, Britain's reputation 'as a country that believes in human rights, justice, fairness and the rule of law – indeed for much of what the Services exist to protect – risks being tarnished'.

Cameron told MPs that one question to be asked by the inquiry was whether Britain should 'have realised sooner that what foreign agencies were doing may have been unacceptable and that we shouldn't be associated with it'. It appeared that nobody had told the new prime minister about MI6's secret renditions to Libya, details of which would emerge almost by accident the following year.

In July 2010, the man appointed to head the inquiry was named as Sir Peter Gibson, a retired judge. It is possible that MI5 and MI6 had a hand in his selection; certainly they could not have hoped for a better choice. For the previous four years Gibson had served as the Intelligence Services Commissioner and his responsibilities included oversight of the use of the Section 7 authorisations that indemnified officers against prosecution for committing crimes overseas. Year after year he would sign off his annual reports with the same exuberant mantra of endorsement of the intelligence agencies: 'It is my opinion that all staff in this difficult and challenging area of work continue to be trustworthy, conscientious and dependable.'

It began to appear that senior figures in government and the intelligence world had found a way of securing another whitewash; that the inquiry would follow the same path as the Bad Nenndorf courts martial in post-war Germany, the Bowen Inquiry into torture in Aden, the Compton Commission and the majority finding of the Parker Report on the Five Techniques.

Binyam Mohamed's lawyers suggested that Gibson should be appearing before the inquiry as a witness rather than presiding over it. In July 2011, most major international and British human rights groups, including Amnesty International, said they would be boycotting the inquiry. The following month, lawyers representing victims of Britain's torture operations announced they too would have nothing to do with it.

Six months later, Scotland Yard announced that the winding up of the Operation Hinton and Operation Iden investigations did not signal the end of the work of its detectives, who would be looking at other allegations of complicity in torture before those cases were examined by Gibson. At this point, the government gave up and announced that the Gibson inquiry was being scrapped.

Instead, the government moved forward with plans to change the law in a way that would prevent evidence of complicity in torture being aired in the courts in the future. It brought forward a green paper that suggested a need for greater courtroom secrecy and also proposed to abolish the legal doctrines that had been employed by Binyam Mohamed's lawyers. At the time of writing, the law has not yet been changed. If new legislation is brought forward, it could prevent the public from learning about any evidence in civil proceedings that government ministers deem sensitive.

After coming to power with a pledge to get to the bottom

of the UK's involvement in torture and rendition, the coalition government faced accusations that it wanted to conceal as many dirty secrets as possible by effectively codifying a cover-up.

When he had announced the establishment of the Gibson Inquiry in July 2010, the Prime Minister had said that the secret interrogation policy had been rewritten in order to give 'greater clarity about what is and what is not acceptable in the future'. The new guidance to intelligence officers, he said, 'makes clear that our Services must never take any action where they know or believe that torture will occur'.

On close examination of the new interrogation guidance, however, it became apparent that it been crafted in a way that could still allow intelligence officers to question people who were at risk of being tortured. It says that MI5 and MI6 officers are prohibited from interrogating prisoners or handing over questions only if they 'know or believe' the prisoners are being tortured. There is no such prohibition if they believe there is a lower risk of cruel or inhuman treatment. In some instances, the guidance says intelligence officers can proceed if the risks can be mitigated through 'caveats or assurances', or if government ministers have been consulted.

Furthermore, the document says that hooding or other methods of obscuring vision should not be regarded as inhuman treatment 'where these do not pose a risk to the detainee's physical or mental health and is [sic] necessary for security reasons during arrest or transit'. This provision was eventually scrapped after a legal challenge. But it was one that would have been immediately recognisable to Sir Dick White.

In September 2011, ten days after Tripoli had fallen to the rebel forces that drove Muammar Gaddafi from power, details emerged of one of the darkest secrets of Britain's counterterrorism operations. MI6 had been running its own rendition operations, in which Libyan dissidents and their families had been abducted and taken to Gaddafi's torture chambers.

An investigator from Human Rights Watch found the evidence of Britain's Gaddafi Connection when he identified the government office block from which Moussa Koussa, the dictator's former spymaster, had commanded the hated Mukhabarat el-Jamahiriya intelligence agency.

Among the detritus of a panicked departure the investigator found a file full of letters and faxes that made clear the Mukhabarat's close contacts with intelligence agencies in the US, UK, Denmark and Austria. Critically, the papers showed that MI6 and the Libyans had cooperated on a number of operations which saw Libyan dissidents – and their wives and children, including a girl as young as six – delivered to Gaddafi.

In November 2003, for example, the papers showed MI6 to have approached the Syrian authorities to ask if they would secure the Chinese government's cooperation with the rendition of Abu Munthir al-Saadi, a leading member of the Libyan Islamic Fighting Group, or LIFG, an Islamist organisation dedicated to the overthrow of Gaddafi.

Al-Saadi was in exile in China with his wife and four children, aged six to fourteen, and had asked MI5, via an intermediary, whether they could return to London, where he had lived as an asylum seeker for four years in the 1990s. He was told that he must first undergo the formality of being interviewed by British diplomats in Hong Kong. In fact, he was about to be delivered up to the Libyans at the climax of the delicate three-way negotiations between Tripoli, London and Washington over oil, Libya's weapons of mass destruction programme and the future of the man convicted of the Lockerbie bombing, Abdelbaset al-Megrahi. To ensure that the talks reached a satisfactory conclusion, al-Saadi and his wife and children were to be presented as a gift to Gaddafi.

On arrival in Hong Kong the al-Saadi family was detained

immediately. A few days later, on 23 March 2004, the CIA sent a fax to the Mukhabarat agency. That document, found inside the file recovered from Moussa Koussa's office, made clear that the Americans had just learned that the British and Libyans were planning the rendition of al-Saadi and his family, and were keen to become involved.[32]

Two days after the fax was sent Tony Blair flew to Tripoli to meet Gaddafi. The two men embraced and declared that they wished to make 'common cause' in counterterrorism operations. The Libyans then announced that they had signed a £110 million gas exploration deal with Shell, the Anglo-Dutch oil giant.

Three days later, Libyan intelligence agents bundled al-Saadi and his family aboard a plane in Hong Kong. They were alone on the chartered airliner but for its Egyptian crew and several officers of the Libyan Mukhabarat, who told the dissident and his wife that they were going to be killed. Instead, on arrival in Tripoli the couple were handcuffed and hooded, and their legs bound together with lengths of wire. The entire family was then thrown in jail.

Al-Saadi's wife and children were released after two months of being subjected to what he describes as 'psychological torture'. Al-Saadi himself was held for six years and was repeatedly beaten, subjected to electric shocks and threatened with death. One day Moussa Koussa visited in person to boast about the way in which MI6 was helping to round up Gaddafi's LIFG opponents around the world. Al-Saadi says that he was interrogated frequently about Libyans living in the UK and shown photographs of a number of them.[33]

Al-Saadi and his family were not the only victims of a UK-Gaddafi rendition operation. Shortly before they arrived in Tripoli, another leading member of the LIFG, Abdul Hakim Belhaj, who was in exile in Malaysia, asked the British if he could seek asylum in the UK. He was advised to fly to London, and he and his pregnant wife were allowed to board a British

Airways flight at Manila airport despite having no visas for the UK. When the aircraft stopped off at Bangkok they were detained and Belhaj was tortured by the CIA for several days. The couple were then rendered to Tripoli.

The file contained page after page of questions that MI5 and MI6 wanted the Mukhabarat to put to Belhaj and al-Saadi. After the revolution, with Moussa Koussa in exile and Gaddafi in hiding, Belhaj explained how the questioning happened. 'In Bangkok I was injected with something, hung from a wall by my arms and legs and put in a container surrounded by ice,' he said. 'In Tripoli I wasn't allowed a bath for three years and I didn't see the sun for one year. They hung me from the wall and kept me in an isolation cell. I was regularly tortured. I'm surprised that the British got involved in what was a very painful period in my life.'[34]

All this was carried out by British agencies that could be criticised, according to the official oversight body, the ISC, only for being 'slow to detect the emerging pattern' of rendition by the US. The ISC even included in one of its reports this assurance from the Cabinet Office, given while the two dissidents were being tortured in Tripoli: 'The Secret Intelligence Service and Security Service operate in a culture that respects human rights. Coercive interrogation techniques are alien to both services' general ethics, methodology and training.'

MI6 in particular was badly shaken by the exposure of the secret rendition programme, one that had been concealed from ISC and, it seemed, an incoming prime minister.

Tony Blair and Jack Straw sought to distance themselves from the rendition of Libyan dissidents, their wives and several children, the youngest being a girl aged six. 'You don't know everything that is happening, what the security forces are doing,' said Blair. Straw added: 'No foreign secretary can know all the details of what its intelligence services are doing at any one time.'

MI6 was livid, making clear privately that everything that had been done vis-à-vis the Gaddafi regime had been 'ministerially authorised government policy'. The message was twofold: not only did the agency wish the public to know that it was executing government policy, it was also signalling that its officers had the protection of Section 7 authorisations. Sir Richard Dearlove, who had been chief of MI6 at the time, went public to place the blame firmly at the feet of ministers. 'It was a political decision, having very significantly disarmed Libya, for the government to cooperate with Libya on Islamist terrorism,' he said.[35]

Asked whether they still maintained that they were unaware of the Libyan rendition operations and whether they possibly knew the identities of the ministers to whom Dearlove was referring, Blair and Straw chose to remain quiet.[36]

Al-Saadi announced that he was suing the British government. Belhaj followed suit after his demand for an apology from London was ignored. A few months later, Scotland Yard announced that it was mounting another criminal investigation, Operation Lydd, into the Libyan connection.

There was more to come. In the former residence of the British ambassador to Tripoli, journalists found another cache of abandoned documents. Among them was an intelligence briefing that explained that the detention of Belhaj had pushed the LIFG towards a more pan-Islamic agenda, one inspired by al-Qaida. The two groups later merged.

The rendition operations had strengthened al-Qaida and had done nothing to protect Britain.

In May 2010, a general election in the UK had led to the creation of a coalition government that was committed, in the new prime minister's words, to examining the past activities of MI5 and MI6 in order to restore the UK's reputation 'as a country that believes in human rights, justice, fairness and the rule of law'.

Four months later there was a startling scene in Badru House shopping arcade on Moi Avenue in downtown Nairobi. Shop assistants and customers were alarmed to see a number of muscular, well-dressed young men grab a shopper and bundle him, kicking and shouting, into a station wagon with tinted windows. As they watched open-mouthed, the vehicle sped away.

The victim of the snatch was Omar Awadh Omar, aged thirty-six, a businessman, community activist and prominent figure in the city's Muslim community. He was suspected of being involved with al-Shabab, the Islamist militant group fighting to overthrow the government of Somalia.

Awadh was driven straight to the Ugandan border and handed over to the Rapid Response Unit, a police brigade notorious for torturing and even murdering its prisoners. He was told he had been detained for questioning over two suicide bombings that had claimed seventy-nine lives and injured more than seventy people in Kampala earlier that year.

At his first interrogation session, however, he found himself face to face with a group of white men who proceeded to beat him while questioning him not about Kampala, but about Kenya and Somalia. The men said they were from the FBI. But one of them, a chubby, bald man who said he was called Frank, spoke with an English accent and asked questions about Awadh's British associates. At one point, according to Awadh, this man began stamping on his bare feet while asking him about two suspected British jihadists.

When Awadh managed to see a pair of lawyers who talked their way into the prison in May 2011, he told them about 'Frank' and the Americans. Immediately, the Foreign Office was anxious to pass the buck. This was a matter for the Home Office, officials said. The Home Office was reluctant to explain what 'Frank' was doing. 'We don't comment on operational security matters,' a spokeswoman said.

But what about the new interrogation guidance, the guidelines that the Prime Minister had said would give 'greater clarity
about what is and what is not acceptable' from now on?

'The guidelines', the spokeswoman said tersely, 'would have
been followed.'

Did Theresa May, the Home Secretary, sign off on this
interrogation? 'We don't comment on operational security
matters . . .'[37]

9

The Final Sifting: The British Military in Iraq, 2003–8

'We have worked very closely with the International Commission [sic] of the Red Cross, who have expressed themselves content with the way we have treated prisoners and detainees throughout the conflict.'

Adam Ingram, Armed Forces Minister,

2 May 2003

With 9/11, the rules of the game changed. Enraged by the audacity of the attack, bewildered by the intangible nature of the threat and panicking over what could strike tomorrow, or the day after tomorrow, the White House put few restraints on the CIA and the US military. As Cofer Black said, the gloves came off.

Britain, through its support for the rendition programme and its subcontracting of torture, had been willing to place any number of terrorism suspects – including its own citizens – in American hands. But the British also showed themselves more than willing to use their own fists to subdue their enemies, to extract intelligence and to persuade prisoners to become informers and double agents. And nowhere was this more obvious than in Iraq.

British Special Forces had been operating inside Afghanistan within weeks of 9/11, and during the first week of 2002 hundreds of Royal Marines flew into the country, an advance party for a UK force that would eventually number tens of thousands. Later that year more British forces flooded into Kuwait, joining the American units awaiting the big push into Saddam Hussein's Iraq.

When the invasion came in March 2003, Tony Blair was clear that it was part of the global conflict over ideas and values, and that it could be justified by the claim that Saddam possessed weapons of mass destruction. The troops were not so certain why they were there. Some talked about 'freeing the Iraqi people'. Others hoped simply that they wouldn't be too unwelcome.[1] Before long they found that they were too poorly equipped and too thin on the ground to deal with the lawlessness and insurgency that the invasion unleashed. Above all, they had too little understanding of their new enemy.

The British military is very proud of the way in which the vast majority of its servicemen and women behaved after the invasion. Despite the difficult circumstances in which they served, the argument goes, most conducted themselves in a professional and humane manner. But during the five and a half years that the British remained in the south-east of the country, hundreds of Iraqi men emerged from British interrogation centres and detention facilities telling strikingly similar stories of systematic and brutal abuse at the hands of their captors. As the British struggled with an Iraqi resistance of unexpected ferocity, one that continually threatened to overwhelm them, they resorted to torture as a means of both punishing their prisoners and extracting intelligence about a hostile people whom they could never quite comprehend.

There were a number of reasons for this. The Intelligence Corps relied on traditional techniques that it had employed in Aden, Cyprus and Northern Ireland. Little control was exerted by ministers or through the chain of command. There was also a belief – usually well founded – that their senior coalition parters, the Americans, thought they were being too soft with their prisoners. And one should never forget the experience of the ordinary British squaddie, who had not initially expected to be plunged into such a protracted and confusing conflict. These young men were often frustrated, sometimes terrified, and usually exhausted and very, very hot.

To understand the structure of the interrogation regime through which the British processed their prisoners in Iraq, one must go back more than sixty years, to the Second World War, when the system was first established.

Towards the end of 1943 a group of officers serving with the Directorate of Military Intelligence at the War Office in London had been instructed to assess the performance and management of the Combined Services Detailed Interrogation Centre and the Prisoner of War Interrogation Service and make recommendations for the future organisation of interrogation that would be 'sufficiently elastic to operate under conditions prevailing with any given force or in any given theatre of war'.

The simple system they devised called for the capturing unit to carry out the first interrogation, known as Interrogation in the Field. At this point the prisoners would be identified and information of immediate value extracted. This would be followed by Detailed Interrogation, to be carried out some distance from the front line by specialist interrogators seeking technical, tactical and strategic intelligence. Finally, a small group of prisoners would be selected for Long Term Examination, in an attempt to meet the specific intelligence requirements of the War Office.

'The various stages can best be compared to a series of sieves of ever-narrowing mesh,' the officers' top-secret report said. 'This will produce, at each appropriate stage, the information bearing requirements of that stage and, at the final sifting, the selected Prisoners of War potentially most interesting for long term Interrogation.'[2]

After the Second World War, CSDIC was renamed the Joint Services Interrogation Wing and its headquarters were moved to Ashford in Kent. Many of its interrogators were soldiers of the Territorial Army, or served with the RAF or Royal Navy Reserve. There were outposts dotted around the country: a plaque outside the TA Barracks in Bloomsbury, central London, declared it to be the home of the Intelligence Corps' Interrogation Company.*

But while the Intelligence Corps' interrogators were kept busy in any number of colonial conflicts, they were rarely called upon to serve in conventional wars. And by the time of the Falklands War, interrogation had become the poor cousin of signals and satellite intelligence.

Guy Bransby, a Spanish-speaking officer with the RAF Regiment who was hastily recruited as an interrogator after the Argentinian invasion of the Falkland Islands, recalls that the British were so eager to repatriate their prisoners that he had little time to do more than note their names and units. Bransby met one Argentinian pilot twice. The man had been shot down, hurriedly questioned and then sent home, whereupon he climbed into another aircraft, took off and was promptly shot down again. 'He shook my hand like an old friend.'[3]

By now, Detailed Interrogation was known simply as Interrogation, while Interrogation in the Field – 'shorter and sharper', according to Bransby – had been renamed Tactical Questioning. Many of the British soldiers on the Falkland Islands regarded the work with distaste. 'Driving two Argentine prisoners from Goose Green ahead of us at forced pace . . . there were murmurings of "Nazis" and some barely audible hisses and boos,' Bransby recalled. 'These observations were not directed at the enemy, but at the Sergeant and myself. The marines and

---

* The plaque was quietly removed during the inquiries into the use of the Five Techniques in Northern Ireland.

paratroopers . . . felt sympathy for fellow infantrymen at the mercy of a sinister and underhand force.'

In 1990, before the Gulf War to drive Saddam Hussein's forces out of Kuwait, British military analysts attempting to evaluate Iraq's capabilities were given instructions – originating, apparently, with Margaret Thatcher in Downing Street – that they were not to use any intelligence thought to have been extracted through torture.[4]

Once war broke out there was little time for interrogation. After the five-week air bombardment finally eased and land forces began to push north into Kuwait, the war lasted precisely 100 hours. A team of British military interrogators found that by the time they had set up their interrogation centre, it was all over.

By now the Intelligence Corps' interrogation unit had been rebranded yet again, as the Joint Services Intelligence Organisation, or JSIO, and in the mid-1990s its headquarters moved, along with other Intelligence Corps units, from Ashford to a former US Air Force base at Chicksands, fifty miles north of London.

Around the time that the JSIO was moving north, senior commanders and defence officials decided an overhaul of British military interrogation doctrine was overdue. Instead of creating a new doctrine for use during wartime, however, they produced one for use in the eventuality of interrogators being called upon to assist the government during internal security operations. It was decided that the doctrine for wartime use should be issued shortly before any hostilities began.[5] This plan was presented to Tony Blair's new government within weeks of the 1997 general election. Inexperienced ministers, who had no expectation of embarking upon a war and had given little thought to the consequences of allowing military interrogators to operate without written instructions, agreed to the plan.

Before long, mid-level officers were attempting to draw up their own doctrine. A Royal Navy lieutenant commander who commanded the reservists at JSIO was asked to come up with a paper on the matter. When he did so, his commanding officer was reluctant to sign off on any policy governing such problematic duties and the matter was put on ice.[6]

In the absence of a revised and clear doctrine, from the mid-1990s the JSIO fell back upon the old traditions. As a result, the JSIO not only practised interrogation techniques that were cruel and illegal but also taught others to do likewise.[7] As well as providing interrogators for use during wartime, the training wing at Chicksands, known as F Branch, instructed soldiers, sailors and airmen in basic interrogation techniques, so that each military unit had its own complement of tactical questioners.

An insight into the way F Branch believed an interrogator should go about his or her work is offered by the unit's credo, which appeared on the front page of some of its training manuals: 'The whole technique of skilled interrogation is to build up an atmosphere in which the initial desire to remain silent is replaced by an urge to confide in the questioner.'[8] They were the words of Lord Diplock, who had been secretary of Churchill's wartime Security Executive when it established Camp 020. He had penned them in 1972, while writing the report that swept away jury trial in Northern Ireland and led to the government passing emergency legislation that encouraged detectives to extract confessions through force.

Trainee interrogators were told at Chicksands that sight deprivation could be used to 'condition' prisoners before interrogation. Because of the sleight of hand employed by the Heath government in 1972, when the Five Techniques were publicly banned and privately condoned, the use of hoods had never been abandoned in the Intelligence Corps. Trainees were also told that prisoners should be kept awake before interrogation, that prisoners should be stripped naked and kept naked until they obeyed orders, and that trainees were permitted to use a technique known as 'harshing': threatening and screaming abuse at high volume at a distance of around six inches from the prisoners' faces. When prisoners were to be moved around an interrogation centre, they should be forced to put their palms together, the trainees were told, and led by a soldier grasping both of their thumbs.

Furthermore, recently trained interrogators would assist with what was known as Conduct After Capture and Resistance to Interrogation training, or CAC and R2I, in which soldiers and airmen were prepared for the event of being captured. This was very similar to the Survival, Evasion, Resistance and Escape training that Guantánamo interrogators had studied at Fort Bragg in North Carolina. Those who had recently undergone interrogation training by F Branch would play the role of the enemy, and subject the CAC and R2I trainees to a range of so-called aids to interrogation, including the Five Techniques that had supposedly been banned decades earlier.[9] In addition to the training conducted by F Branch, individual army units would conduct their own unauthorised CAC training, at which men playing prisoners were subjected to hooding, sleep deprivation, extremely rough manhandling and the use of stress positions.

Before long, then, significant numbers of British military personnel had been trained either directly or indirectly in the use of torture. Meanwhile, the updated detailed interrogation doctrine for use during wartime was still on ice. And it remained on ice, even as the British became engaged in war.

On Monday 14 January 2002, the British Defence Secretary, Geoff Hoon, issued a compulsory mobilisation order which instructed 140 army reservists of the Intelligence Corps, including interrogators, to fly to Afghanistan.

The decision to do this had been taken the previous week. It was the same week in which MI5 and MI6 officers had been issued with the secret interrogation guidance informing them that they could interrogate people who were being tortured as long as they were not seen to condone the mistreatment. It was also the week in which the Foreign Secretary, Jack Straw, had sent the secret telegram which consigned British Muslims taken prisoner in Afghanistan to Camp X-Ray at Guantánamo. At the highest levels of government, it seems, a decision had been taken that the British gloves were also coming off.

Later that year, F Branch received orders to deploy to Kuwait. And still nobody – not even senior officers within the Intelligence Corps – appears to have seen fit to remind ministers that they had agreed to issue detailed guidance on interrogation before the nation's armed forces went to war.

Shortly after the invasion, F Branch would cross the border and set up an interrogation centre south of Basra, under a new name, the Joint Forward Interrogation Team, or JFIT. Before they departed, a senior JSIO officer sent an email to a high-ranking member of the Defence Intelligence Staff at the Ministry of Defence in which he explained that he was fresh from a briefing by American interrogators. 'There was a US Army MP Captain who told us all about what they are doing in Bagram and Guantánamo,' the JSIO officer wrote. What he heard gave him the opportunity to remind his men that they needed to adopt a 'holistic' approach to interrogation and to tactical questioning 'and not to get too wound up in prisoners' rights at the expense of int. [intelligence]'.[10]

Within weeks of the invasion, the enthusiasm with which the downtrodden Shia population in the south-east of the country had greeted the British troops began to evaporate. Before long it was being replaced by suspicion and resentment. Fuel was in short supply, bridges had been bombed and the hospitals were still overflowing with wounded. Electricity cuts meant there was no running water. One day in mid-April, long lines of men clutching buckets formed outside the schools that Royal Marines had commandeered as bases, in the hope that they would be given a drop or two of clean water. It had never been so bad before, the men complained, not in 1991, not even during the bloody eight-year war with Iran. The marines couldn't understand a word they were saying.[11]

The de-Ba'athification of the army and the police led to the disintegration of both institutions. A complete collapse of law and order quickly followed and the prisons were emptied. The British had moved from combat operations to stabilisation, but the number of shooting incidents grew steadily. Parts of Basra descended into anarchy, and car-jackings, kidnappings and revenge killings became rife. 'In a very short space of time,' one British officer noted, 'wealth was being comprehensively redistributed.'[12]

British police commanders decided it was far too dangerous to send any of their officers, which left the British Army as the sole agent for the imposition of law and order. The last time the British military had found itself in this role, as an army of occupation in a strange land, was in 1945 following the end of the Second World War. On that occasion it had had months to prepare.

Battlegroups of around 500 soldiers were given areas of responsibility comprising hundreds of square miles. Some commanding officers found there were no Foreign Office officials to give political, cultural or legal advice: they were expected simply to get on with it.[13]

Before long, soldiers were being ordered that anyone caught looting should be 'wetted' – pushed into the Shatt al-Arab river – so they would be forced to go home and dry off. Some Iraqi boys drowned. At Camp Breadbasket, west of Basra, looters were detained, beaten and sexually humiliated. When the victims' families arrived to demand their release, they too were dragged inside and beaten.

British troops were being expected to deal not only with hordes of looters and significant numbers of serious criminals but also with the menace thought to be posed by former regime loyalists, or FRLs, as they became known. As the year progressed, they were also confronted by the very real threat from the Mahdi Army: the paramilitary force commanded by the Shia cleric Muqtada al-Sadr.

Increasing numbers of suspects were brought in for questioning. And the interrogations were conducted either by trained tactical questioners who believed they had the authority to manhandle and verbally abuse prisoners or by soldiers who had undergone CAC or R2I training.

Iraqis were hooded, threatened and forced into stress positions. Many interrogators favoured the 'ski position', in which the prisoner was placed with his back to a wall and forced to bend his legs, his thighs parallel to the ground, while holding his arms outstretched before him. After a few moments this was excruciatingly painful. As in Northern Ireland, a sixth, unspoken technique – beating – was used to force prisoners to assume the ski position for long periods.

Among the first to be detained was Hussain Hadi Sabir al-Mosawi. On 1 May 2003, a Thursday, Mosawi was walking from his home in Basra to his local pharmacy. It was 10 a.m. and the twenty-two-year-old labourer had been sent to buy some medication for his brother, who had burned himself while repairing a motorbike.

As he was walking down the street, an approaching convoy of British military vehicles came to a halt. The doors of their vehicles opened and troops poured out. 'Soldiers approached me with their rifles,' Mosawi says. 'One of the soldiers kicked me. A soldier pushed me down and handcuffed my hands behind me. The soldiers started kicking me. They were yelling and shouting. It was awful. I couldn't believe what was happening.' A hessian sandbag was forced over Mosawi's head and the drawstring pulled around his neck. 'It was very difficult to breathe.' He was pushed into a Land Rover and driven away.

The soldiers continued to swear at him and kick him, he says. Among them was a man with a Kuwaiti accent, swearing in Arabic. After ten minutes the Land Rover stopped, Mosawi was dragged out, the hood was removed and he was pushed into a dark, windowless cell, five feet square. Around two hours later, two soldiers came into the cell and began beating him with plastic batons. Small round metal rods protruded from the ends of the batons, he says, and when these touched him, on his knees and elbows, he received an electric shock. 'It was like a fire jolting my insides.'

Mosawi was then taken to a larger cell, containing around twenty more Iraqi prisoners. The men were loaded into a truck and driven south to a large barbed-wire enclosure on the edge of the town of Umm Qasr, near the Kuwaiti border. Here Mosawi received medical treatment: his arms and leg were bandaged and a dressing was put on his nose. But he was refused permission to relieve himself. 'I told the interpreter what had happened, but he didn't care.'

He was taken to a large tent where around fifty prisoners were sitting, cross-legged, in rows. The men were each given a small bag containing rice, jam and biscuits, and allowed to sleep. When they woke next morning, one of their number had hanged himself from a rope in the middle of the tent.

Over the next few weeks, Mosawi would be taken away and questioned from time to time, but he seems to have had little information of value. The beatings became less severe and he was never again subjected to electric shocks. Instead, he says, the soldiers would humiliate him. They would force him to lie with his face in the sand or expose themselves in front of him.

After around six weeks, he and a group of other prisoners were put aboard a coach, driven halfway to Basra and dropped off near a mosque. 'They shouted: "Go, go!" I was extremely confused. A car stopped and gave me a lift to my home, about thirty minutes away. I still suffer from my time in detention. I want to understand why I was tortured and why I was so humiliated. I was treated like an animal. Nobody has ever explained to me why.'[14]

Over the summer of 2003, the number of detainees increased rapidly. Some were held and questioned by battlegroup interrogators; others were interrogated at brigade or divisional level. The most unfortunate were those who were dispatched for the final sifting, at the interrogation centre set up by the F Branch trainers from Chicksands: JFIT.

In June, six British military policemen were killed by an Iraqi mob in a police station in the town of Majar al-Kabir, 100 miles north of Basra. Several Iraqi policemen say that a few weeks later they were tortured inside the same building by British troops. Among them were Ali Hamid Lazim, aged thirty-one, and Haidar Yusuf Mohammad, aged twenty-two, two newly recruited officers who say British soldiers − men they had come to view as friends and mentors − forced them into stress positions, beating and whipping them with batons and radio aerials if they attempted to move.

'I was in so much pain and extremely anxious and frightened,' says Mohammad. 'It was very hard to hold this position after a few minutes.' The Iraqis were taken away for questioning one at a time by soldiers who demanded to know the identities of those who had killed the British military policemen. This went on for several hours, while a helicopter hovered low overhead, apparently to drown out the noise of the men's screams. Eventually a large crowd gathered and the men were able to escape by leaping from first-floor windows.[15]

Ali Lafteh Eedan, aged twenty-nine, was one of a group of men detained as suspected FRLs. They spent hours in the wall-standing position with nylon bags over their heads. 'I was beaten on my elbows every time I moved. It was so hot and I felt I was going to suffocate. The soldiers just laughed at us.' Then they were taken for interrogation.

Ahmed Jawad al-Fartoosi, aged thirty-three, a suspected insurgent, was beaten up in front of his family, blindfolded and put aboard an armoured vehicle that rammed both his cars as it left the scene. He was beaten throughout the journey. 'I could tell that the soldiers were enjoying beating me, as they were laughing.' He was then deprived of sleep for several days and interrogated. He was detained for two years.

The list goes on. Haidar Abdul-Karim al-Doori, aged twenty-five, an office manager, was arrested at his home in Basra in December 2003 and accused of hoarding weapons. He was taken away in a pair of blackened goggles and severely beaten. After a quick medical examination he was taken for interrogation. 'They kept asking where Ezzat al-Doori, the vice-president under Saddam, was hiding. Although my surname is the same, I am not related to him. There are thousands of al-Dooris in Iraq.' The interrogations went on for days. In-between each session he was beaten again, or forced into stress positions and prevented from sleeping. The interrogators appear eventually to have believed al-Doori. He was transferred from the interrogation centre to a prisoner of war camp, but it was a further six months before he was released and reunited with his wife and two daughters.

Some captives were handed not to British interrogators but to Americans. British Special Forces operating in the Baghdad area would routinely take their prisoners to Camp Nama, a facility to the west of the city, or to a second interrogation centre at Balad, forty-two miles to the north. As in Aden in the 1960s, however, some members of the SAS became deeply concerned about the way their prisoners were subsequently mistreated.

These concerns were made public by a former SAS trooper,

Ben Griffin, who had been discharged after he refused to return to Iraq. In 2008, Griffin said that he and his comrades had been certain that their prisoners were being tortured after being handed over to US forces. Three of them had seen a prisoner suffering partial drowning and electric shocks. 'I have no doubt in my mind that non-combatants I personally detained were handed over to the Americans and subsequently tortured,' he said. 'My commanding officer at the time expressed his concern to the whole squadron that we were becoming the secret police of Baghdad.'

The Ministry of Defence responded by obtaining an injunction to silence Griffin and insisted that British troops were not handing over prisoners to be abused. The MOD knew this to be false, however: in December 2003, a retired US Army colonel who been asked to inspect Camp Nama had warned the Pentagon that interrogators there appeared to regard the abuse of prisoners as normal. At both Nama and Balad, prisoners were held in cells the size of dog kennels. Conditions at Balad were worse, however, and in late 2004, the UK authorities had told the Americans that the SAS would hand over their prisoners only if there was an undertaking not to send them to Balad.[16]

An unknown number of those handed over by the SAS entered the rendition system and were flown to Afghanistan or elsewhere. Two Pakistani men taken prisoner by B Squadron of the SAS in a raid on a house in southern Baghdad in February 2004, for example, were subsequently flown to Bagram and were still been there eight years later. How many others suffered a similar fate is unknown.

In the south-east of the country, however, most prisoners detained by British forces for interrogation remained in British hands, many of them at JFIT.

The JFIT interrogation centre operated from March 2003 to late 2008, first inside the large prisoner of war camp that the

British built and the Americans operated at Umm Qasr, and later inside a logistics base near the town of Az Zubayr, south-west of Basra. Finally, in April 2007, the interrogation unit retreated, along with other British forces, to the international airport on the outskirts of the city.

The Iraqi men who emerged from JFIT all say they were badly beaten on arrest and that the beatings continued while they were being taken into detention. On arrival they would be subjected to an examination by a military doctor, often being forced to strip in a manner that they found deeply humiliating. The doctors always followed the same procedure – one that would have been instantly recognisable to the fourteen men who had been subjected to the Five Techniques in Northern Ireland more than three decades earlier. The doctors would ignore the obvious injuries suffered during the prisoner's arrest, including, in the most disturbing cases, broken bones, and instead would check breathing, blood pressure and heart rate. They were establishing whether the prisoner was fit enough to survive what was to follow.

Many of the men say that after this examination and before their first interrogation they would be forced to kneel upright for long periods – sometimes more than twenty-four hours – with hoods over their heads, regardless of the heat, and that they would be beaten if they attempted to relax.

In-between interrogation sessions the prisoners would be hooded, or put in blackened goggles and earmuffs and forced to run in zigzags along obstacle courses, all the time being held by their thumbs while unseen men kicked them or struck them with rifle butts. Many of the prisoners were deprived of sleep, either by being held in brightly lit cells little more than three feet square or by being forced to listen to pornographic films played at loud volume on laptop computers placed outside their cell doors.

The Intelligence Corps interrogators were not the only people who questioned prisoners at JFIT. On at least one occasion, in

October 2004, MI5 interrogators spent several days questioning a British-Iraqi dual national who was being held at JFIT after being detained in Baghdad by US forces, apparently at the request of the British. He was held for three years and then released shortly after his British citizenship had been revoked.

When some of the former inmates of JFIT began court proceedings against the British government, their statements were supported by irrefutable evidence about the manner in which some of the interrogations themselves had been conducted. In 2005, two years after JFIT was established, its staff had received orders that each interrogation should be recorded on film. The interrogators subsequently made 2,616 recordings, some of which were disclosed in court.

The few videos that have since been made public show inmates being led into the interrogation room by their thumbs, wearing earmuffs and blackened goggles. The earmuffs are removed and an interpreter sitting behind the prisoner relays the interrogator's shouted instruction to the prisoner to remove his goggles with his left hand and place them on the ground.

In one video, the prisoner is forced to stand to attention while two interrogators scream abuse and threaten him with death. They ignore his complaints that he is not being fed or allowed to sleep. Subsequent videos show this prisoner's physical condition steadily deteriorating. He appears exhausted, confused and stiff. When he protests that he is in pain the interrogator barks: 'Good. I hope you die of cancer. I hope your kids die.' At the end of that session the prisoner is ordered to replace the goggles and the interrogator shouts an order for a guard to take him away 'for a little run'. The earmuffs are replaced and the prisoner is dragged away by his thumbs.[17]

Not all the videos show scenes of abuse and not all the interrogators and guards at JFIT were brutal. Ahmed Jawad al-Fartoosi tells of one man, a Scotsman called 'Sergeant Mike', who would come and chat to him in his cell and bring the prisoners chilled water. 'He was very sympathetic to me.'

Sergeant Mike seems to have been in a minority, however. Officials of the International Committee of the Red Cross were complaining to the British government about the treatment of prisoners within days of the invasion in March 2003. As the year wore on they repeatedly raised concerns about JFIT. In a confidential report submitted to the British government early in 2004, the ICRC said that inmates at JFIT 'were routinely treated by their guards with general contempt, with petty violence such as having orders screamed at them and being cursed, kicked, struck with rifle butts, roughed up or pushed around'. They spent long periods handcuffed and hooded. 'Hooding appeared to be motivated by security concerns as well as to be part of standard intimidation techniques used by military intelligence personnel to frighten inmates into cooperating.'[18] The report, which was eventually leaked, changed little.

In time, it was clear that this was because responsibility for what was happening stretched beyond the tactical questioners and even beyond the army chain of command. It extended all the way to the Ministry of Defence at Whitehall, where ministers and senior officials chose to turn a blind eye to a number of the abuses being suffered by prisoners. Some also sought to conceal what they knew.

In May 2004, a military lawyer asked senior MOD legal advisers whether the Attorney General should be asked for an opinion on the legality of hooding prisoners. The ministry's deputy legal adviser, Vivien Rose, replied by email: 'I would not be in favour of asking the AG at this point.'[19] Asked about this later, Rose's superior, Martin Hemming, the MOD's most senior lawyer, said: 'I would have agreed not to go to the attorney at that time.' It was, he said, 'an academic question', as he believed the use of hooding by British troops had been banned by then and the Attorney General was 'a very busy' man.[20] Rose, however, eventually admitted that one of the reasons that the Attorney General was not consulted was that he might have banned the use of hoods.[21]

Later that month, Adam Ingram, the Armed Forces Minister, claimed in a letter to a fellow MP that the Red Cross had 'expressed themselves content with the way we have treated prisoners and detainees'.[22] He made similar claims to constituents, but this was completely untrue. Just weeks earlier, the Red Cross had privately told the British government that it was deeply concerned about the manner in which UK forces were treating their prisoners. When the use of hooding was raised in Parliament in June 2004, Ingram told MPs: 'We are not aware of any incidents in which United Kingdom interrogators are alleged to have used hooding as an interrogation technique.'[23] Ingram repeated this claim when giving evidence to Parliament's Joint Committee on Human Rights. In fact, the previous September he had been aware of information that detailed the use of hoods during tactical questioning. When the truth finally emerged, Ingram conceded only that he 'should have been more specific' when answering the question.[24]

Several British officers lodged complaints about what they saw at JFIT, but were informed that the interrogation centre operated outside the usual chain of command, answering to senior commanders in London.

One visitor, Lieutenant Colonel Nick Mercer, a senior army lawyer, was shocked to see around forty handcuffed Iraqis being forced to squat on the ground, with their hands cuffed high behind their backs. Dark blue hoods covered their heads and in the background a generator was running. Later, Mercer described what he saw as 'repulsive' and added: 'It's a bit like seeing a picture of Guantánamo Bay for the first time. It is quite a shock.'[25]

Mercer believed the generators were intended to muffle

the sound of whatever was happening inside the tents where interrogations took place. He immediately warned the interrogators that the use of hooding had been banned and that it would impair the detainees' breathing. He was told, however, that the use of hoods and stress positions 'was in accordance with British Army doctrine on tactical questioning'.[26]

Another visitor, a senior intelligence officer at Divisional HQ, had concerns about hooding and forcing prisoners to sit in the sun. But he decided that he should focus on the broader military mission and warn that measures should be taken to prevent anyone photographing JFIT: 'I remember saying . . . it would be preferable to put a screen around the facility so that practices which might alienate the local population were not publicly exposed.'[27]

Public exposure was not the only danger. With all the beatings, the sleep deprivation and the starvation, the stress positions and the hooding, it was only a matter of time before prisoners started to die.

Early in May 2003, soldiers of the Black Watch, the proud Highland regiment that had fought its way into Basra the previous month, were asked to help with a raid on the home of a convicted child killer. This man had been among the many criminals sprung from jail during the invasion. There was no sign of him at the house, but his father, Radhi Nama, was arrested after a quantity of ammunition was found. Nama's daughters say that their father was hooded, his hands cuffed behind his back, and he was then picked up and hurled into the back of a truck.

Nama was taken to a Black Watch base at a compound formerly used by Saddam Hussein's secret police. It was named Camp Stephen, after a soldier killed during the invasion. Soldiers at Camp Stephen appear to have believed that Nama, rather than his son, was the child killer. Tam Henderson, the warrant officer who ran the detention facility, says he left Nama under guard and went to the operations room.

Henderson says that before going to Iraq he had been told that prisoners should be 'softened up for interrogation' by the use of hooding and stress positions, and forcing them to run between two rows of screaming soldiers.[28] Some of Henderson's former comrades dispute this and also deny his assertion that they had been warned to be wary of Red Cross officials as they 'might try to poke their noses in where they're not wanted'.

What is not disputed is that a few hours after Nama was detained and taken to Camp Stephen he was dead.

The death appears not to have caused too many problems for the men who were guarding Nama. An Iraqi hospital assistant with no medical qualifications recorded that he had suffered a heart attack and an Iraqi doctor signed a death certificate accordingly. The Royal Military Police then prepared a report in which they concluded that Nama had died of natural causes.

There had been a slight problem with the removal of the corpse from Camp Stephen, as a Scottish reporter was visiting the base at the time. 'The last thing we wanted was the journalist sniffing around,' Henderson later recalled. The reporter was invited by Henderson to sit down for a chat, while behind him Nama's corpse was strapped, upright, into a Land Rover. Before the vehicle moved off, one of the soldiers took hold of the dead man's head and moved it, like a ventriloquist's dummy, in an attempt to make Henderson laugh.[29]

Five days later a second prisoner died at Camp Stephen. Abdul Jabbar Musa Ali, aged fifty-five and a head teacher, was suspected of being an FRL. When a raid on his home uncovered a firearm, he and his son Bashar were detained for tactical questioning. Bashar says that before being put aboard a truck, a soldier repeatedly struck his father on top of his head with a heavy piece of military equipment, and that they were both beaten en route to Camp Stephen.

Henderson says that by the time they arrived, Ali's nose was broken. The men were examined by military medical staff, who made no record of any injuries, and they were then hooded and forced to assume a kneeling position. Bashar says he and his father were severely beaten inside the detention facility and were taken to other locations around Camp Stephen where they were beaten again. At one point, he says, he heard his father say that he was going to die.[30] He did so within two hours of his arrival at Camp Stephen.

At least one man detained for questioning did not get as far as a detention facility before being beaten to death. Tariq Sabri, a man in his late thirties, was among a group of sixty-four men detained by Australian Special Forces at a roadblock west of Baghdad in April 2003. The prisoners were restrained by having strips of plastic wound around their thumbs before being hooded with sandbags by troops of the RAF Regiment and loaded aboard an RAF Chinook helicopter to be flown to a captured Iraqi airfield for questioning by a joint task force of British and American Special Forces and CIA officers. The prisoners were guarded by several men of the RAF Regiment, who are alleged to have kicked and punched a number of them.[31] By the time the helicopter landed, Sabri was dead. The following day, the alleged killers' commanding officer, a squadron leader in the RAF Regiment, told his superiors that a second prisoner had been unconscious on arrival, while a third, a disabled man, had somehow parted company with both his prosthetic legs.[32]

A decision was taken that the RAF police would be allowed to investigate the matter. These officers waited more than a year before asking an RAF pathologist whether Sabri's body should be exhumed. The RAF pathologist said such an examination was pointless. The RAF officer supervising the inquiry then informed the RAF prosecutor that the cause of Sabri's death was unknown. Upon hearing this, the RAF prosecutor concluded that no RAF personnel should face criminal or disciplinary charges.[33]

The investigation was so superficial that it failed even to establish that the dead man was named Tariq Sabri, and his family has never been told what became of him.[34]

Inquiries into allegations of torture and murder by the British military in Iraq were conducted by military police who were often under-staffed and poorly resourced. Nevertheless, some of the investigations appeared designed to carefully bury evidence rather than unearth the truth.

The father of one young man who was tortured to death by British soldiers was not prepared to countenance such corruption. His name was Daoud Mousa and he was a uniformed colonel in the Iraqi police, a man whom the British permitted to carry a pistol. When a British officer came to Daoud and told him his son Baha had died in their custody, he demanded to see the body.

Baha Mousa's nose had been broken and his face was bloodied and bruised. There were more bruises around his ribs and thighs and the skin was ripped from his wrists. Daoud could see his son had suffered an appalling death. The British offered him $3,000 in compensation.

Instead of taking the money, Daoud embarked upon a series of meetings with British officials, officers, journalists and lawyers, demanding that those responsible be brought to justice. His efforts led eventually to a court martial, then civil proceedings in the High Court in London, and finally, despite bitter resistance from the army and the Ministry of Defence, a public inquiry.

The court proceedings and the inquiry shed stark light not only on the thirty-six hours during which Baha Mousa and nine other men were systematically mistreated – and the role that senior officers, doctors and even a padre played in those events – but also on the way in which young British soldiers believed they had a right, a duty even, to torture civilian prisoners undergoing tactical questioning.

In September 2003, Baha Mousa was twenty-six and working as a hotel receptionist in Basra. He had two sons, aged five and three. Their mother had died of cancer six months earlier. In the early hours of Sunday 14 September, men of the 1st Battalion the Queen's Lancashire Regiment took part in a series of raids on hotels in the city, searching for FRLs. In those lawless days, hotel staff routinely kept firearms in order to reassure their guests and the Hotel Ibn al Haitham was no exception. When the troops found a number of weapons, they began assaulting the staff and removing money from the safe. Mousa and the other men were taken to the detention facility at Camp Stephen.

1 QLR had taken over from the Black Watch a few weeks earlier and they had just lost a popular young officer, Captain Dai Jones, the first British victim of a roadside bomb. Some of the troops were told, wrongly, that Baha Mousa and his colleagues were suspected of involvement in the death of Jones. The beatings began immediately.

The prisoners were hooded and forced to kneel in a circle while their captors struck them in turn. As each of the victims made a different noise, the soldiers called them 'the choir' and before long others were putting their heads around the door to witness the recital. Some of the men were forced to dance. They were all made to assume the ski position, being beaten and verbally abused whenever they slid to the floor. One of the soldiers filmed this part of the tactical questioning process.

The abuse went on throughout the night and into the Monday. Although the temperature inside the small detention facility was almost unbearable, from time to time a prisoner would be forced to sit next to a running generator outside. Occasionally they would be taken away to another building to be interrogated.

On at least one occasion 1 QLR's padre, Father Peter Madden, a Roman Catholic priest who had joined the army on the eve of the invasion, came in to see what was happening. He made no complaint, either to the men beating the prisoners or to any of 1 QLR's officers, although he could see the state the prisoners were in.[35]

By this time the soldiers found that they no longer needed to hit the prisoners to inflict pain: they needed only to touch them. One of the soldiers carrying out the assaults, Private Gareth Aspinall, later told the public inquiry that the unfortunately named Corporal Donald Payne, the man orchestrating the 'choir', had punched the prisoners so often in the lower back that he needed only to prod the area to hurt them: 'The detainees would be stood up and he would move about the room poking them, just basically with his finger, and they would – every one of them would scream out in pain.'

Aspinall admitted that he had been laughing: 'To be honest, when he first did it, I was uncomfortable and there was – I can't remember who was present, other people were there, and other people laughed and maybe I just laughed along with them. I think maybe deep inside I knew it was wrong and it was upsetting, so I just went along with it.

'And I just remember it because I thought, well, even the Padre has visited and even he – is he going to say anything? And he didn't mention anything. So when people like that have come in, of high authority, you start to think, well, if I was going to report it who – is anyone bothered? I don't know. So that's why I was worried about reporting it.'[36]

Father Madden was not the only authority figure who either encouraged the abuse or failed to halt it. The section commander knew that the prisoners were being beaten, the company commander admitted that they were being hooded in order to 'break' them, the battalion's adjutant knew that they were being forced into stress positions and a major serving with

1 QLR who was, in theory, responsible for the prisoners' welfare knew that they were being severely beaten. Meanwhile, the commanding officer of 1 QLR, Lieutenant Colonel Jorge Mendonca, knew that his men 'conditioned' their prisoners by hooding them, forcing them into stress positions and depriving them of sleep.[37]

On Monday evening, after thirty-six hours of 'conditioning', Baha Mousa collapsed and died. The cause of death was later determined by the public inquiry to be twofold. He was suffering from starvation, dehydration, heat, exhaustion, fear, multiple injuries, acute renal failure and damage to skeletal muscle tissue. Having been weakened by all these factors, he then died after being punched and being thrown across a room.

He was tortured to death.

The Regimental Medical Officer, Dr Derek Keilloh, tried unsuccessfully to revive Mousa. The dead man had suffered at least ninety-three separate injuries, including fractured ribs and a broken nose, and post-mortem photographs showed his face and chest to be a mass of cuts and bruises. Despite this, Keilloh recorded that he could see no trace of any injuries, other than a small amount of blood under Mousa's nose. Keilloh then examined two more prisoners who were complaining of being in pain. He gave them pain relief and anti-inflammatory injections and sent them back to the detention facility, where the beatings continued through the night and into the next day.[38] One of the men had a visible hernia.

Seven soldiers went on trial in September 2006. Payne was cleared of manslaughter and perverting the course of justice, but admitted a charge of inhumanely treating civilian detainees. He became the first British soldier to be convicted of a war crime. He was jailed for a year and dismissed from the army.

Three other soldiers were cleared of inhumane treatment

or assault, while three, including Mendonca, were cleared of negligently performing a duty.

The public inquiry ran for over a year and at its conclusion the chairman, Sir William Gage, a retired Court of Appeal judge, concluded that what had happened to Baha Mousa and the other men had not been a one-off incident at 1 QLR's detention facility and that there was 'more than a hint' that such mistreatment of prisoners was more widespread among the British Army in Iraq. Gage made seventy-three recommendations, including the need for clear prohibition of hooding and a ban on sight deprivation and the use of noise.

During the inquiry, it emerged that the US military and the CIA had been concerned that the British were not extracting sufficient intelligence during the interrogation of prisoners. As a result, senior British officers were aware that any restrictions on their interrogation practices could lead to British troops being excluded from joint operations. The day after Mousa's death, Lieutenant Colonel Ewan Duncan, the UK's most senior military intelligence officer in Iraq, sent an email to an army lawyer in which he warned that a ban on hooding would lead to 'a growing diversion of opinion with the US and the adverse impact on interrogations [and] UK involvement in US ops where blindfolding is the milder end of the spectrum'. Duncan told the inquiry: 'My recollection is that there was no pressure as such from the US, rather a view that we could have done better.'[39]

After that inquiry, the Ministry of Defence braced itself for a second public inquiry into disputed allegations that a dozen or more Iraqi prisoners were killed at a separate detention facility in May 2004. There were also demands that a third inquiry should be held into the events at JFIT. In an attempt to persuade the courts that no such inquiry was needed, the MOD assembled a team of forty former civilian detectives, assisted by around the same number of Royal Military Police investigators, to investigate the complaints. That investigation is expected to last a number of years. Whether it results in anyone being prosecuted remains to be seen.

In May 2006, more than two years after the death of Baha Mousa, the Ministry of Defence finally issued the interrogation doctrine that should have been promulgated before the country went to war. At this point, with a public inquiry looming, the Joint Services Intelligence Organisation at Chicksands might have been expected to undergo a period of introspection, perhaps even to arrange a legal audit of its practices, not only in the light of events in Iraq, but to ensure that the laws of armed conflict and international human rights were being observed by its interrogators. Instead, it was business as usual.

In September 2005, a classified PowerPoint training aid with the jokey title 'Any Questions?' had been prepared at Chicksands. It explained to trainee tactical questioners that they needed to arouse 'anxiety, fear, insecurity, humiliation, disorientation' and exhaustion among their prisoners. Enforced nakedness was to be encouraged: 'Get them naked . . . keep them naked if they do not follow commands.' They should then be searched in a manner calculated to increase that fear: 'Pull back foreskin, spread buttocks.'

Any sleep deprivation must not be 'intentional', the training aid cautioned. But blindfolding was permitted as a means of creating stress. And the legal status of the detainees? 'Let the judicial process deal with them after you have finished.'[40]

It didn't end there. In April 2008, a secret training manual was produced at Chicksands that again highlighted the usefulness of enforced nakedness and said that interrogators should aim to employ physical discomfort, noise and intimidation, and create an 'atmosphere of ruthlessness'. It hinted that threats might be made against the families of 'Cpers', or captured personnel. Sight deprivation as a means of creating stress was still encouraged, blindfolds and earmuffs were described as essential equipment, and trainees were informed that sensory deprivation was lawful 'if there is a valid operational reason'.[41]

What is more, the training material made clear that student interrogators were to be taught that they were joining an elite military discipline, one whose skills had been honed over decades, in wars and internal security operations around the globe, 'in Borneo, Malaya, South Arabia, Palastine [*sic*], Cyprus, Northern Ireland . . .'

Conclusion

> '. . . it is your civilization, it is you . . . The suet
> puddings and the red pillar-boxes have entered into your
> soul. Good or evil, it is yours, you belong to it, and this
> side the grave you will never get away from the marks
> that it has given you.'
> George Orwell, 'England, Your England', 1941[1]

In the summer of 2011, I went to see my contact James again. We
met at a small cafe in London's East End, found a table outside
in the sun and slipped the batteries out of our mobile phones.
I had recently obtained a copy of the British government's
highly classified interrogation policy. This was the document
that instructed MI5 and MI6 officers to balance 'the level of
mistreatment anticipated' against 'the operational imperative'
of seeking information from prisoners held in foreign torture
chambers. It was a document that had resulted in many, many
people being tortured. Week by week, as men came forward
to talk about the British who had interrogated them in prisons
across the Muslim world, as details of rendition flights continued
to emerge and as the courts slowly extracted the truth about
the ordeal of Binyam Mohamed, the true extent of Britain's
participation in some of the worst horrors of the 'war on terror'
was beginning to become clear.

I asked James if he recalled our conversation in that cafe near

Liverpool Street Station when he'd asked me whether it was possible that the British government had a secret torture policy, one that it was determined nobody should ever know about. 'Well,' I said, 'it did.'

'That's right,' James replied, stirring his tea. 'You weren't listening properly, were you?'

I also simply hadn't wanted to hear.

Faced with questions about involvement in torture, British officials responded in the post-9/11 era as they had for decades: with denial, obfuscation, ridicule, threats and lies. But, even as I was helping to unearth the evidence, there was a self-imposed handicap: I hadn't wanted to accept that figures of authority in British public life would arrange for their fellow citizens to be tortured.

Back then, I hadn't realised how strongly rooted my assumptions about my country and its values had been. But, as my inquiries went on, I was forced to realise that I had underestimated the capacity of the British government and its senior servants to exercise power with unremitting ruthlessness at times of crisis. I had also failed to appreciate their consummate ability to conceal the truth. The sheer *efficiency* of their efforts had taken me by surprise.

But now I had spent enough time tracing the all but hidden contours of the secret state and could comprehend far more, not just about the abuses of the post-9/11 years but also about the years that had gone before. I understood that far from being a nation that doesn't 'do' torture, Britain had been employing such cruelties for generations, and for a multitude of reasons.

We British have repeatedly resorted to torture as a consequence of our fear of enemies we barely understood, as with the 'fifth columnists' in the summer of 1940 and the Mahdi Army in Iraq in 2003, and enemies we found completely incomprehensible, such as the Mau Mau detainees.

Sometimes Britain's use of torture has been inordinately successful. After the calamitous evacuation from Dunkirk, for example, when the nation's very survival was at stake, the speed with which the Abwehr's invasion spies were turned into pliant and convincing double agents by the interrogators of Camp 020 played a crucial role in protecting Britain and restoring her fortunes.

But its use has also frequently been disastrous. In Aden and Cyprus, the British exposed the depth of their ignorance of their adversaries when they resorted to torture. And in Northern Ireland they plunged headlong into a conflict whose causes were rooted in centuries of fear, distrust and discrimination, and thought they could glean game-changing intelligence by hooding and beating a handful of men and forcing them to assume excruciating positions against a wall for days at a time.

We British have resorted to torture not boastfully, not routinely, and rarely with obvious relish. But we have been ready to resort to torture when we have come to believe that the country's situation was desperate: when an invasion of the south coast of England was thought imminent; when one prized colonial possession after another was being lost; when part of the United Kingdom appeared to be on the brink of civil war; or when an imperfectly understood terrorist organisation showed itself capable of mounting simultaneous mass-casualty attacks upon the country's most powerful ally.

Once we have resorted to torture, however, once we have established techniques that we believe work, identified the people prepared to employ those techniques and constructed the web of deception and denial needed to conceal what we are doing, we British have shown ourselves to be remarkably reluctant to abandon the calculated use of brutal force and pain while questioning our enemies.

So what seemed a necessary evil in 1940, when the Wehrmacht invasion barges were massing at Dunkirk and Ostend, was not halted in 1945 when Allied victory over Nazi Germany had long been assured. Nor did it end with the cessation of hostilities: years after the war, defenceless German men and women were still held at the whim of bullying British officers 'for purposes of revenge'.

Long after the Troubles in Northern Ireland had ceased to resemble civil war and had become a more manageable low-intensity operation for British forces, coercive interrogations remained at the cynical heart of the UK's counterterrorism strategy, being used to extract confessions from hundreds of suspected paramilitaries who could then be convicted by the no-jury courts.

And years after 9/11, when much of the core leadership of al-Qaida had been killed, captured or driven into the mountains along the Afghan-Pakistan border, young British Muslims detained in Pakistan were still having their fingernails prised slowly from their fingers while being asked questions about their associates in Yorkshire.

And while the web of deception that must accompany the use of torture may have deceived few in Cyprus, or parts of Ireland, or south-east Iraq, the British public has remained willing to believe that their nation does not practise torture. One important reason why these crimes have been committed with impunity over the years is that the British public tends not to believe that it has been happening, and the British media is reluctant to make them any the wiser. On the isles of fair play, it is assumed, the use of torture cannot be possible, because it is unthinkable.

But delve a little deeper, observe a little more clearly, and far from being alien, torture can be seen to be as British as suet pudding and red pillar-boxes.

Notes

Chapter One: The Secrets of My Prison House

1. The National Archive (TNA) WO 208/3458.
2. Ibid.
3. Nigel West, *MI5: British Security Service Operations, 1909–1945*, pp. 116–17.
4. Tom Bower, *The Perfect English Spy*, p. 40.
5. Christopher Andrew, *Defence of the Realm: The Authorized History of MI5*, p. 223.
6. West, *MI5*, p. 122.
7. Ibid., p. 332.
8. Bower, *The Perfect English Spy*, p. 41.
9. Robin Stephens, *Camp 020*, p. 10.
10. Ibid., p. 11.
11. *Union*, 19 June 1948.
12. A. W. Brian Simpson, *In the Highest Degree Odious*, p. 242.
13. Ibid., p. 243.
14. Miles Hudson, *Soldier, Poet, Rebel*, pp. 178–80.
15. Terry Crowdy, *Deceiving Hitler*, p. 37.
16. West, *MI5*, p. 247.
17. Kevin Jones, 'From the Horse's Mouth', *Intelligence and National Security*.
18. Andrew Roberts, *The Storm of War*, p. 88.
19. A. P. Scotland, *The London Cage*, p. 11.
20. TNA WO 208/5381.
21. Scotland, *The London Cage*, p. 28.
22. TNA WO 208/4294.
23. TNA TS 50/3.
24. Robin Stephens, *Camp 020*, p. 243.

25. TNA WO 71/1176B.
26. West, *MI5*, p. 146.
27. Stephens, *Camp 020*, p. 367.
28. Ibid., p. 109.
29. J. C. Masterman, *The Double Cross System in the War of 1939 to 1945*, p. 3.
30. TNA WO 208/3456.
31. Matthew Barry Sullivan, *Thresholds of Peace*, p. 52.
32. TNA WO 208/3248.
33. Dominic Streatfeild, *Brainwash*, pp. 379–80.
34. TNA KV 2/1311.
35. TNA WO 208/4970.
36. TNA WO 208/3463.
37. Archives du Comité international de la Croix-Rouge, CSC, Service des camps, Grande-Bretagne, Prisons, RT.
38. *Daily Express*, 9 July 1947.
39. TNA WO 208/4685.
40. Ibid.
41. Cyril Jolly, *The Vengeance of Private Pooley*, p. 198.
42. *Sunday Pictorial*, 30 January 1949.
43. TNA WO 208/4685.
44. Ibid.
45. *Sunday Pictorial*, 30 January 1949.
46. TNA WO 208/5381.
47. Ibid.
48. TNA TS/50/3.
49. Email from MOD to author, 20 November 2005.
50. TNA WO 208/3548.
51. Stephens, *Camp 020*, p. 118.
52. West, *MI5*, pp. 146–9.
53. William Crocker, *Far from Humdrum*, p. 220.

Chapter Two: For Purposes of Revenge

1. TNA FO 1030/275.
2. Ibid.
3. TNA FO 1005/744.
4. TNA FO 1030/275.
5. TNA FO 1060/735.
6. Ibid.

7. Richard J. Aldrich, *The Hidden Hand*, p. 181.
8. Ibid., pp. 181–2.
9. Robin Stephens, *Camp 020*, p. 22.
10. Ibid.
11. Patricia Meehan, *A Strange Enemy People*, pp. 133–4.
12. Richard Bessel, *Germany 1945*, p. 187.
13. TNA KV 4/327.
14. TNA WO 71/1176B.
15. Author interview, Bad Nenndorf, November 2005.
16. Stephens, *Camp 020*, p. 82.
17. Author interview, Bad Nenndorf, November 2005.
18. Statement of Robert Buttlar-Brandenfels to Court of Inquiry, April 1947, TNA FO 371/70830.
19. Ibid.
20. *Quick*, 3 March 1952.
21. Ibid.
22. TNA FO 1030/280.
23. Author interview, Lindau, July 2006.
24. TNA FO 1005/1744.
25. TNA PREM 8/794.
26. TNA WO 71/1176B.
27. Adam Sisman, *Hugh Trevor-Roper*, pp. 131–42.
28. Diaries of Nicolaus von Below.
29. TNA FO 371/70828.
30. TNA FO 1030/279.
31. *Recruiting the Reich*, BBC Radio 4, 9 January 2006.
32. TNA FO 1030/272.
33. TNA FO 1005/1744.
34. TNA FO 371/53.
35. TNA FO 371/53.
36. TNA FO 371/70828.
37. TNA PREM 8/794.
38. *Daily Express*, 11 March 1948.
39. *The Times*, 8 April 1948.
40. *The Times*, 29 May 1948.
41. *The Times*, 17 June 1948.
42. TNA FO 371/70830.
43. Author interview, Lindau, July 2006.

44. TNA WO 71/1176B.

45. Ibid.

46. www.mi5.gov.uk/output/bad-nenndorf.html.

47. TNA WO 71/1176B.

48. TNA FO 371/70830.

49. TNA WO 71/1176B.

50. TNA PREM 8/794.

Chapter Three: Soiling the Honour of the Country

1. Richard Cahill, 'Going Berserk', *Jerusalem Quarterly*.

2. Douglas Duff, *Bailing with a Teaspoon*, p. 168.

3. Jan Morris, *Farewell the Trumpets*, p. 516.

4. Caroline Elkins, *Imperial Reckoning*, pp. 20–25.

5. *South London Press*, 13 March 1953.

6. Elkins, *Imperial Reckoning*, pp. 46–61.

7. Ibid., p. 48.

8. Ibid., pp. 220–21, 226–7.

9. Ibid., p. 323.

10. Peter Benenson, *Gangrene*, p. 31.

11. *The Times*, 13 December 2008.

12. Elkins, *Imperial Reckoning*, p. 52.

13. TNA WO 32/15834.

14. David Anderson, *Histories of the Hanged*, p. 295.

15. Josiah Mwangi Kariuki, *Mau Mau Detainee*, p. 77.

16. 'End of Empire Kenya', transcripts, Rhodes House Library, Oxford, quoted in Elkins, *Imperial Reckoning*.

17. Robert Edgerton, *Mau Mau*, p. 155.

18. TNA CO 822/1251.

19. Elkins, *Imperial Reckoning*, p. 347.

20. *Guardian*, 5 October 2006.

21. Cary Review of Release of Colonial Documents, May 2011.

22. Lawrence Durrell, *Bitter Lemons*, p. 190.

23. Christopher Andrew, *Defence of the Realm*, p. 462.

24. Archives du Comité international de la Croix-Rouge, BAG 225.049/002-003.

25. Ibid.

26. Kirsten Sellars, 'Human Rights and the Colonies', *Commonwealth Journal of International Affairs*.

27. Richard J. Aldrich, *The Hidden Hand*, p. 576.

28. Ibid., p. 577.

29. Author interview, London, November 2010.

30. Andrew, *Defence of the Realm*, p. 465.

31. European Commission of Human Rights, Greece v. the United Kingdom, Application No. 176/56.

32. TNA DEFE 23/109.

33. Andrew, *Defence of the Realm*, p. 475.

34. ACICR B AG 225.001-001.

35. TNA PREM 13/1294.

36. Ken Connor, *Ghost Force*, p. 193.

37. TNA PREM 13/1294.

38. Sellars, 'Human Rights and the Colonies'.

39. TNA PREM 13/1294.

40. 'Report by Mr Roderic Bowen, QC, on the Procedures for the Arrest, Interrogation and Detention of Suspected Terrorists in Aden'.

41. TNA DEFE 24/252.

42. TNA LOC 2/8097.

43. TNA FO 8/155.

44. TNA DEFE 24/252.

45. *Observer*, 15 January 1967.

Chapter Four: A Barbaric Assault on the Mind

1. Dominic Streatfeild, *Brainwash*, p. 111; Alfred W. McCoy, *A Question of Torture*, p. 34.

2. Report of Special Meeting, Montreal Meeting, 1 June 1951, A/B, 1, 38/5, No. 184422.

3. John Marks, *The Search for the Manchurian Candidate*, p. 24.

4. Streatfeild, *Brainwash*, p. 111.

5. Ibid., p. 112.

6. Ibid., pp. 115–16.

7. Max Hastings, *The Korean War*, p. 417.

8. Cyril Cunningham, 'International Interrogation Techniques', *RUSI Journal*.

9. Marks, *The Search for the Manchurian Candidate*, p. 101.

10. Alfred McCoy, 'Confronting the CIA's Mind Maze', *Huffington Post*, 8 June 2009.

11. Lawrence E. Hinkle, 'The Physiological State of the Interrogation Subject as It Affects Brain Function'.

12. www.dtic.mil/cgi-bin/GetTRDoc?Location=U2&doc=GetTRDoc. pdf&AD=AD0670999.

13. Don Gillmore, *I Swear by Apollo*, pp. 85–105.

14. Ibid., p. 124.

15. TNA WO 71/1176B.

16. Streatfeild, *Brainwash*, p. 41.

17. Ibid., p. 41.

18. Dick Craig, 'A Short Account of the Malayan Emergency'.

19. TNA DEFE 70/211.

20. Ibid.

21. Alexander Kennedy, 'The Scientific Lessons of Interrogation'.

22. Ibid.

23. TNA KV2/1311.

24. *Daily Mail*, 9 March 1960.

25. TNA PREM 11/2900.

26. *Hansard*, 17 March 1960.

27. TNA WO 208/5572.

28. TNA CAB 21/3184.

29. www.gwu.edu/~nsarchiv/NSAEBB/NSAEBB27/01-01.htm.

30. TNA DEFE 23/109.

31. See, for example, Stephen G. Rabe, *US Intervention in British Guiana*.

32. TNA DEFE 23/109.

Chapter Five: The Five Techniques

1. David McKittrick, Seamus Kelters, Brian Feeney and Chris Thornton, *Lost Lives*, p. 64.

2. TNA WO 32/21776.

3. Chris Ryder, *The Fateful Split*, pp. 213–14.

4. Statement to Association for Legal Justice.

5. Edward Heath, *The Course of My Life*, p. 429.

6. Tim Pat Coogan, *The Troubles*, p. 126.

7. John McGuffin, *The Guineapigs*, p. 102.

8. Statement to the Association for Legal Justice.

9. Ibid.

10. Ibid.

11. Ibid.

12. Ibid.

13. John Conroy, *Unspeakable Acts, Ordinary People*, p. 38.

14. McGuffin, *The Guineapigs*, p. 75.

15. Sunday Times Insight Team, *Ulster*.

16. Liz Curtis, *Ireland*, p. 33.

17. McGuffin, *The Guineapigs*, p. 99.

18. Author interview, Belfast, June 2010.

19. 'Report of the Inquiry into Allegations against the Security Forces of Physical Brutality in Northern Ireland Arising out of Events on the 9th August, 1971'.

20. TNA PREM 15/485.

21. *Guardian*, 17 November 1971.

22. Statement in House of Commons, 16 November 1971.

23. 'Report of the Committee of Privy Counsellors Appointed to Consider Authorised Procedures for the Interrogation of Persons Suspected of Terrorism'.

24. Ibid.

25. Ibid.

26. Ibid.

27. Ibid.

28. Author interview, Belfast, June 2010.

29. *Observer*, 21 November 1971.

30. Bew and Gillespie, *Northern Ireland*, pp. 36–7.

31. 'Report of the Bloody Sunday Inquiry', Vol. I, Chapter 8.

32. Taylor, *Beating the Terrorists?*, p. 24.

33. Ireland v. The United Kingdom, Application No. 5310/71, 18 January 1978.

34. Ibid.

35. Samantha Newbery, 'Interrogation, Intelligence and the Issue of Human Rights', *Intelligence and National Security*.

36. TNA WO 32/21776.

37. TNA DEFE 23/108.

38. TNA DEFE 13/919.

39. TNA CAB 164/329.

40. TNA DEFE 13/919.

41. Ibid.

42. Ireland v. United Kingdom, Application No. 5310/71, 18 January 1978.

43. TNA CAB 164/329.

Chapter Six: Plenty of Slap and Tickle

1. Statement to Father Raymond Murray, published in *State Violence*.
2. Author interview, Belfast, May 2010.
3. Statement to Father Raymond Murray.
4. *Belfast Telegraph*, 20 April 1973.
5. Frank Kitson, *Bunch of Five*, p. 281.
6. Frank Kitson, *Low Intensity Operations*, p. 69.
7. Public statement of Police Ombudsman for Northern Ireland, 24 August 2010.
8. R. v. Flynn and Leonard, 24 May 1972.
9. Author interview, Belfast, September 2010.
10. Author interview, Belfast, August 2010.
11. Statement to Father Raymond Murray.
12. Ibid.
13. *Guardian*, 25 June 1977.
14. *Daily Mirror* and *Daily Express*, 15 March 1977.
15. Johnston Brown, *Into the Dark*, p. 117.
16. Author interview, Antrim, February 2010.
17. Author interview, Belfast, August 2010.
18. Author interview, Belfast, August 2010.
19. Author interview, Belfast, August 2010.
20. John Potter, *Testimony to Courage*, p.176.
21. Author interview, Monaghan, February 2010.
22. Tony Geraghty, *The Irish War*, p. 113.
23. R. v. McCormick and Others [1977] NI 105.
24. Ibid.
25. Taylor, *Beating the Terrorists?*, pp. 71–7.
26. Author interview, Belfast, August 2010.
27. Author interviews, Belfast and Antrim, August 2010.
28. Taylor, *Beating the Terrorists?*, p. 108.
29. Ibid., p. 111.
30. Author interview, Monaghan, February 2010.
31. http://cain.ulst.ac.uk/proni/1977/proni_NIO-25-1-10_1977-10-24.pdf.
32. Taylor, *Beating the Terrorists?*, p. 286.
33. Ibid. See: http://cain.ulst.ac.uk/proni/1978/proni_NIO-25-1-10_1978-04-05.pdf.
34. *Irish News*, 30 December 2008.
35. *Daily Telegraph*, 16 March 1979.

36. House of Commons, 28 March 1979.
37. Author interview, Belfast, February 2010.
38. Author interview, Belfast, August 2010.
39. Author interview, Belfast, May 2010.
40. Reuters News, 13 November 1991.
41. Author interview, Belfast, May 2010.

Chapter Seven: Standing Shoulder to Shoulder on the Dark Side

1. George W. Bush, *Decision Points*, pp. 126–7.
2. George Tenet, *At the Center of the Storm*, p. 165.
3. Tony Blair, *A Journey*, pp. 345–6.
4. Bob Woodward, *Bush at War*, p. 53.
5. Author interview, London, May 2011.
6. Jane Mayer, *The Dark Side*, p. 38.
7. Ibid., p 33.
8. Mayer, *The Dark Side*, p. 41.
9. 'Alleged Secret Detentions and Unlawful Inter-State Transfers Involving Council of Europe Member States', Second Report of Senator Dick Marty.
10. Ron Suskind, *The One Percent Doctrine*, pp. 82–7.
11. Stephen Grey, *Ghost Plane*, pp. 21–3.
12. *Guardian*, 12 September 2005.
13. Grey, *Ghost Plane,* p. 207.
14. Author interview, Kabul, January 2002.
15. http://humanrights.ucdavis.edu/resources/library/documents-and-reports/tipton_report.pdf.
16. Moazzam Begg, *Enemy Combatant*, p. 9.
17. FO position paper, 10 January 2002. See: www.reprieve.org.uk/static/downloads/2010_07_15_PUB_Binyam_Mohamed_Civil_Case-_Exhibit_LC13.pdf.
18. Intelligence and Security Committee, 'The Handling of Detainees by UK Intelligence Personnel in Afghanistan, Guantanamo Bay and Iraq'.
19. *Guardian*, 29 September 2010.
20. Minutes dated 26 February 2002. See: www.guardian.co.uk/law/interactive/2010/jul/14/torture-files-downing-street-role.
21. Minutes of John Gieve's Meeting with Sir Michael Jay, 12 April 2002.
22. Composite statement of Shafiq Rasul, Asif Iqbal and Rhuhel Ahmed, July 2004.

23. Ibid.
24. Statement to the Center for the Study of Human Rights in the Americas, December 2004.
25. Intelligence and Security Committee, 'The Handling of Detainees by UK Intelligence Personnel in Afghanistan, Guantanamo Bay and Iraq'.
26. *Secret War on Terror*, BBC Two, 14 March 2011.
27. Binyam Mohamed v. Secretary of State for Foreign and Commonwealth Affairs, 29 July 2008.
28. R. v. Secretary of State for Foreign and Commonwealth Affairs, Court of Appeal, 26 February 2010.
29. Philippe Sands, *Torture Team*, p. 57.
30. Ibid. p. 58.
31. See: www.cwsl.edu/content/benner/Laws101_Spr05_TortureMemo. pdf.
32. *The Times*, 8 November 2010.
33. Gareth Peirce, *Dispatches from the Dark Side*, p. 22,
34. *Hansard*, 13 December 2005.

Chapter Eight: The Fruits of the Poisoned Tree

1. Statement of Eliza Manningham-Buller, 20 September 2005, A and Others v. Secretary of State for the Home Department.
2. *Observer*, 17 April 2005.
3. http://news.bbc.co.uk/1/hi/uk/4442479.stm.
4. *The Times*, 10 May 2005.
5. Author interview, HM Prison Whitemoor, April 2009.
6. *Today Programme*, BBC Radio 4, 1 March 2006.
7. Human Rights Watch interview with Pakistani intelligence officials (date, names and place withheld).
8. *Secret War on Terror*, BBC Two, 14 March 2011.
9. Evidence to Foreign Affairs Committee, 16 June 2009.
10. 'Agency Policy on Liaison with Overseas Security and Intelligence Services in Relation to Detainees Who May Be Subject to Mistreatment', July 2006.
11. The policy can be seen at www.guardian.co.uk/law/interactive/2011/ aug/04/mi6-torture-interrogation-policy-document).
12. *Guardian*, 22 September 2010 and 18 January 2011.
13. *Guardian*, 12 October 2010.
14. Author interview, London, June 2008.

15. Human Rights Watch interview with Pakistani security official (date, name and place withheld).
16. *Sunday Times*, 7 August 2005.
17. *Guardian*, 27 July 2009.
18. *Guardian*, 27 July 2009.
19. A (FC) and others (FC) (Appellants) v. Secretary of State for the Home Department.
20. Evidence of Rangzieb Ahmed, Manchester Crown Court, 8 and 9 September 2008, edited.
21. Author interview, HM Prison Manchester, June 2009.
22. *Hansard*, 7 July 2009.
23. Author interview, Islamabad, December 2007.
24. *Guardian*, 16 March 2009.
25. *Guardian*, 18 January 2011.
26. Ibid.
27. Letter to *Guardian*, 19 January 2011.
28. Scheinin, Martin, 'Report of the Special Rapporteur on the Promotion and Protection of Human Rights and Fundamental Freedoms while Countering Terrorism'.
29. *Guardian*, 11 March 2009.
30. Human Rights Joint Committee, 23rd Report, 'Allegations of UK Complicity in Torture'.
31. Intelligence and Security Committee, 'Rendition', HMSO, July 2007.
32. Some of the documents can be seen at: www.hrw.org/sites/default/files/related_material/2011_Libya_External_Security_Building_Documents.pdf.
33. Author telephone interview, October 2011.
34. *Guardian*, 5 September 2011.
35. *Guardian*, 16 September 2011.
36. *Guardian*, 7 October 2011.
37. Author's conversations with Home Office officials, June 2011.

Chapter Nine: The Final Sifting

1. Author interviews, Kuwait and Iraq, March 2003.
2. TNA WO 208/3458.
3. Guy Bransby, *Her Majesty's Interrogator*, p. 80.
4. Evidence to the Parliamentary Joint Committee on Human Rights, 28 April 2009.

5. Sir William Gage, 'The Report of the Baha Mousa Inquiry'.
6. Ibid.
7. JSIO I Branch Manual, April 2008, 'Any Questions?' PowerPoint presentation, 30 September 2005.
8. For an example see www.bahamousainquiry.org/linkedfiles/baha_mousa/baha_mousa_inquiry_evidence/evidence_071209/bmi02775.pdf.
9. Gage, 'The Report of the Baha Mousa Inquiry'.
10. See: www.bahamousainquiry.org/linkedfiles/baha_mousa/baha_mousa_inquiry_evidence/evidence_020610/mod037459.pdf.
11. Author interviews, Basra, April 2003.
12. Brigadier Nick Carter, quoted in Robert Aitken, 'The Aitken Report'.
13. Richard Holmes, *Dusty Warriors*, p. 113.
14. Witness statement of Hussain Hadi Sabir al-Mosawi to the High Court, London, 25 February 2010.
15. These accounts and those that follow are from statements to the High Court, London, made between January 2009 and May 2010.
16. Mark Urban, *Task Force Black*, pp. 53–6, 67–9.
17. Some of the videos can be seen at www.guardian.co.uk/uk/2010/nov/06/iraq-prisoner-abuse-court?intcmp=239.
18. 'Report of the International Committee of the Red Cross on the Treatment by Coalition Forces of Prisoners of War in Iraq during Arrest, Internment and Interrogation'.
19. www.bahamousainquiry.org/linkedfiles/baha_mousa/baha_mousa_inquiry_evidence/evidence_130510/mod020228.pdf.
20. Baha Mousa Inquiry, 10 June 2010.
21. Baha Mousa Inquiry, 13 May 2010.
22. Letter from Adam Ingram to Michael Foster, 2 May 2003, see: www.bahamousainquiry.org/linkedfiles/baha_mousa/baha_mousa_inquiry_evidence/evidence_060510/mod050331.pdf.
23. *Hansard*, 28 June 2004.
24. Baha Mousa Inquiry, 2 June 2010.
25. Statement to the Baha Mousa Inquiry.
26. Baha Mousa Inquiry, 16 March 2010.
27. Statement to the Baha Mousa Inquiry, 8 July 2009.
28. Tam Henderson, *Warrior*, p. 151.
29. Ibid., p 154.
30. www.bahamousainquiry.org/f_report/vol%20iii/Part%20X/ch5/MOD055768.pdf.

31. Author interviews with MOD officials, May–July 2010.

32. Restricted Report, EPW Incident, 11 April 2003.

33. Author interviews with MOD and RAF personnel, police and Iraqi officials, 2010 and 2011.

34. Ibid.

35. Gage, 'The Report of the Baha Mousa Inquiry'.

36. Baha Mousa Inquiry, 9 November 2009.

37. Gage, 'The Report of the Baha Mousa Inquiry'.

38. Ibid.

39. *Guardian*, 31 March 2010.

40. 'Any Questions?', JSIO, 30 September 2005.

41. JSIO I Branch Manual, April 2008.

Conclusion

1. Orwell's essay formed Part 1 of *The Lion and the Unicorn: Socialism and the English Genius*, which he co-edited with T. R. Fyvel. The book was published on 19 February 1941 by Secker and Warburg, London.

Bibliography

Books

Aldrich, Richard J., *The Hidden Hand* (John Murray, London, 2001)

Anderson, David, *Histories of the Hanged* (W. W. Norton, New York, 2005)

Anderson, David, and Killingray, David, *Policing and Decolonisation: Politics, Nationalism, and the Police, 1917–65* (Manchester University Press, Manchester, 1992)

Andrew, Christopher, *Defence of the Realm: The Authorized History of MI5* (Allen Lane, London, 2009)

Balmer, Albert, *A Cyprus Journey: Memoirs of National Service* (Athena, London, 2008)

Begg, Moazzam, *Enemy Combatant* (The Free Press, London, 2006)

Bell, J. Bowyer, *The Secret Army* (Poolbeg Press, Dublin, 1990)

Benenson, Peter, and various authors, *Gangrene* (John Calder, London, 1959)

Bessel, Richard, *Germany 1945: From War to Peace* (Simon & Schuster, London, 2009)

Bew, Paul, and Gillespie, Gordon, *Northern Ireland: A Chronology of the Troubles* (Gill and Macmillan, Dublin, 1993)

Biddiscombe, Perry, *The Last Nazis* (Tempus, Stroud, 2006)

Blair, Tony, *A Journey* (Hutchinson, London, 2010)

Bower, Tom, *The Perfect English Spy* (William Heinemann, London, 1995)

Bransby, Guy, *Her Majesty's Interrogator* (Leo Cooper, London, 1996)

Brown, J. A. C., *Techniques of Persuasion* (Penguin, Harmondsworth, 1981)

Brown, Johnston, *Into the Dark: 30 Years in the RUC* (Gill and Macmillan, Dublin, 2006)

Bush, George W., *Decision Points* (Virgin Books, London, 2010)

Callwell, C. E., *Small Wars* (HMSO, London, 1906)

Campbell, Alastair, *The Blair Years* (Hutchinson, London, 2007)

Carle, Glenn L., *The Interrogator: An Education* (Nation Books, New York, 2011)

Cesarani, David, *Major Farran's Hat* (Heinemann, London, 2009)

Churchill, Winston, *The Second World War* (Cassell, London, 1949)

Comber, Leon, *Malaya's Secret Police, 1945–60* (Monash University Press, Victoria, 2008)

Connor, Ken, *Ghost Force* (Cassell, London, 1998)

Conroy, John, *Unspeakable Acts, Ordinary People* (Vision, London, 2001)

Coogan, Tim Pat, *The Troubles: Ireland's Ordeal 1966–1995 and the Search for Peace* (Hutchinson, London, 1995)

Crocker, William, *Far from Humdrum* (Hutchinson, London, 1967)

Crowdy, Terry, *Deceiving Hitler* (Osprey, London, 2008)

Curtis, Liz, *Ireland: The Propaganda War* (Sasta, Belfast, 1998)

Curtis, Mark, *Web of Deceit* (Vintage, London, 2003)

Danner, Mark, *Torture and Truth* (Granta, London, 2004)

Deacon, Richard, *Spy!* (BBC, London, 1980)

Dearden, Harold, *The Technique of Living* (Heinemann, London, 1924)

Dearden, Harold, *Aspects of Murder* (Staples Press, London, 1951)

Deeley, Peter, *Beyond Breaking Point* (Arthur Barker, London, 1971)

Dillon, Martin, *The Dirty War* (Arrow, London, 1991)

Donohue, Laura K., *Counter-Terrorist Law and Emergency Powers in the United Kingdom 1922–2000* (Irish Academic Press, Dublin, 2007)

Dorril, Stephen, *MI6: Fifty Years of Special Operations* (Fourth Estate, London, 2000)

Dorril, Stephen, *Blackshirt* (Penguin, London, 2007)

Drumheller, Tyler, *On the Brink* (Methuen, London, 2007)

Duff, Douglas, *Bailing with a Teaspoon* (John Long, London, 1959)

Durrell, Lawrence, *Bitter Lemons* (Faber and Faber, London, 1964)

Edgerton, Robert, *Mau Mau: An African Crucible* (Free Press, London, 1989)

Elkins, Caroline, *Imperial Reckoning* (Henry Holt, New York, 2005)

Farrar-Hockley, General Sir Anthony, *The Edge of the Sword* (Star, London, 1981)

Fleming, Peter, *Invasion 1940* (Rupert Hart-Davis, London 1957)

French, David, *The British Way in Counter-Insurgency, 1945–1967* (Oxford University Press, Oxford, 2011)

Fry, Helen, *Churchill's German Army* (The History Press, Stroud, 2009)

Geraghty, Tony, *The Irish War* (HarperCollins, London, 2000)

Gillmore, Don, *I Swear by Apollo* (Eden Press, Montreal, 1987)

Grey, Stephen, *Ghost Plane* (Hurst, London, 2006)

Grinker, Roy, and Spiegel, John, *Men under Stress* (McGraw-Hill, New York, 1963)

Grob-Fitzgibbon, Benjamin, *Imperial Endgame* (Palgrave Macmillan, London, 2011)

Hastings, Max, *The Korean War* (Pan, London, 2010)

Heath, Edward, *The Course of My Life* (Hodder and Stoughton, London, 1998)

Henderson, Tam, *Warrior* (Mainstream, Edinburgh, 2008)

Hewitt, Steve, *The British War on Terror* (Continuum, London, 2008)

Hinsley, F., et al., *British Intelligence in the Second World War*, Vols. 1–5 (HMSO, London, 1979–90)

Hoffman, Bruce, *Inside Terrorism* (Columbia University Press, New York, 2006)

Holmes, Richard, *Dusty Warrors: Modern Soldiers at War* (HarperPress, London, 2006)

Holt, Thaddeus, *The Deceivers* (Phoenix, London, 2004)

Hudson, Miles, *Soldier, Poet, Rebel* (Sutton, Stroud, 2007)

Jagan, Cheddi, *Forbidden Freedom* (Lawrence & Wishart, London, 1954)

Jeffery, Keith, *MI6: The History of the Secret Intelligence Service, 1909–1949* (Bloomsbury, London, 2010)

Jolly, Cyril, *The Vengeance of Private Pooley* (Heinemann, London, 1956)

Kariuki, Josiah Mwangi, *Mau Mau Detainee* (Oxford University Press, Nairobi, 1963)

Kitson, Frank, *Low Intensity Operations* (HMSO, London, 1971)

Kitson, Frank, *Bunch of Five* (Faber and Faber, London, 1977)

Knightley, Phillip, *The Second Oldest Profession* (Pimlico, London, 2003)

Lagouranis, Tony, *Fear Up Harsh* (Caliber, New York, 2008)

Levinson, Sandford (ed.), *Torture: A Collection* (Oxford University Press, Oxford, 2004)

McCoy, Alfred W., *A Question of Torture* (Metropolitan, New York, 2006)

McGuffin, John, *The Guineapigs* (Penguin, Harmondsworth, 1974)

Macintyre, Ben, *Agent Zigzag* (Bloomsbury, London, 2007)

Mackey, Chris, with Miller, Greg, *The Interrogator's War: Inside the Secret War Against Al Qaeda* (John Murray, London, 2004)

McKittrick, David, and McVea, David, *Making Sense of the Troubles* (Penguin, London, 2001)

McKittrick, David, Kelters, Seamus, Feeney, Brian, and Thornton, Chris,

Lost Lives (Mainstream, Edinburgh, 2000)

Marks, John, *The Search for the Manchurian Candidate* (Time Books, London, 1979)

Masterman, J. C., *The Double Cross System in the War of 1939 to 1945* (Yale University Press, New Haven, 1972)

Mather, Carol, *Aftermath of War* (Brassey's, London, 1992)

Mayer, Jane, *The Dark Side* (Anchor Books, New York, 2009)

Mayne, Richard, *In Victory, Magnanimity, In Peace, Goodwill: A History of Wilton Park* (Frank Cass, London, 2003)

Meehan, Patricia, *A Strange Enemy People: Germans Under the British, 1945–50* (Peter Owen, London, 2001)

Moore, Bob, *Prisoners of War and Their Captors in World War II* (Berg, Oxford, 1996)

Morris, Jan, *Farewell the Trumpets* (Faber and Faber, London, 1998)

Murphy, Dean E., *September 11: An Oral History* (Doubleday, New York, 2002)

Murray, Craig, *Murder in Samarkand* (Mainstream, Edinburgh, 2007)

Murray, Raymond, *State Violence* (Mercer Press, Cork, 1998)

Newsinger, John, *The Blood Never Dried* (Bookmarks, London, 2010)

Obama, Barack, *Dreams from My Father* (Canongate, Edinburgh, 2007)

Omand, David, *Securing the State* (Hurst, London, 2010)

Owen, Frank, *The Eddie Chapman Story* (Panther, London, 1955)

Peirce, Gareth, *Dispatches from the Dark Side* (Verso, London, 2010)

Potter, John, *Testimony to Courage: The History of the Ulster Defence Regiment, 1969–1992* (Leo Cooper, Barnsley, 2001)

Rabe, Stephen G., *US Intervention in British Guiana: A Cold War Story* (University of North Carolina Press, Chapel Hill, 2005)

Rejali, Darius, *Torture and Democracy* (Princeton University Press, Princeton, 2007)

Roberts, Andrew, *The Storm of War* (Penguin, London, 2009)

Ryder, Chris, *The Ulster Defence Regiment* (Mandarin, London, 1992)

Ryder, Chris, *The Fateful Split* (Methuen, London, 2004)

Sands, Philippe, *Torture Team* (Penguin, London, 2009)

Sargant, William, *The Battle for the Mind* (Heinemann, London, 1957)

Scotland, A. P., *The London Cage* (Evans Brothers, London, 1957)

Sillitoe, Percy, *Cloak without a Dagger* (Pan, London, 1956)

Simpson, Alan, *Duplicity and Deception: Policing the Twilight Zone of the Troubles* (Brandon, Dingle, 2010)

Simpson, A. W. Brian, *In the Highest Degree Odious* (Oxford University Press, Oxford, 1992)

Sisman, Adam, *Hugh Trevor-Roper: The Biography* (Weidenfeld & Nicolson, London, 2010)

Stafford Smith, Clive, *Bad Men* (Phoenix, London, 2007)

Stephens, Robin, *Camp 020: MI5 and the Nazi Spies,* introduced and edited by Oliver Hoare (Public Record Office, Richmond, 2000)

Streatfeild, Dominic, *Brainwash* (Hodder, London, 2007)

Sullivan, Matthew Barry, *Thresholds of Peace* (Hamish Hamilton, London, 1979)

Sunday Times Insight Team, *Ulster* (Penguin, Harmondsworth, 1972)

Suskind, Ron, *The One Percent Doctrine* (Simon & Schuster, New York, 2006)

Taylor, Peter, *Beating the Terrorists?* (Penguin, Harmondsworth, 1980)

Tenet, George, *At the Center of the Storm* (HarperCollins, New York, 2007)

Thiessen, Marc A., *Courting Disaster* (Regnery, Washington, DC, 2010)

Townshend, Charles, *Britain's Civil Wars: Counterinsurgency in the Twentieth Century* (Faber and Faber, London, 1986)

Townshend, Charles, *Political Violence in Ireland* (Clarendon, Oxford, 2001)

Trevor-Roper, Hugh, *The Last Days of Hitler* (University of Chicago Press, Chicago, 1992)

Tyrie, Andrew, Gough, Roger, and McCracken, Stuart, *Account Rendered* (Biteback, London, 2011)

Urban, Mark, *Big Boys' Rules* (Faber and Faber, London, 1992)

Urban, Mark, *Task Force Black* (Little, Brown, London, 2010)

Warburton, John, and Watts, Charlie, *The Hell of Ham Common* (European Action Publications, Ramsgate, 2010)

Watson, Richard, *The Rise and Fall of the British Jihad* (Granta, London, 2008)

West, Nigel, *MI5: British Security Service Operations, 1909–1945* (Military Heritage Press, New York, 1981)

West, Nigel, *The Guy Liddell Diaries,* Vols. 1 and 2 (Routledge, London, 2005, 2009)

Wheatley, Ronald, *Operation Sea Lion* (Oxford University Press, Oxford, 1958)

Woodward, Bob, *Bush at War* (Simon & Schuster, New York, 2002)

Worthington, Andy, *The Guantanamo Files* (Pluto, London, 2007)

Zimmerman, David, *Top Secret Exchange: The Tizard Mission and the Scientific War* (McGill-Queen's University Press, Montreal, 1996)

Other Sources

Aitken, Robert, 'The Aitken Report: An Investigation into Cases of Deliberate Abuse and Unlawful Killing in Iraq in 2003 and 2004', Ministry of Defence, London, January 2008

Allegations of Brutality in Cyprus, Government House, Nicosia, June 1957

Von Below, Nicolaus, private diaries

Cahill, Richard, 'Going Berserk: Black and Tans in Palestine', *Jerusalem Quarterly*, Summer 2009

Cary Review of Release of Colonial Documents, May 2011, published at: www.fco.gov.uk/resources/en/pdf/migrated-archives

Central Intelligence Agency, 'Kubark Counterintelligence Interrogation Manual', July 1963

Craig, R. J. W. (Dick), 'A Short Account of the Malayan Emergency', cyclostyled booklet, September 1964.

Cunningham, Cyril, 'International Interrogation Techniques', *RUSI Journal*, September 1972

Gage, Sir William, 'The Report of the Baha Mousa Inquiry', HMSO, London, September 2011

Hinkle, Lawrence E., 'The Physiological State of the Interrogation Subject as It Affects Brain Function', in O. Biderman and H. Zimmer, *Manipulation of Human Behavior* (Wiley, New York, 1961)

Human Rights Watch, 'Cruel Britannia: British Complicity in the Torture and Ill-treatment of Terror Suspects in Pakistan', New York, November 2009

'Instructions for British Servicemen in Germany', Foreign Office, London, 1944

Intelligence and Security Committee, 'The Handling of Detainees by UK Intelligence Personnel in Afghanistan, Guantanamo Bay and Iraq', HMSO, London, March 2005

Intelligence and Security Committee, 'Rendition', HMSO, London, July 2007

Jones, Kevin, 'From the Horse's Mouth: Luftwaffe POWs as Sources for Intelligence', *Intelligence and National Security*, Vol. 15, No. 4, Winter 2000

Kennedy, Alexander, 'The Scientific Lessons of Interrogation', Royal

Institution, London, February 1960

Marty, Dick, 'Alleged Secret Detentions and Unlawful Inter-State Transfers Involving Council of Europe Member States – Part II', Council of Europe, Strasbourg, June 2006

Mumford, Andrew, 'Minimum Force Meets Brutality: In-depth Interrogation and Torture in British Counter-insurgency Operations', paper by Dr Andrew Mumford, Department of Politics and International Studies, University of Hull

Newbery, Samantha, 'Interrogation, Intelligence and Ill-treatment in Northern Ireland', in 'Interrogation, Intelligence and the Issue of Human Rights', edited by Samantha Newbery, *Intelligence and National Security*, Vol. 24, No. 5, October 2009

'Report by Mr Roderic Bowen, QC, on the Procedures for the Arrest, Interrogation and Detention of Suspected Terrorists in Aden', HMSO, London, November 1966

'Report of the Inquiry into Allegations against the Security Forces of Physical Brutality in Northern Ireland Arising out of Events on the 9th August, 1971' (Compton Report), HMSO, London, November 1971

'Report of the Commission to Consider Legal Procedures to Deal with Terrorist Activities in Northern Ireland' (Diplock Report) HMSO, London, December 1972

'Report of the Committee of Privy Counsellors Appointed to Consider Authorised Procedures for the Interrogation of Persons Suspected of Terrorism' (Parker Report), HMSO, London, March 1972

'Report of an Amnesty International Mission to Northern Ireland', Amnesty International, London, June 1978

'Report of the Committee of Inquiry into Police Interrogation Procedures in Northern Ireland' (Bennett Report), HMSO, London, March 1979

'Report of the International Committee of the Red Cross on the Treatment by Coalition Forces of Prisoners of War in Iraq during Arrest, Internment and Interrogation', ICRC, Geneva, February 2004

'Report of the Bloody Sunday Inquiry' (Saville Report), HMSO, London, June 2010

Scheinin, Martin, 'Report of the Special Rapporteur on the Promotion and Protection of Human Rights and Fundamental Freedoms while Countering Terrorism', United Nations, February 2009

Sellars, Kirsten, 'Human Rights and the Colonies', *Commonwealth Journal of*

International Affairs, Vol. 90, No. 358, 2001

Smith, Stanley, 'Effects of Sensory Deprivation', *Proceedings of the Royal Society of Medicine*, June 1962

Wark, Wesley K., 'Coming in from the Cold: British Propaganda and the Red Army Defectors, 1945–52', *International History Review*, February 1978

Acknowledgements

I owe an enormous debt to the great many people who talked and corresponded with me while I was researching and writing this book, helping me to understand what measures have been taken to defend Britain and protect British interests, and how, and why. A few, in government, provided unwitting assistance. Many more people knew exactly what they were doing but, given the nature of their own positions and the subject matter being explored, would not welcome being named here. This applies particularly to those former detectives of the Royal Ulster Constabulary who agreed to talk candidly about their work. You know who you are and I am very grateful.

Many colleagues at the *Guardian* gave me a great deal of support while researching the news reports that preceded this book. They include Richard Norton-Taylor, who was generous with advice that drew upon immense good sense and decades of experience. Nick Hopkins, Paul Johnson, Ian Katz and Alan Rusbridger gave me every encouragement. Jan Clements and Gill Phillips were among those who kept me out of trouble. Owen Bowcott planted the first seed for the book, suggesting that there may be dots to be joined between my research into the wartime work of CSDIC and my reporting on some of the darker aspects of the UK's counterterrorism initiatives in the post-9/11 world.

It was Kate Shaw of the Viney Agency who had the imagination to see that my work for the *Guardian* could be developed into a book and who did so much to talk me into writing it. My good friends Jackie and Julian Birch gave me the final nudge.

I am indebted to a number of historians and journalists whose work has touched upon matters that are similar to those explored here. They include David Anderson, Liz Curtis, Caroline Elkins, Stephen Grey, Jane Mayer, Patricia Meehan, Alfred W. McCoy, Samantha Newbery, Brian Simpson, Dominic Streatfeild and Peter Taylor. I am particularly thankful for the pioneering work of the late John McGuffin.

I am grateful for the kindness and patience of countless archivists and librarians, including those at the British Library, the British Library Newspaper Library, the *Guardian*, the Imperial War Museum, the Irish Defence Forces, the Linen Hall Library, the Metropolitan Police, the National Archives and the Royal Institution. Thanks go in particular to Fabrizio Bensi at the ICRC.

This book simply would not have happened without the keen intellect, skill and discipline of Laura Barber, my editor at Portobello Books.

I am grateful for the help of Martin Soames, the care that he took when reading the manuscript and the good advice that he offered.

The details of the UK's involvement in torture and rendition since 9/11 and the abuses committed by some British soldiers serving in Iraq have not emerged as the result of the work of any one journalist, lawyer or parliamentarian. Each piece of the jigsaw has been extracted painstakingly, in the face of official secrecy, obfuscation and denial. The number of people engaged in this task has been surprisingly small, but a significant part of the puzzle has now been assembled, allowing the public to gaze at a picture that may be incomplete, but is nonetheless disturbing.

For this I would like to offer my heartfelt thanks to Brad Adams, Tayab Ali, Louise Christian, David Davis, Andrew Dismore, Clara Gutteridge, Hashmat Ali Habib, Ali Dayan Hasan, Imran Khan, Stuart McCracken, Sapna Malik, Craig Murray, Peter Oborne, Gareth Peirce, Tom Porteous, Asim Qureshi, David Rose, Philippe Sands, Phil Shiner and his colleagues at Public Interest Lawyers, Clive Stafford Smith and his colleagues at the legal charity Reprieve, Richard Stein and Andrew Tyrie.

Waqar Kiani, who assisted me in Pakistan, was not only enterprising but brave.

Others have helped in many different ways. My thanks go to Rangzieb Ahmed, Shahidul Alam, Rupert Allason, Fauzia Amin, Salahuddin Amin, Fanoulla Argyrou, Damien Austin, Steve Ballinger, Moazzam Begg, Claus Dirk von Below, Huw Bennett, Mick Browne, Jason Burke, Susanne Burri, Duncan Campbell, Alex Carlile, Patricia Coyle, Michael Culbert, Abby d'Arcy-Hughes, Martin Dearden, Omar Deghayes, Martin Dillon, Stephen Dorril, Heppilena Ferguson, Alam Ghafoor, Guy Grandjean, Ingrid Groth, Noelle Grothier, Saghir Hussain, Dr Robert Irwin, Fariha Karim, Dominic Kennedy, Dan Leader, David List, Bill Lowther, Eamonn McCann, Eamonn McDermott, Henry McDonald, Professor Kieran McEvoy, Raheed Mahmood, Tommy McKearney, Charlie McMeneman, Gerhard Menzel, Rabia Mohamed, Dr Paul Moore, Dr Andrew Mumford, the late Walter Münstermann, Father Raymond Murray, Petros Petrides, Faisal Qureshi, Professor Stephen G. Rabe, Jamilur Rahman, Iftikhar Sattar, Clare Schulenburg, Tahir Shah, Liam Shannon, Mick Smith and Declan Walsh. I apologise to anyone I have inadvertently left out.

Finally, I would like to acknowledge the officers and former officers of the security and intelligence services, the soldiers of the Intelligence Corps and, most especially, the men and women who served with the RUC, who may be aggrieved that this book has concentrated on specific aspects of the actions of the British state and has not examined other efforts and sacrifices that have been made over many years on behalf of the British people.

Index